You Gotta Have Heart

You Gotta Have Heart

A History of Washington Baseball from 1859 to the 2012 National League East Champions

Frederic J. Frommer

Taylor Trade Publishing

Lanham • New York • Boulder • Toronto • Plymouth, UK

To my father, Harvey, who taught me how
to play baseball and to how to be an author.
Your example of hard work has been an inspiration to me.

Published by Taylor Trade Publishing
An imprint of The Rowman & Littlefield Publishing Group, Inc.
4501 Forbes Boulevard, Suite 200, Lanham, Maryland 20706
www.rowman.com

10 Thornbury Road, Plymouth PL6 7PP, United Kingdom

Distributed by National Book Network

British Library Cataloguing in Publication Information Available

Library of Congress Cataloging-in-Publication Data
Frommer, Frederic J.
  You gotta have heart : a history of Washington baseball from 1859 to the 2012 National
League East champions / Frederic J. Frommer.
    pages cm
  Includes bibliographical references.
  ISBN 978-1-58979-843-4 (pbk. : alk. paper) — ISBN 978-1-58979-844-1 (electronic)
1. Baseball—Washington (D.C.)—History. 2. Washington Senators (Baseball team)—History.
3. Homestead Grays (Baseball team)—History. 4. Washington Nationals (Baseball team)—
History. I. Title.
  GV863.W18F78 2013
  796.357'6409753—dc23
                                                            2013014109

♾™ The paper used in this publication meets the minimum requirements of American
National Standard for Information Sciences—Permanence of Paper for Printed Library
Materials, ANSI/NISO Z39.48-1992.

Printed in the United States of America

CONTENTS

CONTENTS

ACKNOWLEDGMENTS

My wife, Michele, a talented writer, was an invaluable editor for this project, reading every word of the manuscript, tightening and sharpening the writing, and proofing with an eagle's eye for details. She also helped with a great deal of the research and offered invaluable advice and support throughout the process.

My parents, Myrna and Harvey, both accomplished authors, offered important critiques, which improved the book immeasurably, as well as encouragement and mentoring as good as any big-league manager's.

Phil Hochberg, a Washington attorney and former Senators public address announcer, provided crucial institutional memory. He fact-checked the historical material and suggested important details that helped provide a fuller context and offered his own memories that can be found throughout the book.

Thanks to Bob Schieffer for his wonderful foreword to the book.

Thanks to Rick Rinehart, Janice Braunstein, and Karie Simpson at Taylor Trade Publishing for their excellent work on this project.

Thanks also to Bill Gilbert; Lara Potter, and the rest of the Washington Nationals organization; Charlie Brotman; Frank Howard; the staff at the Washingtonian Division of the Martin Luther King Jr. Memorial Library; and the staff at the Historical Society of Washington, D.C.

Thanks to my young sons, Alexander and Ethan; my sister Jennifer; my brother Ian; and my Aunt Caroline for their love and support.

FOREWORD

BOB SCHIEFFER, CBS NEWS CHIEF WASHINGTON CORRESPONDENT

I got to Washington in 1969, just in time to wave good-bye to the Senators. I got to see them a few times, but by the time they left in 1971, I wasn't as upset about it as some people. The reason was, they were moving to my hometown, Fort Worth (or at least out on the Turnpike, halfway between Fort Worth and Dallas), and I was glad to see my hometown get a major-league club.

I grew up watching the Fort Worth Cats. In the years after World War II, the Cats were the Double-A farm club of the Brooklyn Dodgers in the old Texas League, and, from the age of ten, when I wasn't eating or sleeping, I played, worried, or thought about baseball. The Dodgers' general manager, Branch Rickey, had put together the first great minor-league farm system, and we saw some great ballplayers come through Fort Worth on the way to the Big Show. They included the likes of Carl Erskine, Duke Snyder (he was still Eddie when he played in Fort Worth), Dick Williams, and later Maury Wills.

Bobby Bragan, who had been the backup catcher in Brooklyn, was sent down to manage the Cats, and he was my hero. He was a catcher, and I was a catcher, and we played the position for the same reason. In those days, they always put the slowest guy behind the plate, and Bobby was said to be the slowest guy ever to make it to the bigs. I pretty much held the slow title around Fort Worth.

We didn't play football in my neighborhood, just baseball, year-round, but the honest reason our family became such fans was because of the Texas heat. There was no air conditioning in Fort Worth in those days, and the coolest place in town was LA Grave Field, where the Cats played, so most nights our mom would gather up the kids, and we'd go to the ballpark to cool off. From those days onward, baseball was always a part of my life.

It was not until the Senators left Washington that I realized a town without a baseball team just isn't quite complete. Sure, Washington had the Redskins and some other teams, but I just never got into football, except when it involved my TCU Horned Frogs, and I have never watched a basketball game from start to finish. For me, sports season begins when pitchers and catchers report in February and ends with the World Series.

There must have been a few people around Washington who felt the way I did. How could a city be the capital of the free world and not have a baseball team, they would ask. We needed one, came to believe we deserved one, and saw it as a matter of credibility, maybe even national security—how could Washington be Washington, an example to the world, without a ball club? I actually heard people take that line, and they sounded like they believed it. I more or less believed it myself.

We hoped, prayed, and argued for a team, so when baseball finally returned, we were pushovers. We were like teenagers on their first car date. We fell in love with the new team—the Nationals—before they took the field, and the field was, how shall I say it, no walk in the park. The Nat's first home was old RFK Stadium, not that pretty, not that modern, not much actually, but old and creaky. But for us it became a holy place right up there with the Coliseum in Rome, for it was the home field to our already beloved Nationals.

I bought season tickets behind the home team dugout and was there every night. You can watch baseball on television, you can listen on the radio, but if you've been away from baseball for a while, you forget that nothing matches the experience of being in the ballpark, where you can hear the crack of the bat, the smell of the grass—where the game just envelops your senses from the moment you come through a stadium portal and see the green of the grass.

That's the thing about baseball, it's great on television, it can be exciting on the radio, but being at the ballpark is an experience unto itself. You can watch it on so many levels. If you played the game when you were young, you see more in that panorama that unfolds before you than someone who didn't play. But if you watch it with a former pro, he'll see a lot more than you do. On the other hand, if you know nothing of the game, or even if you do, you can watch the girls and other such activities, which is also not such a bad way to spend an evening.

Joe Garagiola, the late catcher and broadcaster, once pointed out that the bullpen was a lot more than the place where pitchers warmed up. It's also the place, he used to say, where baseball philosophers did some of their best thinking, while players would while away an afternoon assembling an all-star ugly team, or list the goofiest, or strangest, or most superstitious. Baseball gives you time to do that.

Because baseball's action comes in spurts, the observer can use the interval between pitches to offer observations, criticisms, tall tales, and comment—and not just about the game, about everything. No other sport provides that luxury, which is why sports literature is dominated by baseball books. No surprise there, most sports stories are about baseball. Think about it, ever heard a good joke about basketball? Is it any wonder, then, that a sport that encourages storytelling and comment would be a favorite in Washington, a town that runs on talk?

Washington's baseball-starved fans would have settled for anything, and, for a while, that looked like what we got. In the old days, the Washington battle cry had been "first in peace, first in war, and last in the American League." The new team was in the National League, but last place was beginning to look like home.

Then the Lerner family bought the team, built a ballpark, and began to build a team. The new park opened, Davey Johnson was coaxed out of retirement to manage an exciting bunch of kids who loved the game as much as the fans, and, in 2012, a date that will live forever in our hearts, we didn't just have a team, we won the National League East. A city that couldn't agree on much of anything had something everyone could love. We had a winner!

The playoffs that fall didn't come out exactly the way we wanted, but that's baseball, and when the season came down to that final game with the Cardinals, I wrote the following commentary in rhyme for my *Face the Nation* broadcast, which for me, summed up how we all felt about our team:

Things were looking mighty good for our beloved Nats.

Harper found his batting eye, Zimmerman his bat.

Can this be right? Is it true? Are we having too much fun?

We were leading three to zip, and it was only inning one.

The innings really rolled along. We could not believe our eyes.

From Morse the Beast and Harper: homers Big Boy size!

God is great and so are we. We sing Hip, Hip Hurrah!

At the end of three: the Nats are six, the Cardinal lads, Na-da.

It was very close to freezing, but no one there was cold.

World Series fever kept 'em warm, if the truth be told.

With victory in the offing, tomorrow'll be a glorious day.

But then the Cardinals—being birds—began to peck away.

Their first score in inning four put no damper on our glee.

Shortly then, they got two more, but we still led six to three.

By inning nine, it's 7–5, we're comfortably ahead.

But suddenly these Cards seemed risen from the dead.

Our closer guy is throwing heat, but Cardinal bats got hot.

We don't know how or why, but leading now, we're not.

We had ourselves believing we were on the way to heaven.

But dreams became reality. We lost it, nine to seven.

In Casey's famous epitaph, the sun did still shine bright.

Bands still played, children sang. Somewhere hearts were light.

Skies were blue as blue, and somewhere bells were ringing.

But there was no joy in Mudville when Casey went down swinging.

And so it was in Washington on a cold and windy eve.

Yes, baseball is our greatest game, that I still believe.

But know like love, it brings a risk, and that's the other part.

If you take it seriously, it just may break your heart.

Congratulations to the Cardinals. Thanks to the Nats for a really great year!

Bob Schieffer was a sore-armed catcher at TCU whose baseball career ended his freshman year, when Dizzy Dean's nephew, SMU Pitcher Paul Dean Jr., hit him in the eye. Schieffer later joined CBS News and still works in the Washington Bureau.

INTRODUCTION

In a city filled with some of the most competitive people on the planet, waiting eight years for the Washington Nationals to have a winning season must have felt like a lifetime. But they didn't have to wait nearly as long as previous generations of Washington baseball fans. In 1912, a hundred years before the Nationals posted their first winning record and made the playoffs, the Washington Senators broke .500 for the first time in their history, following eleven straight losing seasons. But it would be another twelve years before the Senators made the postseason—when the team won the World Series in 1924.

The Roaring Twenties—a time of rising prosperity, when Americans fell in love with jazz, drank alcohol at illegal speakeasies during Prohibition, and drove cars in greater numbers—also marked the high point for the Washington Senators, who repeated as American League pennant winners in 1925. The team added its final pennant in 1933, when Prohibition came to an end and FDR began his presidency. At the time, black players were still banned from baseball. When Washington returned to the postseason seventy-nine years later, Americans were gearing up to reelect a black man as president.

The Nats' successful 2012 season ended a couple of other droughts as well. Washingtonians hadn't seen a bona fide pennant race since 1945, when the Senators finished one-and-a-half games out of first place. They hadn't seen a winning team of any kind—forget about a contender—since 1969, when Ted Williams managed the team to a fourth-place finish. That was a huge success by Washington standards, especially coming off a last-place finish the year before. The 1964 Senators had an even lower bar. The team's yearbook that year boldly predicted, "Off the Floor—in '64!" Washington met the challenge by losing one hundred games and finishing in ninth place—second-to-last in the American League.

For decades, the closest that Washington baseball fans could get to seeing the Senators win was in fiction. Tired of waiting for his favorite team to make it back to the World Series, native Washingtonian Douglass Wallop wrote a 1954 novel called *The Year the Yankees Lost the Pennant*, in which a middle-aged man named Joe Boyd accepts an offer to sell his soul to the devil to play for the Senators. "You can be Moses and lead them out of the wilderness, to use a metaphor I've never particularly cared for," the devil character, Applegate, tells Boyd.

Boyd is transformed into twenty-one-year-old slugger Joe Hardy, who helps lead the team to the pennant. Nearly sixty years later, long-suffering Washington baseball might have thought they were seeing a modern-day Joe Hardy in the body of Bryce Harper. Harper, like Hardy, joined the team during the season and provided a jolt that helped catapult the team to the postseason.

The story is more well known as *Damn Yankees*, the musical based on the novel. Before he breaks into the song "You Gotta Have Heart," Senators manager Benny van Buren tells his players, "Baseball is only one-half skill." As if channeling van Buren, Nats manager Davey Johnson made a similar observation in explaining the decision to shut down phenom pitcher Stephen Strasburg in 2012: "I'm a firm believer that this game is 90–95 percent mental. And he's only human."

Whatever happens in the coming seasons, Nats fans should take solace in having a team—good or bad. Twice, Washington teams moved away, and the city was without baseball from 1972 to 2004. When the second Senators team left for Texas, manager Ted Williams supported the move. "Basically, Washington is a city of transient people," he said. "Most people don't give a damn." Major League Baseball pretty much shared those views for three decades, passing up the city for several expansion teams.

For most of the twentieth century, Washingtonians enjoyed the rhythm of a baseball season: the reliable company of a radio broadcast on the front stoop; a relaxing evening stretched out on the couch in front of the television, perhaps dozing through the fourth inning; watching the flight of a ball at a game against a blue afternoon sky or starry night; checking the local team's box score in the next day's newspaper. A generation of baseball fans in Washington never got to experience those pleasures with the home team. Hopefully a century from now, the three decades without a baseball team will merit only a footnote in a proud 200-year Washington baseball tradition.

Frederic J. Frommer
February 2013
Washington, D.C.

ONE

Beginnings

BEGINNINGS

The Montreal Expos moved to Washington in 2005 as wards of the state. Major League Baseball owned the vagabond franchise, deciding the team's fate, from how much it spent to where it played. Nationals fans may have seethed over the outside control, but the arrangement actually mirrored Washington's first modern-era team a century earlier.

When the American League started play in 1901, league president Ban Johnson controlled 51 percent of every team, including the original Washington Nationals, known more popularly as the Senators. Two years later, the league tightened its grip on the infant Washington franchise by buying out team president Fred Postal's stock. Only in 1904 did the team finally have independent ownership, when a group, including Thomas C. Noyes, whose family published the *Washington Star*, bought the team.

Although 1901 marked the beginning of the city's first lasting franchise, Washington baseball went back at least forty years before. In 1859, a group of government clerks formed the "Potomacs," winning this approving description from the *Washington Star*: "It is good to see health-promoting exercises taking the place of insipid enervating amusements."

That same year, other government workers started up the National Base Ball Club of Washington, D.C., or "Nationals." The team included Arthur Pue Gorman, a twenty-one-year-old pitcher who went on to become a U.S. senator and the inspiration for the name Washington Senators. The club's constitution still exists today at the Washington Historical Society, laying out the club's bylaws. Players were required to pay a fifty-cent initiation fee and monthly dues of twenty-five cents. The members were mostly government clerks—upper-middle-class gentlemen— and they envisioned a gentlemen's game. As such, there would be fines for antisocial behavior: ten cents for "profane or improper language," twenty-five cents for disputing an umpire's call, and even a ten-cent fine for expressing an opinion on a close call before the umpire made his decision. Such fines would wipe out today's players, even at those rates.

On May 5, 1860, six months before Abraham Lincoln was elected president, the Nationals and Potomacs squared off for a game on the "White Lot," a field near the White House now known as the Ellipse, where recreational softball games are played today. The score was like a softball game, with the Potomacs winning, 35–15, thanks to rules that allowed a batter to dictate where the pitch would be thrown. A month later, the Nationals avenged the loss with a 46–14 victory. And so a friendly rivalry was born.

Newspaper accounts of the games between the Nationals and Potomacs offer a glimpse of the gentlemanly game envisioned by the Nationals' constitution. One story notes, "The game was witnessed by a large number of spectators, including nearly 400 ladies, representing the beauty and fashion of the capital."

Apparently, both teams had developed something of a home-field advantage, although neither one wanted to acknowledge it. The Nationals played on Capitol Hill, while the Potomacs called the White Lot their home. Being able to win games away from "home" became a point of pride. A newspaper story described the subtext: "The Base Ball fraternity and the sympathizing public began to say that each club had the advantage on its own grounds, and the Potomacs, unwilling to admit this, yielded to the wish of the Nationals to play on their grounds the game deciding the championship of Washington, and probably the South." The Potomacs made their point. They won that late October game, an ancient Fall Classic, 32–16, on the Nationals' home field. "The result has been a triumph for the Potomac by more handsome odds than ever," this reporter added.

The piece provoked an angry response from both teams. A letter to the editor signed by "National" retorted that both teams had agreed ahead of time that whoever won the pregame coin toss would choose to play on the opponents' field. A member of the Potomacs also wrote in, saying that his team had chosen to play on the Nationals' grounds after winning the coin toss "to disabuse the public of an idea [that] has gained credence that a club could play best on their own ground, and not for any other reason." He also apologized for some of his teammates, who "were betrayed into expressions of triumph, and disposed to be a little more boastful than either good taste or sober second thought would permit." One can assume there wasn't any trash talking or high fives, but celebrations didn't fit in with the game as it was played back then.

One of the first fans was President Lincoln. A November 1860 editorial cartoon shows him vanquishing his three opponents in the presidential race on a baseball diamond. Each candidate holds a bat with his political position: "fusion," "nonintervention," "slavery extension," and, in Lincoln's case, "equal rights and free territory." The president-elect is standing on home plate.

The Potomacs, despite their "championship," soon faded from view, while the Nationals continued to play baseball through the Civil War. In the summer of 1865, they played a tournament against the Brooklyn Atlantics and Philadelphia Athletics at the Ellipse. Lincoln's successor, President Andrew Johnson, let government clerks out early to catch the action. (What a cool boss!) He attended one of the games himself, along with six thousand other fans.

The local team made a poor showing. The Nationals lost the first game, 87–12, to Philadelphia, and then fell to Brooklyn, 34–19. But the game continued to increase in social stature, as players from all teams visited Johnson at the White House. In October, Washington took on another team from Brooklyn, the Excelsiors, and earned a matter of East Coast respect by beating them, 36–30. That night, the home team feted their guests with a "complimentary dinner" of mock turtle soup, baked bluefish with port wine sauce, boiled ham, tongue, leg of mutton with caper sauce, and other old-school entrees.

The rivalry with New York continued the next season. An 1866 newspaper story observed: "This game is becoming a matter of national importance. As New York is the centre of the fraternity of the North, Washington is the baseball city of the South." In fact, the Nationals' only losses in 1866 were in New York, according to "The Washington Nationals and the Development of America's National Pastime," a historical paper by Frank Ceresi and Carol McMains. "As much of a mark as the Nationals had made in the capital region, even being dubbed 'champions of the South,' New York was still the baseball capital," they write. Also in 1866, the Nationals accepted a challenge from the American Cricket Club. The Nationals smoked their bat-and-ball cousins, 70–10.

The following season, 1867, the Nationals took off on a tour of what was then considered the West—cities like Cincinnati, Louisville, Indianapolis, Chicago, and St. Louis. Winning big, the Nationals walloped opponents by margins as large as 53–10, 88–12, and 90–10, before being upset by the Forest City Club of Rockford, Illinois, 29–23, their only loss of the trip. Washington rebounded by throttling the Chicago Excelsiors, 49–4.

The gentlemanly era of the sport was passing. In 1870, a poolroom owner named Mike Scanlon laid the groundwork for more organized baseball by building a ballpark at the corner of 17th and S Streets, N.W., complete with five hundred seats. His team, the Olympics, entered the National Association of Professional Base Ball Players the following season, winning 16 of 31 games. The Nationals joined them in the league in 1872. But setting a pattern of Washington baseball futility, both teams finished at the bottom of the league—the Nationals last in the eleven-team league, and the Olympics eighth.

The league disbanded in 1875, replaced by the National League of Professional Base Ball Clubs in 1876, which did not include a Washington franchise. But D.C. teams did make several appearances in the 1880s: the Washington Statesmen in the American Association, the Washington Nationals in the Union Association, and a four-year stint by the Washington Nationals in the National League. None of them were any good. The Nationals, for example, finished last three times in the eight-team National League, and seventh once, before hanging up their spikes after the 1889 season.

But the Nats did feature some notable players in their short big-league run. One was Cornelius Alexander McGillicuddy, an excellent defensive catcher and fan favorite. Sportswriters shortened his name to Connie Mack, and the young catcher went on to make his mark as a Hall of Fame manager. He managed the Philadelphia Athletics an amazing fifty years, covering the first half of the twentieth century.

In 1888, a deaf-mute player named William Hoy, known as "Dummy" Hoy, stole eighty-two bases as a rookie outfielder for Washington. According to legend, umpires began to use hand signals to accommodate his disability. Seventy-three years later, at the age of ninety-nine, he threw out the first ball of the 1961 World Series. His life story was turned into a play called *The Signal Season of Dummy Hoy*.

Visiting ballplayers in Hoy's days stayed at the downtown Willard Hotel, where they would sit in armchairs in front of the building, chew tobacco, and fraternize with fans on a street nicknamed "Boulevard de Base Ball." A *Washington Star* story described an interaction one day between player Mike Kelly and a local fan.

"Why is it that Washington can't win any pennant?" the fan asked.

"Because you are so damned busy making money in that place across the street," Kelly responded, pointing to the Treasury Building, "that you don't give time enough to the honest occupation of playing baseball right."

A new Washington team was admitted to an expanded twelve-team National League in 1892. Unfortunately, this early version of the Senators wasn't much better than its predecessors, finishing higher than ninth only once, and never playing over .500 in its eight years of existence.

The Senators were owned by a pair of brothers from Philadelphia, George and J. Earl Warner, who did little to advance baseball's cause in Washington. The National League bought out the Senators after the 1899 season, returning to eight teams again, as the league also folded franchises in Louisville, Baltimore, and Cleveland. When Ban Johnson started the American League in 1901, Washington was given another chance. This new team was named the Nationals, to avoid confusion with the 1890s team, but fans would continue to refer to them as the Senators.

Washington got off to a bad start. It finished with a .449 winning percentage, sixth place in the eight-team league, blowing one game to Cleveland after leading, 13–5, with two outs in the ninth inning. The team's luck would not improve any time soon. In 1902, Washington signed outfielder Ed Delahanty away from the Philadelphia Phillies of the rival National League, giving him a $1,000 bump in salary to $4,000. Coming off a season in which he batted .354 for the Phillies, Delahanty was one of the best hitters in the game, and he turned it up a notch for the Senators in 1902, hitting .376. But just two months into the 1903 season, Delahanty, who drank heavily, was suspended for missing a game. He boarded a train from Detroit to New York and was ejected near Niagara Falls for threatening riders. His body was found a few days later in the Niagara River. He was thirty-five.

That 1903 season, Washington stumbled to a last-place finish, one of many, with a 43–94 record (.314). In 1904, the Nationals lost their first thirteen games on their way to the franchise's worst season ever, 38–113 (.252), and another last-place finish. The team averaged only 1,689 fans a game that year, last in the American League. The team would finish no higher than seventh place until the 1912 season.

A turning point came in 1907. That season, manager Joe Cantillon sent the team's catcher, Cliff Blankenship, on a western scouting trip to check out some prospects. One was speedster Clyde Milan, who made the team that year and became the Senators' starting center fielder for the next decade and a half. The other was a young player pitching in Idaho who had come recommended by a traveling salesman.

Walter Perry Johnson, just nineteen years old, impressed Blankenship immediately. "You can't hit what you can't see," the catcher telegraphed Cantillon. "I've signed him and he is on his way."

The Nationals acted just in time. The New York Highlanders' manager, Clark Griffith, had also gotten word from a friend in Idaho to check out the flame-throwing teenager. By the time Griffith wrote back to send Johnson to New York for a tryout, Washington had already signed him. It worked out well for Griffith, who took over the Senators a few years later.

Johnson was quickly labeled a can't-miss by Washington sportswriters. "SECURES A PHENOM," a *Washington Post* headline declared on June 30, 1907. A subhead explained, "Johnson His Name and He Hails from the Wooly West." The story reports that Johnson had pitched seventy-five scoreless innings in the semipro Idaho State League and averaged more than fifteen strikeouts a game. Cantillon helped fuel the hype, perhaps tongue-in-cheek, by saying, "If this fellow is what they say he is we (will) have to use only two men in a game, a catcher and Johnson. He strikes out most of the men, so why have an infield and an outfield? I shall give all the boys but the catchers days off when Johnson pitches."

That was just barely hyperbole. Johnson posted a 1.88 ERA in 110 innings for the Senators that year. The team was so awful, finishing with a .325 winning percentage in 1907, that Johnson's pitching prowess was good for just a

5–9 record. But the "Big Train" was on his way. The next year, his first full season, Johnson managed to go 14–14 for another bad Senators team, this time with a 1.65 ERA. He "slumped" to a 2.22 ERA in 1909, the only time in his first ten years with an ERA that topped 2.00.

Not only was Johnson an exceptional athlete, he was an exception to one of sports' unfortunate truisms: Arrogance and greatness go hand in hand. A nonsmoker and nondrinker, Johnson's strongest expression was, "Goodness gracious sakes alive." He hated to hit batters; Ty Cobb admitted that he took advantage of Johnson's good nature by crowding the plate, knowing Johnson would not brush him back.

Sportswriters nicknamed him "Sir Walter" and the "White Knight." Teammates called him "Barney," for the race car driver Barney Oldfield. Another of his many nicknames was "The Big Swede," even though Johnson hailed from German stock, but he never bothered to correct the record. "There are a lot of nice Swedish people, I guess," he said. "I don't want to offend anybody."

Hitters sure found him offensive. Once, Johnson blew two fastballs by Cleveland's Ray Chapman, and the batter started walking back to the dugout. When the umpire told him he had only two strikes, Chapman responded, "I know, and you can have the next one. It won't do me any good."

Folks also called Johnson the "Kansas Cyclone," playing off his birthplace of Humboldt, Kansas. Legend has it that he developed his pitching speed by pitching hay on the farm back in Kansas. Johnson wasn't your classic power pitcher. He actually threw more with a sidearm delivery and didn't mix in many off-speed pitches. "Walter's idea of a changeup was to just throw harder," said Cobb, arguably the best hitter in baseball history. "The first time I faced him, I watched him take that easy windup—and then something went past me that made me flinch," Cobb writes in his book, *My Life in Baseball*. "I hardly saw the pitch, but I heard it. The thing just hissed with danger. Every one of us knew we'd met the most powerful arm ever turned loose in a ballpark."

William McCarty watched Johnson as a young fan. "He had a windmill windup, and when he got through with it, he'd throw it as hard as anyone at the time," recalls McCarty, who became team mascot and ball boy in the early 1930s, when Johnson was manager. "But he was a very soft guy. He set a great example, telling me the things I needed to do to succeed in life."

Johnson set the all-time strikeout record of 3,508 (later broken by Nolan Ryan) and led the league in strikeouts a dozen times. His 417–279 record (.599) puts him second in career wins, behind Cy Young. He still holds the record for career shutouts, with 110, which surely will never be matched in today's obsessive pitch count era. Once, he shut out the New York Highlanders (later renamed the Yankees) three times in four days. He probably could have thrown four shutouts, except that there was no Sunday baseball played back then in New York.

Johnson could do it all. In those days, when starting pitchers often came in to relieve on their days "off," Johnson went 40–30 with thirty-four saves out of the bullpen. He had a career batting average of .235, with twenty-four home runs, and hit an astonishing .433 in one season.

But Johnson played for lousy teams early on, and he didn't have a winning record until his fourth year in the big leagues. That season, 1910, he had a breakout year—a 25–17 record, 1.36 ERA, and a career-high 313 strikeouts. Johnson may have been a nice guy, but he knew his value. Holding out before the next season, he demanded that the team double his salary to $9,000. He finally settled on a three-year deal at $7,000 a year.

Despite having the game's best pitcher, the Senators continued to struggle. In Johnson's first five seasons, the Nationals finished in seventh place three times and last twice, including a 42–110 record in 1909—a .276 winning percentage. The team was so bad that year that in Johnson's five starts in July, Washington failed to score even one run for him. It's no wonder that he lost a career-high twenty-five games in 1909.

The franchise's fortunes changed dramatically in 1912, when Clark Griffith took over as manager. The Griffith name became synonymous with Washington baseball for the next half-century. Griffith was born in a log cabin in Clear Creek, Missouri, in 1869. His father was shot and killed when Clark was just two years old, mistaken for a deer while hunting. Griffith later claimed that outlaw Jesse James had been a friend of his father's and slept in his home one night.

Young Clark and his siblings spent time growing up with relatives. "My early life made me very sympathetic toward orphans," he wrote years later. Griffith and his wife, known as "Aunt Addie," would adopt the children of her late brother, Jimmy Robertson, and the children would work for the team in one capacity or another, including Griffith's ultimate successor, Calvin.

That sympathy was manifested in other parts of his life as well. *Washington Post* sports editor Shirley Povich recalled years later being in Griffith's office one day when the newspaper ran photos of a widow and two small children on the sidewalk after being evicted. "The tough little former pitcher who in one season had been thrown out of more baseball games than any other player in history reacted to the eviction picture," Povich wrote.

Griffith told the team secretary, "Find these people and bring them to my house and rent them a house of their own before the day is over and pay the rent for six months and call some of our friends in Congress and get the lady a job." Then he turned to Povich and said, "If this gets in the paper I'll take you out in the woodshed and give you what you deserve."

At the age of seven, Griffith got his first taste of baseball as a mascot for a local team, and he became bat boy two years later. After four years of semipro ball, he began his big-league career with the St. Louis Browns of the American Association, at the age of twenty-one.

Griffith's build was all wrong for pitching. He was just five feet, six inches tall, weighing 156 pounds, and the mustard on his fastball was definitely of the mild variety. Still, by cunning and grit—and no hesitation in scuffing up the ball—he became a good pitcher, winning twenty games seven times and finishing his career with a .619 winning percentage and a 3.31 ERA. His best years were in the 1890s for Cap Anson's Chicago Colts (an early name for the team that would become the Cubs).

But Griffith's true calling was not pitching, and, in December 1900, he helped change the course of baseball. Ban Johnson, president of a minor circuit called the Western League, and Charles Comiskey, a Western League team owner, plotted along with Griffith to upgrade to big-league status—the American League.

Griffith's main charge was to lure players away from the National League, giving the upstart organization instant credibility. Griffith, one of Comiskey's former players, prevailed upon thirty-nine National Leaguers to switch leagues, according to a 1940 *Saturday Evening Post* profile.

When the league started up in 1901, Griffith became a player-manager of Comiskey's Chicago White Stockings and led them to a first-place finish and the league's inaugural pennant. (The first World Series was still two years away.) Griffith also went 24–7 with a 2.67 ERA. In 1903, he became the first manager of the New York Highlanders. Griffith piloted the New York team for five and a half years but quit in 1908, as the team was on its way to a last-place finish. Returning to his old league, he managed three years for the Cincinnati Reds but was unhappy in the senior circuit. He would later refer to his time with the Reds as his "exile back in the National League."

Then a dream job opened up, although only in his eyes: managing in Washington. It wasn't exactly a plum gig, and many friends tried to talk Griffith out of taking a job in what was considered a baseball graveyard. Washington had yet to have a winning record in eleven seasons and was coming off its second straight seventh-place season entering the 1912 campaign. Griffith signed for $7,500 a year and paid $27,000 to buy a 10 percent ownership in the team, making him the single largest stockholder. He mortgaged his six-thousand-acre Montana ranch for $20,000 to come up with most of the money.

Griffith immediately cleaned house. He traded catcher Gabby Street to New York and unloaded several veteran players as part of a youth movement. On May 30, 1912, Griffith purchased twenty-four-year-old first baseman Chick Gandil for $12,000. The Senators immediately reeled off seventeen straight wins. Gandil would hit .305 that year, with fifteen triples in just 117 games. He would later be suspended for life for his role in the infamous Chicago Black Sox scandal in the 1919 World Series.

Clyde Milan, the outfielder who was discovered along with Walter Johnson in 1907, became the team's spark plug. Milan batted .306 in 1912, with a league-best eighty-eight stolen bases and eleven triples. Johnson, still just twenty-four years old, went 33–12, with a 1.39 ERA and 303 strikeouts.

Under Griffith's guidance, the Senators catapulted in the standings to second place. Not only did they have their first .500 season, they played at nearly a .600 clip, finishing at .599. Griffith led the team to another second-place finish in 1913, when Johnson, at the age of twenty-five, would have his best year ever—36–7, 1.14 ERA, eleven shutouts, and the first of his two Most Valuable Player Awards. That season, Griffith offered the Detroit Tigers $100,000 for Ty Cobb ($2.3 million in 2012 dollars) but was rebuffed. With Cobb and Johnson on the same team, there's no telling how good the Senators could have become.

But after the Senators slipped to a disappointing third place in 1914, they almost lost Johnson. In the offseason, the Big Train signed a contract with the Chicago team of the upstart Federal League. Griffith traveled to Kansas City to meet with Johnson, gave him a guilt trip about American League loyalty, and, more importantly, agreed to match the salary. Johnson remained a Senator.

Griffith would never win a pennant as manager of the Senators, but the "Old Fox" did lay the groundwork for the team's first pennant through smart trades and signings. In 1915, he landed outfielder Sam Rice for $600 and got first baseman Joe Judge as a throw-in as part of another deal. Judge anchored Washington teams as an excellent defensive first baseman and perennial .300 hitter. Rice, a future Hall of Famer, would hit .322 for his career.

As if an early proponent of Moneyball, Griffith continued to get young, cheap players who would pay dividends in the team's glory years of the 1920s. He bought second baseman Bucky Harris, who, as a "boy wonder" manager, would lead the team to its first pennant in 1924, for $4,000. He landed future Hall of Fame outfielder Goose Goslin, who blossomed into a .316 career hitter, for $6,000. Griffith also traded for shortstop Roger Peckinpaugh, who became the glue on Washington's steady infield. These players helped form the nucleus of the 1924 Senators World Series championship team.

On the field, Griffith wasn't able to sustain the managerial magic of his first two seasons, when the team finished in second place. The next five years, Griffith-managed teams finished no better than third, and as low as seventh. After the 1919 season, Griffith found a wealthy backer, Philadelphia exporter William Richardson, and the two men bought a controlling interest in the team, with Griffith becoming team president. He managed one season after that, but the team finished in sixth place, and Griffith decided to replace himself as skipper with shortstop George McBride. Griffith changed managers each of the next three seasons after that, trying to find the winning formula. In 1924, he would finally find his man.

TWO

Washington's Only Championship

WASHINGTON'S ONLY CHAMPIONSHIP

By 1923, all but two of the American League's eight teams had gone to the World Series at least once. The sad-sack St. Louis Browns and the Washington Senators were the only exceptions. Coming off two straight losing seasons and four managers in four years, the Nats gave no indication they would be pennant contenders in 1924. Owner Clark Griffith, who had been the first of those four managers, realized he needed to make a bold move and offered the manager's job to his twenty-seven-year-old second baseman, Bucky Harris.

Griffith knew something about young managers. He had started his own skipper career at the age of thirty-one, as player-manager of the Chicago White Sox in 1901, and led the team to an American League pennant that season. Still, sportswriters derided Harris's hiring as "Griffith's Folly." "Those boys are going to get somewhere this year," Griffith insisted at the team's spring training facility in Tampa, Florida.

In fact, Washington had a pretty talented team, despite its mediocre record the previous couple of years. Its outfield featured two future Hall of Famers, Goose Goslin and Sam Rice, along with Nemo Leibold, all of whom hit .300 or better in 1923. Harris and fiery shortstop Roger Peckinpaugh provided a solid double-play combination, and first baseman Joe Judge provided outstanding defense and offense, batting .314 in 1923. Catcher Muddy Ruel hit .316, giving the team five .300 hitters. The only thing the offense lacked was power, as no regular had hit more than nine home runs in 1923.

Walter Johnson, one of the greatest pitchers of all time, anchored a pitching staff that also included a pair of talented southpaws, George Mogridge and Tom Zachary, and a rubber-armed young reliever, Firpo Marberry. Johnson, now thirty-six years of age, was not quite the unhittable pitcher he had been in the first ten years of his career, when he had an ERA over 2.00 only one year. Still, he was the ace of the staff, and his 1923 numbers had been good by mortal standards—a 17–12 record and 3.48 ERA.

In the beginning of the season, it looked like another typical Washington baseball season. After twenty-eight games, the Senators were 12–16, the same record as the previous season, and the hiring of Harris as manager appeared to make no difference. Ty Cobb, the player-manager of the rival Detroit Tigers, made it tougher on the young manager by calling him "baby face" and "snookums."

Washington struggled to play .500 baseball for the first two months of the year, and by mid-June, the Senators fell into sixth place, with a 24–26 record. But the team won its next five games, providing some momentum heading into a four-game series against the first-place Yankees in New York.

The Nationals barged into Yankee Stadium by sweeping a Monday afternoon doubleheader, 5–3 and 4–2. They took the third game of the series the next day, 4–3, and completed the stunning four-game sweep by squeaking past the New Yorkers, 3–2. Looking up, the Senators found no one above them in the standings. "Washington got hot quicker than almost any club I ever saw," Babe Ruth would write years later in his autobiography.

Eight thousand fans welcomed the team home upon its return to Union Station after the series. "Oh You Nationals!" the *Washington Post* declared. "Washington fans for the first time in their lives will experience the thrill of seeing the home representatives take the field tomorrow afternoon as the official defender of first place."

The Nationals extended their winning streak to ten games the next day, as Johnson blanked the Athletics, 5–0, in the first game of a doubleheader at Griffith Stadium. But the streak ended in the second game, when Ed Rommel shut out the Senators, 1–0.

By the time Washington and New York met again for a five-game series starting on July 4, the Nationals had opened up a four-game lead over their rivals. But the Yankees quickly stormed back into the race, taking four of the five games to pull within one game of the Senators. A few days later, the Yankees reclaimed first place. They would hold on to it for most of July and August, while Washington kept close, never falling more than three games back. By the time the two teams met again in late August for another pivotal four-game series in New York—the teams' last matchup of the year—the Nationals had shaved the lead to half a game.

In the opener, Babe Ruth smacked two home runs. But Goose Goslin hit for the cycle, and the Nationals rallied for eight eighth-inning runs en route to an 11–6 victory, propelling the team into first place. The Senators took the second game, 5–1, but saw their pennant hopes flash before their eyes when a line drive off the bat of Wally Schang slammed into Walter Johnson's pitching hand. The Big Train "crumpled up like an accordion," in the words of *Washington Post* sportswriter Frank H. Young. The game was delayed for five minutes as players from both teams gathered around Johnson, who was lifted from the game. Luckily for the Nats, the injury was not serious.

Although New York won the third game, 2–1, behind the pitching of Waite Hoyt, the Senators came back to take the series finale, 4–2, on a two-run double by Sam Rice in the top of the tenth inning, disappointing forty-five thousand fans in the Bronx. By winning three of the four games, Washington claimed the season series, 13–9. Even more impressive, the Nationals had won nine of eleven games played between the two teams at Yankee Stadium.

But the Yankees kept the pressure on their southern rivals. On September 1, Washington swept a doubleheader against the Philadelphia Athletics but couldn't widen its lead, as the Yankees won both games of a twin billing against the Red Sox. Two days later, New York pulled within one game, beating the Red Sox while the Nationals had the day off.

For the first two weeks of September, the two teams battled to a near standstill in the standings, with New York gaining no more ground, but Washington failing to pull more than two games ahead. The deadlock broke on September 15, when the Yankees finally caught the Nats by defeating the Chicago White Sox, 2–0, while Washington lost by an identical score to the Tigers in Detroit. Not only did the Senators fall into a tie with New York, they found themselves with only a four-game lead over third-place Detroit, the only other team still in the pennant race.

Washington's trip to Detroit kicked off a crucial four-city western road trip, which would also take the team to Cleveland, St. Louis, and Chicago. But the Senators did not face the usual road-field disadvantage. Fans across the country had taken to the Nats, the sentimental favorite that year, partly because the team had never won a pennant. More importantly, fans wanted to see Johnson finally make it to the World Series after so many years spent playing for lousy teams. "There is more genuine interest in him than there is in a presidential election," Will Rogers wrote in a syndicated column in September, entitled "Everybody Is Pulling for Walter."

Harris understood the dynamic and urged the team from Washington to be politic. "Let's not make any enemies if we can help it," he told the players. "Most of the western clubs would rather see us win the pennant than the Yankees. Let's beat 'em, but treat 'em nice."

On September 19, the Senators pulled a game ahead of the Yankees, with a 15–9 victory over the St. Louis Browns, while the Yankees lost to the Tigers, 6–5, in Detroit. Sam Rice, Goose Goslin, and Earl McNeely paced Washington with four hits apiece. The Tigers, meanwhile, were reduced to playing spoiler; despite their victory, they had fallen seven games off the pace.

The prospect of the team's first pennant had Washington in a state of crazed excitement. Fans couldn't turn on ESPN or check their cellphones for updates, but they could see the scores posted by the half-inning on walls of office buildings and groceries. "Base ball in D.C. Classed Disease in Epidemic Form," declares a headline in the September 20 *Washington Evening Star*. The hyperbole continued in the story as follows:

> Base ball in the National Capital no longer is a national game. It is a disease, a flaming epidemic, and if something doesn't happen soon to ease the strain on the faithful fans, half the population of the District of Columbia will be dead of heart failure.
>
> No army fighting in foreign lands ever had the support that the old home town is giving to the Nationals in their dazzling fight for the American League pennant out there in the West, where men are men, where base hits are a blessing and errors the saddest words of tongue or pen.

Back then, the manly West referred to such rugged outposts as Cleveland, Detroit, and Chicago. St. Louis constituted the baseball frontier, with no major-league teams south or west of the city.

Even gray federal bureaucrats were getting swept up, the *Star* said: "In the government departments, Uncle Sam is losing thousands of dollars a day through the utter helplessness of his employees. They've got the base ball palsy."

If fans were truly on the verge of heart attacks, the Senators' next game would have sent them into cardiac arrest. A day after scoring fifteen runs, Washington found that fourteen just didn't cut it, losing to the Browns, 15–14, in ten innings. Protecting a 14–13 lead with one out and the bases loaded in the bottom of the tenth, the Nationals had a chance to win when St. Louis pinch hitter Herschel Bennett tapped one back to the mound for a potential double play.

But rather than throw home to start a one-two-three twin killing, pitcher Firpo Marberry turned around and threw the ball to second base. Unfortunately, no one was covering the bag, and the ball sailed into the outfield, allowing the tying and winning runs to score. Marberry's miscue was the team's sixth error of the game, and it helped nullify three Washington comebacks. Starting pitcher Walter Johnson lasted just one inning, getting hammered for four runs (three earned). "The Nationals made a terrible showing, especially for a team with pennant aspirations," the *Post* commented. The loss prevented the team from getting some breathing room from the Yankees, who also lost. The lead stayed at just one game.

"We were never so surprised in our lives at the way those western teams fought us—fought us in the face of the boos and protests of their own fans," Joe Judge recalled a few weeks later. "You know we knocked St. Louis out of the pennant race two years ago, and I guess they just smacked their lips in anticipation when we landed in town, needing that series like we never needed anything else in our lives. Man, they came at us like an avalanche."

But Washington rebounded from the tough loss, winning the rubber game in St. Louis the next day, while the Yankees again lost in Detroit and widened the lead to two games. That set the stage for the final few games of the season. Washington would travel to Chicago for a three-game series against the White Sox and then finish the season at Fenway Park with a four-game set against the Red Sox—two of the league's bottom-feeders. New York's schedule was nearly equally soft—three games on the road against Cleveland, followed by a four-game series in Philadelphia against the Athletics, also among the league's weaker teams.

But the seventh-place White Sox were not content to play out the string. "The Nationals now realize they have a hard fight on their hands," the *Star* reported after Washington won the first game, 8–3, behind Walter Johnson's thirteenth consecutive victory. The Sox ran the bases as if they, and not the Senators, were in a pennant race, "and when forced to slide did not hesitate to make the National infielders keep a sharp outlook for spikes." Washington trailed for most of the game, but rallied for six runs in the seventh inning to turn a 3–1 deficit into a 7–3 lead. New York kept pace by beating the Indians, 10–4, in Cleveland.

The two American League pennant leaders continued to keep the heat on one another the next day. Washington eked out a 7–6 victory over the White Sox, nearly blowing a 7–3 lead, while New York beat Cleveland, 8–2. On September 24, the Nationals completed a three-game sweep of Chicago, with a 6–3 victory, but the Yankees again stayed even, beating the Indians, 2–0. Washington had finished its western tour by winning nine of twelve games.

"That the Yankees have been so persistent in their efforts to remain around the top of the heap has not bothered the Bucks greatly," the *Star* wrote, turning the Nats' nickname into one named for the team's manager. "They have shaken off the Gotham horde three times this season and have no fear of it."

After a day off Thursday, both teams began their season-ending series on Friday. Washington immediately heightened tensions by losing to Boston, 2–1, while New York hammered the Philadelphia Athletics, 7–1. The loss snapped Washington's four-game winning streak, Johnson's thirteen-game winning streak, and Sam Rice's thirty-one-game hitting streak. Now Washington led by just one game with three to go.

In the loss to Boston, the Senators had a chance to tie the game in the ninth inning but ran themselves out of a rally. With runners on first and third and two outs, Washington base runner Roger Peckinpaugh took off for second base on a delayed steal, but he was tagged out in a rundown before the runner on third, Ossie Bluege, could score.

A tie in the standings looked like a distinct possibility. In that case, New York and Washington would play a best-of-three playoff series to determine the pennant winner. Manager Bucky Harris encouraged his depressed players to shake off the loss: "We'll win our games and let those Yankees take care of themselves. Don't expect them to waver. Just see to it that we don't and we'll take the championship back to Washington Wednesday. We are good enough to win, and if we play our game we will win."

The team responded with a 7–5 victory the next day, which brought Washington tantalizingly close to its first pennant. Coupled with the Yankees' 4–3 loss in Philadelphia, Washington now had a two-game lead with just two games to go. The phrase "magic number" had not yet been coined, but people still grasped the concept. The Nats needed just one victory or one Yankees loss to clinch the pennant. Meanwhile, in the National League, the New York Giants had iced their fourth straight pennant by beating the Philadelphia Phillies, 5–1.

Both the Nationals and Yankees had to cool their heels the next day. Neither Boston nor Philadelphia played home games on Sundays during that time because of blue laws. Trying to stay relaxed, Senators' players used the day off to sightsee around Boston, attend football games, or go fishing.

Although a Yankees loss would clinch a Nationals pennant, Manager Harris was not banking on it: "We are going to put every ounce of fighting strength into tomorrow's game and pack away the old American League pennant; we are not depending on the Athletics beating the Yankees in Philadelphia either tomorrow or Tuesday, for I feel positive that we will experience little difficulty in disposing of the Red Sox in one of the remaining two games here, one victory assuring us of the first championship ever won by a Washington ball team."

Washington started Tom Zachary, the pitcher who had come out of the bullpen to save the previous game, but he didn't have it this time, surrendering two runs in three innings. Zachary did contribute offensively, going 2-for-2, and was lifted in the fourth inning for a pinch runner, with Washington clinging to a 3–2 lead.

So once again, the Nationals were forced to turn to their rubber-armed reliever, Firpo Marberry, although that rubber had been stretched thin of late. Marberry was making his fiftieth appearance of the season (including fourteen starts), and his tenth in the team's last nineteen games. Just the day before, he had complained of a sore arm, which was diagnosed as a slight muscle strain.

Marberry's arm had some elasticity left after all. He pitched five straight scoreless innings, giving up only three hits, and then started the ninth inning with a 4–2 lead. But with one out, pinch hitter Danny Clark singled off Marberry, and Denny Williams, who had collected two hits on the day, came up with a chance to tie the game. But this time, he managed just a ground ball to second baseman Bucky Harris, and the player-manager stepped on second base and threw to first, for a pennant-clinching double play.

The celebration at Fenway Park that followed must have made the Senators feel like they had been playing on their home field. The fifteen thousand Red Sox fans were caught up in the national craze for the nation's capital team, with a little extra incentive, as Washington's pennant denied Boston's hated rival, the Yankees, a chance to repeat as American League champions.

Hundreds of fans rushed onto the field to mob the Senators, and thousands more cheered the team as it left the field. They tossed straw hats into the air and waved handkerchiefs, and some lifted Nats owner Griffith from his seat in the stands and ferried him down to the dugout. Griffith, Harris, and Johnson received standing ovations.

Meanwhile, back in Washington, in the days before fans could gather in sports bars to see their teams on the road, thousands had congregated in the drenching rain to watch the mechanical scoreboards register updates from Boston. More fortunate fans listened to the game indoors on the city's first radio station, WRC, which had just begun broadcasting two months earlier.

In Philadelphia, rain washed out the scheduled Yankees–Athletics doubleheader, and the meaningless games were not made up. New York's season was over. But having vanquished one New York team, Washington now had to take on another—the ten-time National League champion New York Giants. Washington's pennant broke up a Big Apple baseball monopoly—the previous three World Series had been New York–New York affairs.

"Naturally we are a happy lot, just like one big family, everybody tickled," Griffith said. He continued, saying,

> We are going after the World Series and realize in that connection that we are going up against the hardest club in the majors. The Giants have a wonderful ball club and are at their very best when the stakes are heaviest.

I have no fear of the ball club cracking even though we are not as experienced as the Giants. We will give our best, and it will be a series [that] Washington, at least, will long remember.

He added that the pennant "vindicated" his much-maligned decision to hire the young and unproven Harris as manager. "I knew he could do it and he did," Griffith declared.

For Harris, it was business as usual. Before leaving Boston to return to Washington, the player-manager told his players, "Winning the pennant means just another hard job for us, fellows, so after you land in Washington Wednesday get all the rest you can before reporting at the ball yard at one o'clock for practice."

The next day's *Star* ran a three-column cartoon featuring a smiling and celebrating Uncle Sam; the Washington Monument turned into semihuman form with outstretched arms, one hoisting a pennant; and even the Capitol Dome shaped like a baseball, with the bronze female statue on the top yelling, "Hooray!"

"The champions are not Washington's alone," wrote sportswriter John B. Keller. "They belong to the country, as typified in its National Capital, and the entire Nation insists upon sharing with Washington the joy and pride that follows the Griffmen."

President Calvin Coolidge, a Yankee in the literal sense (hailing from Vermont), sent a telegram to Manager Harris, saying, "Heartiest congratulations to you and your team for your great work in bringing Washington its first pennant. We of Washington are proud of you and behind you. On to the world's championship."

Other branches of government celebrated as well. "The good news gives me a distinct thrill," said Supreme Court Justice Joseph McKenna. "I am delighted, and I am sure that all of Washington feels likewise."

The U.S. postmaster, James E. Power, traveled three thousand miles from California—in the days before transcontinental flights—to attend the World Series. "Out in California, everybody was rooting for Washington to win," he said. Major League Baseball on the West Coast was more than thirty years away.

Even Ty Cobb, the player-manager of the Detroit Tigers, jumped on the bandwagon. "I didn't win the pennant, but I had the consolation of kicking the Yankees out of the race, and I got quite a kick out of that," he said, referring to Detroit's three-game sweep of New York in the final weeks of the season. He said he was rooting for Washington to win the series. "They are imbued with the competitive spirit, and they'll fight hard."

On the train ride back to Washington, Judge said the team tapped the national affection for inspiration. "We knew that the country wanted us to win, and that's what helped to keep us fighting," he said. But Judge was miffed at a New York newspaper story that predicted easy pickings for the Giants. "This bird is going to be a lot wiser, but sadder, when this series is over," he said of the New York reporter.

If the Nationals needed some confidence, all they needed was a pep talk from their batboy, Frankie, who was practically blasé about the pennant. "What's all the fuss about?" the batboy told a newspaper reporter, adding:

> Goodnight, the time to shout was a month ago. Why, it was a cinch. We had that pennant all ironed out and properly creased with a special place built for it in my bat bag four weeks ago. The Giants? Say, you're not kidding me, are you? If you've got any extra money and want to make a lot more, easy, see, soak it all on the Nats. They're there, I tell you.

Frankie's bravado notwithstanding, the Giants posed a formidable challenge. The team had won its fourth straight pennant and featured future Hall of Fame manager John McGraw, already legendary in baseball circles. McGraw, one of the few managers to wear a suit and tie in the dugout rather than a uniform, had been at the helm of the Giants since 1902, guiding the team to ten pennants.

Despite Walter Johnson, most observers gave New York the edge in pitching—then, as now, crucial in a short series. The Giants' rotation featured two sixteen-game winners, Virgil Barnes and Jack Bentley; talented left-hander Art Nehf, who went 14–4; and Hugh McQuillan, who posted a low 2.69 ERA. They performed especially strongly down the pennant stretch drive.

The offense featured an astonishing six future Hall of Famers: George Kelly, who led the league with 136 RBIs, and whose twenty-one homers were just one less than the entire Washington team; Frankie Frisch, the scrappy team captain and perennial .300 hitter who hit .328, with fifteen triples and a league-high 121 runs; rookie Bill Terry, who later became the last .400 hitter in National League history; Travis Jackson, a .300 hitter and outstanding defensive shortstop; Ross Youngs, who led the team with a .356 batting average; and rookie Hack Wilson, who six years later set the single-season RBI record, with 191.

Washington's offense stressed getting on base and manufacturing runs, with a special emphasis on the hit-and-run. Only one player hit more than three home runs—outfielder Goose Goslin, who finished with twelve. In fact, the Senators' twenty-two homers during the regular season put them dead last in the American League. But the lineup featured a trio of .300 hitters—Goslin (.344), Sam Rice (.334), and Joe Judge (.324)—and no regular batted below .268.

Aside from Johnson, Washington's pitching staff still had some solid "twirlers," as pitchers were often called back then. Southpaw George Mogridge won sixteen games, and fellow lefty Tom Zachary won fifteen, with a 2.75 ERA. Curly Ogden, acquired during the season, rounded out the rotation with a 2.58 ERA. But there was concern that the staff had been spent by the end of the season. Some even expressed concern that Johnson, despite his stellar season, had finished only twenty of his thirty-eight starts. That would be considered a staggering success in modern-day baseball, but not by 1920s standards. The Big Train, who turned thirty-seven after the season, admitted he wasn't the same pitcher he had been in his prime. "I realize that I cannot go much further," he said. "My arm is still good, but I know I haven't got the stuff I used to have. When the season started I had fully made up my mind to retire at the end of this year. Now it all depends on what comes up this winter."

As usual, Johnson carried the capital's aspirations on his big shoulders. "I think we will win the World Series under any circumstances, but I am doubly sure we will win if Walter Johnson is right," Harris said.

Two thousand fans camped out at Union Station to greet the team upon its return to Washington Wednesday morning, the day after the regular-season finale. In the afternoon, one hundred thousand people jammed Pennsylvania Avenue for a parade to celebrate the team's first pennant. The self-importance that marks Washington was dropped for a day, as the *Star* described it, writing, "This debonair old capital of the United States completely forgot to take itself seriously in its eagerness to give its conquerors a welcome befitting champions."

Whistles, car horns, and cheers punctured the air along the procession, which included mounted policemen, a U.S. Cavalry Band, and red-coated members of the Washington Riding and Hunt Club. At the Ellipse by the White House, President Calvin Coolidge told the players, "By bringing the baseball pennant to Washington you have made the National Capital more truly the center of worthy and honorable national aspirations." Coolidge, joined on the stage by Bucky Harris and Walter Johnson, presented the player-manager with a "loving cup" as a gift. He also joked that now that the team had won the pennant, perhaps the city could actually get some work done. "When the entire population reached the point of requiring the game to be described play-by-play, I began to doubt whether the highest efficiency was being promoted," he said.

The president relayed that he had received a telegram from Congressman John F. Miller of Washington State, asking that Coolidge call a special session of Congress that Saturday so that lawmakers could sneak out and go to the ballpark to see Johnson pitch in the series opener. "Mr. Miller has such judgment and his sense of public psychology is so accurate that I do not need to say what party he represents," Coolidge said of his fellow Republican. After the president left, fans crowded around the stage and shouted out, "Three Cheers for Bucky!" "Welcome Home Bucky!" "Hello, Goose."

But word soon came of a scandal that threatened to derail the World Series. Commissioner Kenesaw Mountain Landis banned a player and coach on the National League champion Giants after learning of an alleged bribery plot. According to Philadelphia Phillies shortstop Heinie Sand, Giants outfielder Jimmy O'Connell had offered him $500 to throw a game against the Giants on the last weekend of the season. The Giants locked up the pennant with a victory in that very game. O'Connell then implicated one of his coaches, Cozy Dolan, as the mastermind behind the plan.

Coming only five years after the infamous Black Sox scandal, in which eight White Sox players had allegedly thrown the 1919 World Series, the sport's integrity was once again at stake. There was even a debate about whether the Fall Classic should be played at all. No less a figure than the American League president, Ban Johnson, second-guessed Commissioner Judge Kenesaw Mountain Landis's decision to go forward with it. "In view of the public statements the World Series should have been called off," he said. Johnson also suggested that there was probably a bigger plot to buy off Phillies players than had been revealed publicly. "It is my opinion that others of the Philadelphia players, in addition to Heinie Sand, were approached in an effort to have games thrown," he stated, and called for a federal investigation.

Pittsburgh Pirates owner Barney Dreyfuss joined Johnson in the criticism. He said:

> If this thing is not cleared up properly and to the entire satisfaction of the public by bringing every guilty man to justice—and there must be more than two involved—I will be in favor of eliminating the World Series, for a time at least, as a growing menace to the best interests of the game.

Dreyfuss added, "It is absurd to say that O'Connell and Dolan were the only ones involved."

O'Connell, in fact, had fingered teammates Frankie Frisch, George Kelly, and Ross Youngs, but Landis cleared the three players. And the commissioner told Johnson and Dreyfuss to buzz off: "It seems to be time for those not clothed with responsibility to keep their shirts on," he said.

Ban Johnson telegraphed Griffith to tell him he would not attend the series, sending the Old Fox into a rage against his erstwhile ally. "Johnson is trying to play baseball politics and is taking advantage of an unpleasant situation with which he has nothing to do, to put Judge Landis in a bad light," the Washington owner said. "We have waited years for this world's series and now Johnson wants to call it off, which would be manifestly unfair to the Senators and to the fans of this city, who have so loyally supported the team."

The series went forward, and it was another Johnson—Walter—who would be the focus of attention. Johnson was coming off an excellent regular season—23–7, with a 2.72 ERA, leading the American League in wins, winning percentage, ERA, strikeouts, and shutouts. It was his best season since 1919. He even hit .283, with a .389 slugging percentage. "Outside of the most rabid of Giant partisans, fans throughout this country will root for him in unison," predicted the Associated Press.

"All the sentiment of sentimental Washington is built around Johnson," the *New York Times* declared. "He is bigger than the Washington Monument, broader than the Potomac River." And the Nationals had the nation pulling for them, the *Times* observed: "Harris and his players are liked everywhere because they are young and dashing and enthusiastic. New York is hated because it has won too many pennants and possesses too much money and is too powerful." Some things never change.

More than one hundred fifty thousand fans tried to get tickets for the first two games at Griffith Stadium, which had been expanded to thirty-six thousand seats to accommodate the World Series crowds. Prices ranged from a buck in the bleachers to six dollars for box seats. Some fans managed to gain admittance by securing jobs as peanut and soda vendors.

Bert Abramson, who was an eleven-year-old boy at the time, got to see the first game of the series for free by taking advantage of a policy that let kids under twelve in for free if they were accompanied by an adult. "There was a big tree outside Griffith Stadium, and we used to stay there, and you'd ask: 'Mister, will you take me in? It won't cost you anything,'" Abramson recalls nearly ninety years later.

Abramson, who turned one hundred shortly after the 2012 season, lived at 7th and N Streets N.W. as a child and walked the eight or nine blocks to the ballpark for that first series game. Once he got inside, he sat on the steps in the pavilion. He says the fans were mostly men in coats and ties. "The crowd was very nice," Abramson says. "It wasn't loud. They didn't have waves. No screaming or anything like that. They would wave the hats. I don't remember any booing." He didn't get to see any other games of the series, because after the first game, the Senators changed the policy and wouldn't let anyone into the ballpark without a ticket.

Abramson's most vivid memory from the 1924 Senators was from a regular-season game he attended: "I remember Walter Johnson—he knocked a home run. And that was very interesting. That was my favorite play. I couldn't believe a pitcher was making a home run! Our man now, Stephen Strasburg, he knocked a home run. And I was telling everybody, I saw Walter Johnson hit a home run, back in '24. I grabbed it. People fell over my head. They were trying to catch the ball. I didn't have a glove, like they do nowadays."

Washington, still very much a southern city at the time, drew fans for the World Series from points all across the South; there was not yet a team in Atlanta or Florida, or even Texas. Downtown hotels were filled to capacity. Fans flooded in from the North, too, as New Yorkers made the more than 200-mile trek down to catch their hometown Giants. An advertisement in the *New York Times* touted special World Series express trains to and from Washington.

But other New Yorkers made the trip to make a buck. Some set up "brokerage" offices to resell tickets at many times face value. Local police rounded up several of these scalpers but were soon overruled by federal officials, who decided that brokers registered with the government could legally sell the tickets. Federal law, however, required the resellers to split their profits equally with the U.S. Treasury Department. Brokers who set up shop on "Scalpers Row" on Pennsylvania Avenue, just a few blocks from the White House, hawked tickets for as much as $100—worth more than $1,300 in 2012 dollars.

Meanwhile, thousands of fans lined up outside the ballpark with hopes of landing one of the last-minute bleacher seats, waiting all night for a shot at getting a ticket. Even here, entrepreneurs plied their trade. "Place speculators" sold spots in line for fees of fifty cents to two dollars.

Hundreds of fans who couldn't get into the ballpark paid fifty cents each to watch the first game from the tops of wooden houses surrounding the ballpark. Another twelve thousand gathered outside the *Washington Post* and *Evening Star* buildings to watch the game recreated on scoreboards. New York City, always on the cutting edge, offered fans a chance to watch a reproduction of the game on a "Playograph," a scoreboard-type device that showed the position of the ball as it made its way around a baseball diamond, as well as the base runners.

At Griffith Stadium, the crowd included ordinary fans, alongside cabinet members, congressmen, senators, foreign ambassadors, and President Coolidge. "For once rank and title meant nothing in Washington," observed the *New York Times*. An army band warmed up the fans with "Sidewalks of New York" and "Dixie." Although it was decades before million-dollar contracts, a couple of Washington Senators made out pretty well during the pregame ceremonies. Washington fans, including Coolidge, chipped in to buy Johnson an $8,000 Lincoln car, while shortstop Roger Peckinpaugh received a Peerless touring car from his hometown Cleveland fans. Coolidge threw out the first pitch, but his errant toss sent umpire Tom Connolly leaping for a one-handed grab.

The president's poor aim was a subtle reminder that he was not a huge fan of the game. That distinction belonged instead to his wife, Grace Goodhue Coolidge, who kept score and told him how the players were doing. The president listened, puffing on a cigar, sending smoke up that mingled with that of other fans' cigars and cigarettes, which formed a hazy cloud in the ballpark. Men were decked out in suits, ties, and fedoras, while women wore dresses and fur-collared coats. On the field, Senators players leaned out of the dugout with their front feet on the playing field and bats neatly laid out on the field in front of them.

The pitching matchup featured the iconic Johnson, thirty-six years old and making his first World Series appearance, against the crafty thirty-two-year-old southpaw Art Nehf, who had won the clinching games in the 1921 and 1922 World Series against the Yankees. The Giants struck quickly. George Kelly hit a solo homer to left field off Johnson in the second inning, with the ball dropping into temporary bleachers that had been installed for the series. Bill Terry did the same in the fourth inning, and New York was up, 2–0. Both balls may have been caught had the makeshift bleachers not been there.

Washington pulled within 2–1 in the sixth inning, when Earl McNeely doubled, moved to third on a grounder, and scored on an RBI groundout by Sam Rice. The Nationals went down in the seventh and eighth, however, and came to bat trailing by a run in the bottom of the ninth inning. With one out, Ossie Bluege singled, and Peckinpaugh followed with a double off the left-field wall to tie the score, sending the crowd into a delirious uproar. The game had to be held up for several minutes as excited fans threw coats, hats, cushions, and newspapers onto the field. A newspaper from the upper deck landed on Coolidge's hat, knocking it off-kilter, and the president took the advice of his Secret Service agents and sat down.

The Nationals stranded Peckinpaugh at second, and the game went into extra innings. In the twelfth, Johnson struck Hank Gowdy in the ribs on ball four, putting the potential go-ahead run on first. Next was Nehf, who lifted a fly to center field. McNeely charged and tried to make a shoestring catch, but the ball squirted free. Worse, he fired wildly past second baseman Harris, and now the Giants had runners on second and third with no one out.

McGraw, having already left his pitcher in to bat earlier in the inning, now sent a second pitcher to the plate, Jack Bentley, to pinch-hit. But Bentley, a former National, wasn't your typical weak-hitting hurler. In two seasons with New York, he had hit .342. Washington intentionally walked him to load the bases and set up a force at home plate.

The next batter, Frisch, hit a ground ball to second, and Harris forced Gowdy at the plate. But Young followed with a soft single to center field, giving the Giants a 3–2 lead. Kelly followed with a sacrifice fly to left to make it 4–2.

The Senators scratched back in their half of the inning. Mule Shirley, pinch-hitting for Johnson, reached second base when shortstop Travis Jackson dropped a pop-up. One out later, Harris singled Jackson home to bring the Nationals to within one. Rice followed with another single, sending the potential tying run to third, but he tried to stretch the hit into a double and was thrown out. Now Washington had a runner on third with two outs, instead of first and third with one out. The next batter, Goslin, grounded out to end the game.

The loss was especially disappointing to Johnson. Some longtime Johnson watchers said he seemed nervous and tried too hard. "Walter yesterday worked with a degree of deliberation that caused widespread comment," the *Star* observed. "He seemed from the very outset to be debating with himself at great length over every delivery he made."

In twelve innings, Johnson had thrown 165 pitches, surrendering two homers and a whopping fourteen hits, but also striking out twelve batters. "Walter pitched a great game," said Nehf, who had outpitched the legend. "It was mighty fine to win, of course, but it would not have been hard to lose to the man I opposed today. There were moments when victory hung on a thread." McGraw, in a syndicated column, called it the "greatest World Series game ever played. . . . In all my experience, I never have seen a game harder played."

The next day, Washington sent Tom Zachary to the mound against Bentley, the former Senator. Washington jumped out to an early 2–0 lead, thanks to a two-run homer by Goose Goslin. Bucky Harris made it 3–0 with a solo homer into the temporary bleachers in the fifth. The Giants plated a run in the seventh and entered the ninth trailing, 3–1.

But Zachary, who had held New York to just four hits through the first eight innings, began to falter. He walked the leadoff batter, Frisch, on four pitches. One out later, Kelly singled to right field, and Frisch scored all the way from first base after right fielder Rice bobbled the ball. Kelly moved into scoring position on a groundout, and now Washington needed only one more out to even the series. But Hack Wilson deflated the fans with an RBI single to right field, bringing Kelly home with the tying run. Zachary was done, and Marberry came in to extinguish the rally by striking out Travis Jackson.

Now in danger of falling behind two games to none, the Nationals knew they had to pull this one out. In the bottom of the ninth, Judge worked a leadoff walk and moved to second on a sacrifice. The crowd cheered wildly as Peckinpaugh came to the plate. The Washington shortstop had made the most of his RBI opportunities during the regular season, driving in seventy-three runs, while hitting only two homers. Now he ripped a line drive down the left-field line for a hit, and Judge crossed the plate with the winning run. But Peckinpaugh pulled a tendon in his leg while sprinting to first base, which would cost him playing time in the series.

Back then, there were no off days in the World Series, so the two teams squared off the next afternoon at the Polo Grounds, located in Upper Manhattan. Games 3, 4, and 5 would be played there, while Game 6, if necessary, would be played back in Washington. A coin toss would determine the location of a possible seventh game.

Even in the World Series, the Nationals maintained their road-fan appeal, as many New York fans cheered on the visitors. Some Giants fans even taunted their own team's role in the bribery scandal, shouting, "Where's Jimmy O'Connell?" and "Put Cozy Dolan on the coaching line!" In Washington, meanwhile, some fans who weren't satisfied looking at mechanical scoreboards or listening on the radio watched the U.S. Marines pantomime the game at Griffith Stadium.

Peckinpaugh tried to play through his injury but only lasted into the third inning, forcing Washington to adopt a makeshift defense on the left side of the infield. Third baseman Ossie Bluege moved to shortstop, and Ralph Miller took over at third base. Peckinpaugh's injury proved costly, as Miller made an error in the sixth inning that led to an unearned run.

Washington started Marberry, normally a relief pitcher, but he fell behind, 3–0, and didn't make it out of the fourth inning. By the top of the ninth, the Nationals trailed, 6–3. Washington loaded the bases and pulled within two runs on a one-out walk to Bluege but could get no closer. The Giants held on for a 6–4 victory, and a 2–1 series lead.

The Nationals got better luck from their starting pitcher in the next game, as George Mogridge went seven-plus innings, allowing only three runs (two earned) on three hits. He left the game to an enthusiastic ovation from the New

York not-so-faithful. Goose Goslin fueled the Washington offense, going 4-for-4, with a home run and four RBIs, to pace the Senators' 7–4 victory. "For the country at large the eagle may remain the national bird, but for the National Capital the greatest bird that flies is the goose," the *Post* opined.

Goslin, it turned out, had received some pretty good hitting advice. "Babe Ruth came to me before the game and told me I was swinging wrong," Goose said. "So I started swinging another way, and you could see the result yourself. I sure do owe a lot to the Babe."

Ruth was among several celebrity athletes at the game. Yankees Joe Dugan and Whitey Witt were also there, along with former Giant player and future Yankees manager Casey Stengel, Ty Cobb, Christy Mathewson, Rogers Hornsby, George Sisler, and boxer Jack Dempsey.

With Johnson taking the mound for the pivotal Game 5, Washington was confident it could take command of the series. A win by the ace would send the series back to Washington with the Nats up three games to two. But once again, Johnson didn't have his good stuff. The Giants hammered him for thirteen hits and six runs (four earned) in eight innings, including four hits by eighteen-year-old Freddy Lindstrom, to take the game, 6–2. A Washington castoff, Bentley outpitched the greatest pitcher of the era, and even smacked two hits off him, including a two-run homer in the fifth inning, giving the Giants a lead they would never relinquish.

Johnson's grandson, Henry W. Thomas, recounted an incident that demonstrated the depth of the pitcher's fan appeal. As the Big Train was getting pounded, the stunned crowd was mostly silent, but one fan started yelling, "Take him out! Take him out!" Sitting in the same section of the stadium was umpire Billy Evans, a longtime friend of Johnson's. "Appalled fans around the man were already turning on him in outrage as Evans came charging over, yelling, 'Let him alone, let me have him. He's mine,'" Thomas writes in a biography of his grandfather. Only the intervention of fans prevented a fistfight.

The game was close for seven and a half innings. Trailing, 3–1, Washington pulled within 3–2 on an eighth-inning solo home run by Goslin. But the Giants broke the game open in the bottom of the frame, scoring three runs off Johnson. The zip on Johnson's fastball had faded, and he made matters worse by committing a key error.

Johnson said after the game he would likely retire. With no more starts scheduled in the series, it appeared as if the Big Train had sputtered on his final ride. Scribes from both cities bemoaned such an unfitting end to such a glorious career. The *Times* led its story the next day like an obituary:

Giant bats penned one of the saddest stories ever known to baseball yesterday. After the name of Walter Johnson they wrote "finis," for it was Johnson, before the second greatest crowd of the series, who tried again and failed again. When Johnson's own world's series finally came along he couldn't win a single game. . . . Even for 52,000 New Yorkers it was a tragic affair and Johnson the most tragic figure that ever stalked through a world's series.

The *Post* expresses a similar sentiment: "No sadder scene was ever presented in World Series annals than the one that was played before 50,000 spectators today."

In the clubhouse after the game, Johnson read telegraphs that had come in during the game wishing him success. "I couldn't hold the Giants, I just couldn't hold them," he said. He continued,

These telegrams make me feel worse about it than ever. I've received wires from all over the world telling me how everyone was pulling for me to win, and I couldn't come through for them. I wish I could have. It's not very encouraging to know that I'll finish up my career in the big leagues with two World Series defeats, but I don't think I'll come back next year.

Harris at least brought some good news to the team's clubhouse. He had won a coin toss, meaning if Washington could win Game 6 at home, Game 7 would be played there as well. "We'll get them in the seventh game," the Washington skipper declared. "This series isn't lost yet by any matter or means."

Peckinpaugh, the fiery shortstop whose injury had kept him out of most of Game 3 and all of Game 4 and Game 5, vowed to play again. The team sorely missed his steady defense. "I'll be in there if I have to tear the leg off and throw it away when the game is over," he said. "My leg doesn't feel any too well, but I'll play if I have to stand on one foot."

Facing elimination the next day, Washington fell behind quickly when New York's George Kelly hit an RBI single off Tom Zachary in the first inning. The Washington pitcher settled down after that, but the Nats couldn't get anything going off the Giants' Nehf, who had also handcuffed them in the series opener. When the Senators came to bat in the bottom of the fifth inning, they trailed, 1–0.

Peckinpaugh limped to the plate to lead off and lined a base hit down the left-field line. Muddy Ruel sacrificed him to second, and Zachary's groundout advanced him to third with two outs. McNeely walked and stole second. Then Harris got an outside pitch and went with it, driving a single to right field, scoring both runs and giving Washington a 2–1 lead.

In the top of the ninth inning, Peckinpaugh's vow to play on one foot if necessary was tested. The Giants got the tying run on base with one out, and Irish Meusel bounced a ball up the middle. Ranging to his left, the limping Peckinpaugh raced over to the ball, fielded it, and tossed it to second base for a force play. He immediately went down after landing awkwardly on his bad leg and had to be carried off the field. Peck was finally done for the series. Zachary sealed the victory by striking out Hack Wilson.

Peckinpaugh's double-play partner and manager, Harris, saluted him in a column the next day. "His statement the day previous that he'd play ball yesterday if he had to break his leg was almost borne out," Harris wrote. "He didn't break his leg, but he turned a tendon, opened up an old charley horse, and must have suffered the agonies of the damned. If that isn't gameness, there's no such thing in athletics."

On a Sunday afternoon in Washington, the two teams squared off for the seventh game. New York started Virgil Barnes, who had surrendered five runs in five innings as the starter in Game 4. Washington gave Curly Ogden his first start of the series, but it was actually a ruse by Harris to get Bill Terry, the rookie Giants left-hander, out of the game.

Terry had obliterated the Washington pitching staff for a .500 batting average through the first six games, but he didn't hit left-handed pitchers well, and McGraw often sat him against southpaws. Harris decided to start the right-handed pitcher Ogden and then bring in a left-handed pitcher, Mogridge, in the first inning, forcing Giants manager McGraw to make a choice: leave Terry in to face a left-handed pitcher or take him out and have him unavailable for the reminder of the game.

Ogden, making his only World Series appearance, faced just two batters, striking out one and walking the other, before Harris made the switch to Mogridge, who got the final two outs. Terry was due to lead off the top of the second, and McGraw decided to leave Terry in the game, at least for a while. Harris's gambit worked, as the red-hot Terry went 0-for-2 before being lifted for a pinch hitter in the sixth inning. Harris also enjoyed success as a hitter, smoking one into the temporary bleachers in left field to give Washington a 1–0 lead in the fourth inning. It was Harris's second homer of the series—double his output the entire regular season.

But New York came storming back in the sixth. After putting men on first and third with no one out, the Giants sent right-handed hitter Irish Meusel in as a pinch hitter for Terry. Harris countered with right-handed reliever Marberry, and Johnson began warming up in the bullpen. Meusel greeted Marberry's first pitch for a sacrifice fly to right field, tying the game.

Then Washington's defense became unglued at the worst possible time. After a single by Hack Wilson put runners at first and third, Travis Jackson hit a ground ball to Judge at first base, but Judge fumbled the ball for an error, allowing the go-ahead run to score. The next batter, Hank Gowdy, hit a ground ball to shortstop, and it looked like Washington would get out of the inning with a 6–4–3 double-play. But the ball went through the legs of Ossie Bluege, normally a third baseman who was filling in for the injured Peckinpaugh. Now the Giants were up, 3–1.

Washington went down in order in the sixth inning and managed two hits in the seventh but could not score. With one out in the bottom of the eighth, pinch hitter Nemo Leibold doubled down the left-field line. He moved to third base on Muddy Ruel's first hit of the series. Backup catcher Bennie Tate, pinch-hitting for Marberry, walked on a 3–2 pitch to load the bases.

With one out and the top of the order coming up, Washington would have two shots at tying the game on a base hit. McNeely flied out to left, and the runners stayed put. Up came Harris, whose homer had accounted for all of Washington's offense up to that point. The player-manager smacked a ground ball to third that proved to many that the Senators were a team of destiny—or at least a team with a friendly home infield. The ball took a bad hop over third baseman Freddy Lindstrom's head and sailed into left field, tying the score at 3–3.

The game was stopped for several minutes as Griffith Stadium convulsed in celebration. Confetti, thousands of pieces of ripped-up newspapers, hats, and coats were thrown onto the field. Wild cheers were mixed in with the sounds of whistles, bells, and horns. McGraw then sent in Nehf, the previous day's starting pitcher, who got Rice to ground out to end the rally.

The fans continued to cheer as the Nationals took the field in the top of the ninth inning, because coming in to pitch one last time was Walter Johnson. He had a chance for redemption that no one could have predicted after his Game 5 loss, but equally possible was that he'd lose again—and finish the series with a 0–3 record. After getting the first batter out, Johnson came dangerously close to losing his third World Series game, as Frisch tripled to deep center field.

Washington intentionally walked the next batter, Ross Youngs, who had hit .356 during the regular season. But there was no relief in the Giants lineup, as National League RBI leader George Kelly came to the plate. In the previous matchup in Game 5, Kelly had singled off Johnson to start the eighth-inning rally that put the game out of reach. But this was not the same tired Johnson of just two days ago. The Big Train threw fastballs by Kelly for a crucial strikeout. He then induced Meusel to ground out to third.

In the bottom of the inning, Washington also got a man to third base with one out when Judge singled to center and advanced to third on an infield error. But Ralph Miller grounded into a rally-killing double play off new pitcher Hugh McQuillan. So Game 7 would end just as the opening game had—in extra innings.

Johnson gave up a leadoff walk to start the tenth inning, but a strikeout and double play quickly extinguished the threat. The Senators went down in order in the bottom of the inning, as Harris let Johnson bat rather than lift him for a pinch hitter. Johnson flew out to deep left-center field.

In the eleventh, the Giants again had Johnson on the ropes. With a runner on second and one out, Johnson faced Frisch, who had tripled off him just two innings earlier. This time, Johnson struck out the Giants' captain, and then, for the second straight time, intentionally walked Ross Youngs and struck out George Kelly. In Washington's half of the inning, Goslin doubled with two out off of new Giants pitcher Bentley but was stranded there.

Johnson had his good stuff, but he continued to make the game stressful for the hometown fans. Meusel led off the twelfth inning with a single, the third straight inning the Giants got the leadoff man on against the Washington pitcher. But Johnson struck out Hack Wilson and retired the next two batters on a force out and fly ball. Johnson had pitched his fourth inning of relief, just two days after pitching eight innings.

With one out in the bottom of the twelfth, Ruel popped a foul behind home plate, and it looked like the Senators would go quietly. But catcher Hank Gowdy tripped over his own mask, which he had thrown to the ground to get a view of the ball, and Ruel had another shot. He took advantage, lining a double past third base. Harris again let Johnson bat for himself, and he reached first on an error by shortstop Travis Jackson. Ruel stayed put at second base.

Washington had had good luck with the area around third base back in the eighth inning, when Harris's bad-hop single tied the game. Why not take a shot at the same neighborhood? McNeely did just that, grounding a ball to third, and, incredibly, the ball took another bad bounce and skipped over third baseman Lindstrom's head. Ruel chugged home with the winning run at 5:04 p.m., without drawing a throw.

Fans jumped onto the field and danced on the tops of the dugouts, while police came to rescue players from the masses. The fans surrounded McNeely before he even reached first base on his series-winning hit, and his shirt was torn by the time he got to the dugout. "He was thumped and pummeled and hugged and reached the bench a very crushed young man," the *New York Times* wrote. McNeely was dubbed the "$50,000 man," because the team had paid that princely sum to purchase him in August. Legendary sportswriter Fred Lieb wrote, "Perhaps the millions of fans pulling for Washington to win its first World Series championship influenced the usually fickle goddess of luck to give a little lift to the gallant Nationals."

Meanwhile in the clubhouse, Johnson told a reporter,

> I'm the happiest man in the world—the happiest man in the world. Tell everybody I'm tickled to death and anything else along the same line you can think of. I'll stand back of anything you say, as I can't express my feelings in words at all right now. I can never thank Bucky enough for having confidence in me again after my two other failures, and I'm happy I didn't disappoint him and my friends.

Harris said he believed in his aging ace all along. "Walter was my best bet," he said. "That's why I put him in. Anyone who thought Walter was through was a fool. I knew he was all right." Harris said he also had visions of the game ending in a tie, because "I knew absolutely that they couldn't score on Walter if we played all night, and we didn't seem to be able to get the breaks."

The Giants' losing pitcher, Jack Bentley, suggested there may have been a higher power at work. "The good Lord just couldn't bear to see a fine fellow like Walter Johnson lose again," he said. *New York World* sportswriter Heywood Broun waxed more poetically:

> I was never swept by the Easter story until I saw the seventh game of the World Series. I have seen Osiris die in the darkness and come back from his cavern into the sunlight to conquer. Mithra, Adonis, Krishna, Atlas, Hercules—all these I take to be symbols of the human spirit, and so without incongruity I may add Walter Johnson to the list.

Fans celebrated well past midnight, honking horns, blasting sirens, blowing whistles, and shaking rattles. Cars on Pennsylvania Avenue were forced to drive on streetcar tracks as thousands of fans jammed the street. People threw torn-up newspapers from office buildings.

"In spontaneity and unadulterated enthusiasm the demonstration yesterday afternoon and last night exceeded anything of its kind in the history of Washington," the *Post* reports. "It was an Armistice Day and Mardi Gras blended into one. It was the thrilling outburst of a city's joy [that] knew no bounds. It was wonderful."

Giants manager John McGraw called it the best World Series ever played. "There were more thrills to the square inch in these seven games than any baseball man ever saw," he wrote in a syndicated column. In a follow-up column, he conceded that Washington winning the series was the "greatest thing that could have happened to baseball. It was a popular victory."

THREE

Glory Years

GLORY YEARS

Washington's 1924 World Series championship ushered in the franchise's only true golden age. In a decade covering the Roaring Twenties and the early years of the Great Depression, the team won three pennants, along with a second-place finish and three third-place finishes. Only once did the Senators fail to finish in the eight-team league's top half—known as the "first division" in those days before divisional play. Six times in ten years the team finished with a winning percentage of .597 or better.

Senators owner Clark Griffith did not coast on the success of the 1924 team. He went out and upgraded the starting pitching rotation with two brilliant moves in the off-season. First, he acquired thirty-five-year-old veteran right-hander Stan Coveleski from the Cleveland Indians in exchange for two inconsequential players. Coveleski, a cagey spitballer and future Hall of Famer, eclipsed Walter Johnson as the ace of the pitching staff in 1925, going 20–5 for a league-high .800 winning percentage, along with a league-best 2.84 ERA.

In another steal, Griffith purchased Dutch Ruether from Brooklyn, and the southpaw went 18–7 for the Senators in 1925. Meanwhile, the thirty-seven-year-old Johnson may not have been the staff ace, but he was close, posting a 20–7 record and a 3.07 ERA. He also hit an astonishing .433, with a pair of homers and twenty RBIs.

Several everyday players had great seasons, too. First baseman Joe Judge batted .314; catcher Muddy Ruel hit .310; outfielder Sam Rice stroked a team-best .350, with eighty-seven RBIs; and outfielder Goose Goslin hit .334, with eighteen home runs and 113 RBIs. He also led the league with twenty triples. No regular hit lower than .286.

Backed by great starting pitching and a deep lineup, the Senators cruised to the American League pennant in 1925. This time, the Yankees weren't even in sight, finishing in seventh place, twenty-eight and a half games behind the Senators. New York had to play the first two months without Babe Ruth, who was sidelined with an ulcer. Finishing with a .636 winning percentage, the Senators won the pennant by a comfortable eight and a half games over the Philadelphia Athletics. The Senators also set a franchise record by drawing 817,000 fans, shattering the mark the team had set the year before, when it drew 584,000.

This time, the Senators matched up against the underdog Pittsburgh Pirates in the World Series, but Pittsburgh had a dangerous lineup. The Bucs led the National League in hitting, with a .307 batting average, and also paced the league in doubles, triples, on-base percentage, slugging percentage, and, of course, runs. Only one regular, second baseman Eddie Moore, batted lower than .300, and that was just barely—.298. Four Pirates drove in at least one hundred runs. The lineup featured three future Hall of Famers—outfielder Kiki Cuyler, who led the team with a .357 batting average; third baseman Pie Traynor, who hit .320; and outfielder Max Carey, who hit .343 and led the league with forty-six stolen bases.

It was to be a mirror image of the 1924 series for Walter Johnson. The "Big Train," who had lost his first two starts in the 1924 series, won his first two starts against the Pirates, staking the Senators out to a commanding 3–1 series lead. But his victory in the fourth game came at a cost. In the third inning, Johnson singled to left and strained his leg while trying to stretch the hit into a double.

His teammates couldn't hold the series lead. Coveleski, the Nats' most dependable pitcher in the regular season, lost Game 5 at Griffith Stadium, 6–3, his second World Series loss. The Senators wasted a solid performance by Alex Ferguson in Game 6 at Forbes Field, dropping the game, 3–2.

So again, Washington's season would come down to one game. The Senators turned to none other than Johnson to start Game 7. The conditions in Pittsburgh were not good for a pitcher getting over a leg injury. The game had to be postponed once because of rain, and when the two teams squared off on another cold, rainy day the next afternoon in Pittsburgh, the field was wet and muddy.

The next day's *New York Times* described it as the

> wettest, weirdest, and wildest game that fifty years of baseball has ever seen. . . . Water, mud, fog, mist, sawdust, fumbles, wild throws, wild pitches, one near fistfight, impossible rallies—these were mixed up to make the best and the worst game of baseball ever played in this century. Players wallowing ankle-deep in mud, pitchers slipping as they delivered the ball to the plate, athletes skidding and sloshing, falling full length, dropping soaked baseballs—there you have part of the picture that was unveiled on Forbes Field this dripping afternoon. It was a great day for water polo.

The Senators jumped out to a 4–0 lead in the first inning, but the Bucs rallied for three runs in the third. Washington outfielder Joe Harris doubled in two runs in the fourth to give the Nationals a 6–3 lead. That should have iced the game with the durable Johnson on the mound, who had already pitched two complete games. But the "Big Train" was pitching on a slippery track and could not put the game away.

After pulling within 6–4 in the fifth inning, the Pirates tied the score with two runs in the bottom of the seventh. The rally started with an error by shortstop Roger Peckinpaugh, incredibly the seventh of the series for the normally reliable infielder. Peckinpaugh, who had hit only four home runs in the regular season, made amends for the miscue by slamming a homer into the left-field seats in the top of the eighth, giving Washington a 7–6 lead. But he made yet another error in the bottom of the inning, and the Pirates scored three runs to take a 9–7 lead. Pittsburgh held on to win the game, becoming the first team in history to come back from a 3–1 World Series deficit.

For both Peckinpaugh and Johnson, the series marked a reversal of fortune. Peck had played such a heroic 1924 World Series, overcoming injuries to make clutch plays that helped Washington win its first championship. Now he was a goat. Johnson, who atoned for two losses in the 1924 World Series by winning a dramatic Game 7, now lost a seventh game after winning his first two starts. In the deciding game, he was pounded for fifteen hits and nine runs, although only five runs were earned.

American League president Ban Johnson second-guessed manager Bucky Harris's use of Johnson for three games. "You sacrificed a World's Championship for our league through your display of mawkish sentiment," he lectured the young manager in a telegraph. But Johnson's final line was still good: a 2–1 record, a 2.08 ERA. And Harris replied testily, "You run the American League, and I'll manage the Washington baseball team."

The next year, Washington slipped to fourth place. The bats were still there—six of the eight regulars hit .290 or better, including Buddy Myer, who replaced the aging Peckinpaugh at shortstop and batted .304. Goslin had another monster year, hitting .354, with seventeen home runs and 108 RBIs. But the pitching dropped off considerably.

Walter Johnson started things off brilliantly, winning a 1–0, fifteen-inning pitching duel over the Philadelphia Athletics' Eddie Rommel on opening day, fanning nine batters. But Johnson, now thirty-eight years old, would have his worst season since breaking into the major leagues twenty years earlier. He finished with a 15–16 record and 3.63 ERA and would pitch only one more season.

Coveleski turned in another good year in 1926, winning fourteen games, with a 3.12 ERA, but he was not the dominating pitcher he had been the year before. Overall, Washington posted a poor 4.34 ERA—up from 3.70 the year before. The Senators still finished with a decent winning percentage of .540, but the Yankees were back at the top of the league. Babe Ruth returned to form, batting .372, with forty-seven home runs and 146 RBIs. And a young first baseman named Lou Gehrig chipped in sixteen homers and 112 RBIs.

Washington improved slightly in 1927, finishing in third place, with a .552 percentage, but nobody could compete with the Yankees that year. New York put together its infamous "Murderer's Row," with Ruth setting a single-season record with sixty home runs—more than any other team in the league—and Gehrig batting .373, with forty-seven home runs and 175 RBIs. New York won 110 games and finished twenty-five games ahead of the Nationals.

Meanwhile, a line drive off the bat of Joe Judge in spring training broke Johnson's leg. He pitched only 100 innings that year, going 5–6 with a 5.10 ERA, and decided to retire after the season. Johnson did go out with a bang offensively, hitting .348, with two more home runs. "The fact that he didn't seem to weigh heavily in the team's pitching scheme ultimately decided the issue," writes Johnson's grandson, Henry W. Thomas, in the biography *Walter Johnson: Baseball's Big Train*. "Despite a great deal of speculation in the press as to the veteran's plans, there had been no communication from Griffith, and Johnson took it as a sign that perhaps he was no longer wanted." Griffith insisted later that was not the case.

With Johnson done, Griffith admirably patched up the Senators' starting rotation in 1928. He acquired pitchers "Sad" Sam Jones and Milt Gaston from the St. Louis Browns for outfielder Earl McNeely and pitcher Dick Coffman. Jones would turn in a great season, going 17–7, with a 2.84 ERA.

A trade that Griffith had made in 1926 also paid dividends for the 1928 team. The Old Fox had traded Dutch Ruether to the New York Yankees for Garland Braxton. Ruether was out of baseball by 1928, while Braxton led the American League with a 2.51 ERA that year. At the plate, the Senators got another terrific season from Goslin, who led the league with a .379 batting average, the first time a Senator had won the batting crown since Ed Delahanty's .376 in 1902.

Despite the individual accomplishments, the team slumped to fourth place, with a 75–79 record, its first sub-.500 season since 1923. It was also the first time player-manager Bucky Harris failed to guide the team to a winning record. His playing tanked as well; Harris hit just .204. The home crowd turned on Harris, yelling, "Take him out!"

Griffith did just that after the season, firing the only manager to take the Senators to the World Series. Speculation on a successor focused around first baseman Joe Judge and catcher Muddy Ruel, but, two weeks later, Griffith decided to go for an even bigger name—Walter Johnson.

Some baseball writers wondered if the kindhearted Johnson might be too soft for the job. At his signing, Johnson said he would "go to the whip" when necessary, adding he would not tolerate loafing. "Washington players at least will be expected to give their all, and if they don't, there is no room for them on the team," he said.

Johnson, who would be forty-one by the time the 1929 season started, even held out the possibility of pitching again for the team. "I really believe that I still have a few good games in my arm," he said, but he never pitched again. For Griffith, hiring a Senators player as skipper continued a precedent he had set when he made shortstop George McBride manager in 1921. All five of Griffith's managers, including Johnson, had played for the Senators.

Meanwhile, Harris quickly landed the manager's job with the Detroit Tigers. Although only thirty-two years of age when the season started, Harris was effectively done playing; he appeared in only seven games in his first year as Detroit's skipper that season and four more the rest of his career. Harris now focused exclusively on managing, returning later for two more tours of duty with the Senators.

At first, Johnson had little success as manager. In 1929, the team finished in fifth place, with a .467 winning percentage, thirty-four games out of first place and two games ahead of Bucky Harris's Tigers. Goslin dropped nearly one hundred points from his batting title year, to .288. Sam Jones slumped to 9–9, with a 3.92 ERA. The Senators drew just 355,000 fans, their worst attendance since 1919.

But Johnson turned things around the next year, and Washington zoomed to second place in 1930, finishing with a .610 winning percentage. That record would be good enough to win the pennant most seasons, but not this year. The Senators finished eight games behind the Philadelphia Athletics, a dynasty in the making packed with such future Hall of Famers as Jimmy Foxx, Al Simmons, Mickey Cochrane, and Lefty Grove. Still, 1930 proved to be a success for the Senators both on the field and at the gate. The team drew 614,000 fans, nearly double the year before—even though it was the first season played in the Great Depression.

In a year dominated by offense, the Nats had a league-best 3.96 ERA and tied for the league lead with seventy-eight complete games. Five pitchers won at least fifteen games under Johnson's tutelage—Bump Hadley, Alvin Crowder, Lloyd Brown, Fred Marberry, and Sam Jones. All but one had exactly fifteen wins, with Lloyd Brown leading the staff with sixteen victories. Baseball went nearly seventy years before another team featured five fifteen-game winners—the 1998 Atlanta Braves pitching staff of Denny Neagle, Tom Glavine, Greg Maddux, John Smoltz, and Kevin Millwood.

At the plate, six Washington regulars hit .300 or better, led by outfielders Heinie Manush (.362) and Sam Rice (.349) and shortstop Joe Cronin, who hit .346, with thirteen home runs and 126 RBIs, and won the *Sporting News* American League Player of the Year award. Manush and Cronin were two recent acquisitions Griffith made as he built up Washington's last great team of the twentieth century.

The Senators acquired Manush in a midseason exchange of top-flight hitters with the St. Louis Browns, in which Washington reluctantly parted with Goose Goslin. Two years earlier, Goslin had beaten Manush for the American League batting crown by just one point, .379 to .378. The Browns also kicked in Crowder.

Although Washington did not win the pennant that year, Griffith set the groundwork for the 1933 pennant-winning team. Crowder, Manush, and especially Cronin proved invaluable. In 1928, Griffith had plucked Cronin from Kansas City, a minor-league team, for $7,500. But Griffith didn't think much of him at the time. When he told reporters the team had purchased a "young shortstop, name of Cronin," a reporter asked for a first name. "It don't make no difference, and I don't even know if he's got a first name," Griffith responded. "He's only gonna be around long enough to give (shortstop) Bob Reeves a rest, then we'll ship him to Birmingham. Don't you fellows go writin' your heads off about him now—he's only a fair to middlin' busher." Little did Griffith know that he had himself a future Hall of Fame player, manager, and even son-in-law.

In yet another Kansas City bargain, Griffith picked up Joe Kuhel for $65,000 late in the 1930 season. Kuhel took over for Joe Judge at first base the next year and became yet another key ingredient in the 1933 team.

In 1931, Washington put together another good year under Johnson, finishing with a .597 winning percentage. But the team fell to third place as the Yankees claimed second, and the Athletics won 107 games en route to their third straight pennant. Griffith continued to build up the team's starting pitching by purchasing Monte Weaver from the minor league Baltimore team.

Posting their second .600 season in three years, the Senators won ninety-three games in 1932, but still fell victim to better ball clubs. The team's .604 winning percentage ranked just third in the league, as the Yankees this time won the pennant with 107 wins. The Senators finished fourteen games back, and one game behind the second-place Athletics.

The new Senators continued to develop. Crowder led the league in wins, going 26–13, with a 3.33 ERA, while Weaver won twenty-two games. Heinie Manush batted .342, with 116 RBIs. Cronin hit .318, with 116 RBIs, and led the league with eighteen triples.

Despite piloting the team to another excellent record, Johnson was fired after the 1932 season. The "Big Train" proved the adage "Nice Guys Finish Last" wrong, but some thought he was too nice to finish first. "It was believed in many quarters that Johnson was too easygoing to infuse the fighting spirit held so vital to a pennant-winning club," the *Washington Post* wrote after the manager got sacked. Johnson would go on to manage the Cleveland Indians, and then try an entirely new career. In 1940, he ran for Congress from Maryland as a Republican but lost the race to Democrat William Byron.

Griffith didn't immediately name a replacement for Johnson, and he even considered the possibility of returning to the dugout himself "in case of emergency." But the owner soon settled on a new skipper, deciding to return to the winning formula of the mid-1920s—a player-manager in his mid-twenties. Griffith named Joe Cronin to the post days before the star shortstop's twenty-sixth birthday. Cronin was even younger than Bucky Harris, the "Boy Wonder," had been when Harris took over the 1924 Senators.

"I like these scrappy youngsters as leaders," Griffith said, adding that he was enthusiastic about Cronin's "pep and fight and willingness to take a chance." He maintained realistic expectations for his young manager. "I'm not looking for him to suddenly turn us into a championship team," Griffith stated. But once again he underestimated Joe Cronin.

Griffith had other changes in store for the Senators, making a series of key trades before the 1933 season to fortify the team. In yet another blockbuster trade with the St. Louis Browns, Washington swapped outfielders Sam West and Carl Reynolds for outfielders Fred Schulte and former Senator Goslin. Although Goslin wasn't a batting title threat anymore, he had a good year in 1933, batting .297, with ten triples and ten home runs. Two pitchers also changed hands in the deal. Washington exchanged Lloyd Brown for Lefty Stewart, who went 15–6 for the 1933 Nats.

Griffith also acquired Earl Whitehill from the Tigers, who won twenty-two games for the 1933 Senators, with a 3.33 ERA, and pitcher Jack Russell from the Indians, who won twelve games and saved a league-high thirteen, with a svelte 2.69 ERA.

If the Senators were to win the pennant, they would have to dethrone the New York Yankees, just as they had in 1924. The two teams fought it out between the lines—and sometimes outside them. On April 25, the Yankees and Senators faced off at Griffith Stadium for the third game of a three-game series. Lingering animosity was still pent up from the previous season, when Bill Dickey, the Yankees' catcher, and Carl Reynolds, then a Senators outfielder, had fought it out at home plate.

This time, Yankees base runner Ben Chapman came in spikes flying to break up a double play in the fourth inning, knocking Washington second baseman Buddy Myer's feet out from under him. With Chapman still on the ground, an enraged Myer kicked him several times in the back. The two players exchanged blows as players from both dugouts rushed out to get a piece of the action.

Chapman and Myer were ejected from the game, and Chapman made his way to the Yankee clubhouse. Unfortunately, that required a trip through the Washington dugout, where Senators players didn't exactly greet him with flowers. When Nats pitcher Earl Whitehill made a comment that Chapman found particularly offensive, the Yankee outfielder punched him in the face. Now hundreds of Washington fans stormed onto the field to join the melee. Some got several punches in before Chapman's Yankees teammates could rush to his defense. Police had to come on the field to restore order, arresting five fans, and the game was delayed for fifteen minutes. But the Yankees did the only baseball thrashing that day, whipping the Senators, 16–0. American League president Will Harridge fined Chapman, Myer, and Whitehill $100 each and suspended them for five games.

Chapman was unapologetic about instigating the brawl. "That's baseball and always has been, breaking up double plays," he said. "That's what I'm in there for when I'm running. If this game is Ping-Pong, I don't know anything about it. I'm playing baseball."

Washington dropped to 6–6 with the loss, and the Yankees improved to 8–2. The defeat seemed to ignite the Senators, who won eight of their next ten. They also handled the Yankees well that year, winning the season series, 14–8, which helped decide the pennant. The Senators won the flag by seven games over New York, putting together the finest season in Washington baseball history—a 99–53 record, good for a .651 winning percentage.

Leading the charge was Washington's "boy manager," shortstop Joe Cronin, who hit .309, with a team-high 118 RBIs and a league-high forty-five doubles. "Crossing his early season critics by assuming managerial cares without losing any of the sparkle of his play afield and at the plate, Cronin has been credited with imparting something akin to college-boy spirit to the Senators," wrote the Associated Press.

Cronin was one of four regulars to hit .300 or better, along with first baseman Joe Kuhel (.322 with 107 RBIs), second baseman Buddy Myer (.302 with fifteen triples), and outfielder Heinie Manush (.336 with ninety-five RBIs and a league-high seventeen triples), with Goslin just a tick below, at .297. The lineup featured three future Hall of

Famers: Cronin, Manush, and Goslin. On the mound, Crowder shared the league lead, with twenty-four victories, with Whitehill just two wins behind.

Washington's pennant-winning team in 1933 drew just 437,000 fans, an average of 5,757 fans a game, but attendance was way down in baseball in general because of the Depression. Only the Yankees outdrew the Senators in the American League, with 728,000 fans. The St. Louis Browns, by contrast, drew just 88,000 fans for the entire season, for an average of 1,144 fans per game, in what many consider the best baseball town in the United States. True, St. Louis had two teams back then, but even the more popular Cardinals drew just 256,000 fans.

Despite the low attendance, Washington treated the Senators to a raucous celebration after they clinched the pennant in September. Cronin was "besieged in the clubhouse by a hero-worshiping throng of thousands of fans of both sexes gone mildly mad," the *Washington Post* reported. He slipped out of the clubhouse onto the field, where "shrieking women" ran after him, and the young player-manager had to sprint to escape them, the newspaper recounted.

In the World Series, Washington faced off against the team it had defeated in 1924, the New York Giants. When the teams had last faced one another, Bill Terry was a rookie first baseman for the Giants; now he was their player-manager, and the team's only .300 hitter, with a .322 batting average. But this Giants team was built on pitching.

New York led the National League with an amazing 2.71 ERA, featuring a trio of dominating starting pitchers—southpaw Carl Hubbell, who led the league in wins (23), shutouts (10), and ERA (1.66); Hal Schumacher, who won nineteen games, with a 2.16 ERA; and "Fat Freddie" Fitzsimmons, who won sixteen, with a 2.90 ERA.

In the first two games of the series, played in New York's Polo Grounds, Washington managed just three runs against Hubbell and Schumacher, and fell behind, two games to none. Hubbell set the pace quickly in Game 1 by striking out the side in the first inning, fanning Myer, Manush, and Goslin, and went the distance in a 4–2 victory over Lefty Stewart (both Nationals runs were unearned). Schumacher also pitched a complete game in New York's 6–1 victory the next day over twenty-four-game winner Alvin Crowder.

When the series returned to Washington for Game 3, only 25,727 fans showed up on the rainy afternoon, including President Franklin D. Roosevelt. Those who did were treated to a fine pitching performance by Earl Whitehill in a must-win game for Washington. The first-year Nat mowed down the Giants with a shutout, and the Senators won, 4–0. Leadoff man Buddy Myer went 3-for-4, with a run scored and two RBIs.

Currier and Ives cartoon from 1860 using baseball as a metaphor for Abraham Lincoln's triumph over his opponents in his first presidential election. Courtesy of the Library of Congress.

American League Park in Washington, May 6, 1905. About 9,300 people were in attendance. Courtesy of the Library of Congress.

Walter Johnson, arguably the greatest player to ever play in a Washington uniform. He was inducted into the Baseball Hall of Fame in 1936. Courtesy of the Library of Congress.

Otis Clymer of Washington bats as John Kleinow of New York catches in this photo of a game from April 22, 1909. Courtesy of the Library of Congress.

The Senators in 1913. Courtesy of the Library of Congress.

1924 winners of the American League Pennant. Courtesy of the Library of Congress.

The Senators comedy team of Al Schacht and Nick Altrock entertain fans during the 1924 World Series. Courtesy of the Library of Congress.

Miss Elsie Tydings purchases the first ticket sold for a World Series in the nation's capital, 1924. Courtesy of the Library of Congress.

Goose Goslin, Washington's fabled perennial .300 hitter, who was inducted into the Baseball Hall of Fame in 1968. Courtesy of the Library of Congress.

The Washington Senators make their way through a crowd to meet with President Calvin Coolidge after winning the American League pennant in 1924. Courtesy of the Library of Congress.

The 1924 World Champion Washington Senators with President Calvin Coolidge (standing center-left, black arm band on left sleeve) at the White House. Courtesy of the Library of Congress.

Collection of photos showing ceremonies of the Senators' home opener in 1925, the year after Washington's first World Series championship. Clockwise from upper left: New York Yankees manager Miller Huggins and Senators player-manager Bucky Harris shake hands; President Calvin Coolidge throws out the first ball; Secretary of State Frank Billings Kellogg raises the flag; and Senators players watch batting practice. The Senators won the game, 10–1, behind a complete-game start by Walter Johnson. Courtesy of the Library of Congress.

The 1944 Homestead Grays. Courtesy of the Rucker Archive.

Pitcher Stan Coveleski in 1925. Courtesy of the Library of Congress.

Washington's Earl McNeely slides into home plate safely in front of Boston Red Sox catcher John Bischoff in a game in 1925. Courtesy of the Library of Congress.

Josh Gibson, said to be the greatest power hitter of all time, swings the bat. Courtesy of the Rucker Archive.

Josh Gibson scores. Courtesy of the Rucker Archive.

A Negro League game at Griffith Stadium in Washington. Courtesy of the Rucker Archive.

The 1948 Homestead Grays. Courtesy of the Rucker Archive.

The pivotal game of the series would be next. Once again, Washington had the difficult task of facing Hubbell, this time sending Monte Weaver to the mound for his first start of the series. Weaver surrendered a solo home run to Terry in the top of the fourth, but Washington tied it in the bottom of the seventh inning, when Kuhel reached on an error by Hubbell on a bunt, moved to second on a sacrifice, and scored on a single by Luke Sewell.

The game went into extra innings, and the two starting pitchers continued to battle. In the top of the eleventh, New York went with the small-ball strategy that Washington had used to tie the score four innings earlier. Travis Jackson legged out a bunt; moved ninety feet up on a sacrifice by Gus Mancuso; and scored the go-ahead run on a single by Blondy Ryan, who had hit just .238 in the regular season.

In the bottom of the inning, Washington tried to manufacture the tying run with a similar tactic. Fred Schulte singled to left, and Kuhel reached on a bunt to put runners on first and second with none out. Ossie Bluege sacrificed the runners to second and third. The Giants intentionally walked Sewell to load the bases, and Cliff Bolton came in to pinch-hit for pitcher Jack Russell. All Washington needed was a fly ball to tie the game, and a single would likely win it. But Bolton hit a ground ball to shortstop, and the Giants turned it into a game-ending 6–4–3 double play. New York now led the series, 3–1.

In Game 5, the Giants jumped out to a 2–0 second-inning lead, as the Giants pitcher, Schumacher, knocked in two runs on a single off Crowder. New York made it 3–0 in the sixth, but Washington rallied to tie the score in the bottom of the frame on a three-run homer by Fred Schulte, triggering memories of the come-from-behind victories by the 1924 World Series team. Schulte had hit only five home runs in the regular season.

For the second straight day, the teams lumbered on into extra innings at Griffith Stadium. Jack Russell, who had come in on relief in the sixth inning, stayed on for Washington in the tenth inning. He surrendered a long drive to left-center field by Mel Ott. Center fielder Schulte got a glove on the ball, but it bounced into the stands for a home run, giving the Giants a 4–3 lead.

In the bottom of the inning, after two quick outs, the Senators mounted a threat. Cronin singled to left, bringing up Schulte, whose home run five innings earlier had tied the score. An encore performance would win the game for Washington. But the Giants pitched him carefully and finally walked Schulte, and the move paid off when the next batter, Kuhel, struck out against the Giants' forty-three-year-old Cuban reliever, Dolf Luque. The World Series was over. The Senators would never return to another one.

Red, White, and Gray: Washington's Negro League Team

RED, WHITE, AND GRAY: WASHINGTON'S NEGRO LEAGUE TEAM

Washington may have lost two mediocre Major League Baseball teams in the last century, but it also picked up a great one. In the late 1930s through the 1940s, the Homestead Grays of the Negro National League began splitting games between their original home of Homestead, Pennsylvania, and Washington, D.C. Within a few years, the Grays played primarily in Washington, providing fans there with an outstanding baseball team at a time when the Senators were struggling. The Grays also shined a spotlight on a missed opportunity for the Nats to both make a historical stand for civil rights and better themselves in the process, because literally playing in the Senators' own ballpark were the "Thunder Twins"—Negro League stars Josh Gibson and Buck Leonard.

Before 1940, several Negro League teams had tried to make a go of it in Washington, but none were successful. The Washington Potomacs lasted just a few years in the 1920s, and the Elite Giants decided to skip town for Baltimore after playing in D.C. in 1936 and 1937. There was even a Washington Black Senators team that went 1–20 in 1938, before folding up its tent.

It wasn't that black Washingtonians weren't into baseball. They were, but they enthusiastically supported the Senators, even though Major League Baseball was closed off to black players. Ironically, Griffith Stadium was located in a black neighborhood, close to Howard University, one of the nation's premier black colleges. But as Washington was a segregated southern city, blacks would sit in their own section of the ballpark, in the right-field pavilion. A famous photograph shows black fans leaning over the railing just inches away from an unconscious Babe Ruth, who had slammed into the wall chasing a ball on July 5, 1924.

Shirley Povich, who was named sports editor of the *Washington Post* around this time, described 1920s Washington as a "sadly segregated city." "No newspaper bothered to cover games of the black high schools, and Howard University teams got scant notice," Povich wrote in a retrospective column more than sixty years later. He continued:

> It was an inconceivable age when blacks were denied service in restaurants, admission to downtown movie
>
> theaters and white hotels, and there was almost a common acceptance of that condition that later would call forth
>
> such outrage. The civil rights movement was in its early, feeble stage. Once, after a delegation of black leaders

visited the managing editor of the *Post*, he told me of their complaint: They wanted the *Post*, when we used the word Negro in the future, to use it with a capital N.

In 1938, black fans at Griffith Stadium took angry retribution against a Yankees outfielder who had made a violent racial slur. The outfielder, Jake Powell, had been asked in a WGN radio interview what he did in the off-season. Powell responded that he worked as a police officer in Dayton, Ohio, where he particularly enjoyed "cracking niggers over the head." The interview was immediately terminated, and Commissioner Kenesaw Mountain Landis suspended Powell for ten days.

About two weeks later, Powell made his first start after the suspension in the second game of a doubleheader at Griffith Stadium. Powell had started his career as a Senator, but this was no homecoming. Black fans booed him and threw soda bottles his way, causing the game to be delayed for several minutes. One bottle flew right behind his shoulders when he was on first base; a tin pail came close to hitting him. "Take him out! Take him out!" fans chanted from the black section of the ballpark. Despite their taunts, the Yankees swept the doubleheader, 16–1 and 6–2.

Yankees manager Joe McCarthy stood by his decision to play Powell, a platoon player, at Griffith Stadium. "Powell will play in our outfield against southpaw pitching if they throw a million bottles on him," the defiant skipper declared. "I had to send him out there to face the music. Once Powell got in the game, I wouldn't have taken him out if we'd all been killed."

Some accused Commissioner Landis of hypocrisy in suspending Powell for a racist remark, yet presiding over a sport that closed off its ranks to black players. *Washington Post* columnist Westbrook Pegler wrote, "Judge Landis, who tried the case and imposed the penalty, would thus placate the colored clientele of a business [that] trades under the name of the national game but has always treated the Negroes as Adolph Hitler treats the Jews."

Powell, by the way, was an equal opportunity bigot. Two years earlier, on April 29, 1936, while still a Senator, he collided with Detroit's Jewish first baseman, Hank Greenberg. Many saw anti-Semitism in Powell's dirty play, which broke Greenberg's wrist, sidelining him for the season. Powell, who retired after the 1945 season, would end his life by committing suicide in a Washington police station while being questioned on a charge of writing bad checks.

Around the time of the Powell incident at Griffith Stadium, black fans in Washington were getting their own team to root for—and a winning one at that. The Grays were a perennial pennant winner of the Negro National

League from the late 1930s to the mid-1940s, even posting a phenomenal .746 winning percentage in 1943, according to baseballreference.com.

The team's most recognizable stars were catcher Josh Gibson and first baseman Buck Leonard, nicknamed the "black Babe Ruth" and "black Lou Gehrig," respectively. Gibson, like Ruth, was a monstrous home run hitter, and Leonard, like Gehrig, was an unassuming first baseman with tremendous power. The two usually batted third and fourth in the lineup, just like Ruth and Gehrig did for the Yankees, and they were elected to the National Baseball Hall of Fame in 1972. Gibson and Leonard saw the Senators games as well. "We went to their games," Leonard told an Associated Press reporter in 1994, three years before his death at the age of ninety. "We watched those boys. We imitated them. We wanted to be just like them."

Another Hall of Fame player, James "Cool Papa" Bell, was one of the fastest players ever to play the game. Bell joined the Grays in 1943, when he turned forty, and stayed for three seasons. Gibson famously said, "Cool Papa Bell was so fast he could get out of bed, turn out the lights across the room, and be back in bed under the covers before the lights went out."

Gibson's heroics were legendary, and some of them were, in fact, legends. He was said to have hit a ball out of Yankee Stadium in 1934, which would make him the only player to do so, although no documentation exists of the act. But some feats were documented. At a doubleheader at Griffith Stadium in 1939, he hit three home runs and a triple. One home run "followed the left-field foul line until it went out of sight," the *Post* reported. In 1937, he hit a ball that traveled 580 feet at Yankee Stadium. Once, in a game in Monessen, Pennsylvania, Gibson hit a ball so far over the center-field fence that the mayor stopped the game to measure it, at 512 feet.

"Josh's power came almost completely from strength above his waist: arms, shoulders, and back muscles so awesome that he didn't need the coiled power of his legs or the whiplike action of his wrists," writes William Brashler in *Josh Gibson: A Life in the Negro Leagues*. Brashler elaborates, stating the following:

> With his upper-body power, he could thrash a ball with a motion much like that of beating a rug. He stood
> flat-footed, his heavy bat gripped down to the end and held high above his right shoulder, his feet spread fairly

wide apart, and with the pitch he strode only slightly—some say about four inches, some say not at all, but simply raised his foot and put it down in the same spot when the pitch came.

Gibson started his career with the Grays but left to play for several seasons in the 1930s with the rival Pittsburgh Crawfords before returning to his original team. Years later, Leonard described the unique defensive shift the Grays would employ against the right-handed-hitting Gibson. "The corner outfielders would play toward the gaps, the first baseman and third baseman would play away from the foul lines, and the middle infielders would play deep," Leonard wrote in a 1970 *Washington Star* story with Negro League historian John Holway. "And then the pitcher would throw the ball straight down the middle of the plate," Leonard said. He added:

> He could hit the ball 500 feet to center field and we would catch it—I say 500 feet, but I mean extreme center. We'd gang up right in the center. He couldn't pull it—not a fastball. Throw it straight down the middle of the plate, and just hope we catch it, because he's going to hit it 400-something feet.

Gibson's Hall of Fame plaque states that the slugger hit nearly 800 home runs in league and independent games. In exhibition at-bats against major-league pitchers, Gibson batted .426. At six feet, one inch, 215 pounds, Gibson had the build of a catcher, but his defense was not his strong suit. He had trouble with pop-ups, although he had a cannon for an arm.

For all his hitting prowess, one pitcher had his number: Satchel Paige. At a game in Pittsburgh in 1942, with a runner on third base, the theatrical Paige walked two men intentionally to face Gibson with the bases loaded. "Three fastballs, Josh," Paige said, before fanning the Grays' slugger on three pitches. When the Grays met Paige's Kansas City Monarchs for the Negro World Series that year, Gibson again came up with the bases loaded, and this time with a chance to tie the game, as the Monarchs led, 8–4. But Paige repeated his earlier feat, striking out Gibson on three pitches, and the Monarchs swept the four-game series.

Leonard, meanwhile, was the glue of the Grays' franchise, especially during the 1940–1941 seasons, when Gibson played in Venezuela and Mexico for higher wages. Leonard was such a good fastball hitter that Monte Irvin, who would star in both the Negro leagues and the major leagues, once said, "Trying to sneak a fastball past him was like trying to sneak a sunrise past a rooster." A consistent .300 hitter with pop, Leonard was also an outstanding defensive first baseman. And, unlike Gibson, who was a heavy drinker, Leonard did not consume alcohol.

In 1942, the two stars held out until they got $1,000 a month for the five-month season. "When I started out with the Grays in 1934, I was getting $125 a month—for four and a half months," Leonard wrote in the *Washington Star* article. "My best payday was 1948; I made $10,000 that year all told, summer and winter. And baseball was a rough life back then. We'd play 210 games a year, then go to Cuba or Puerto Rico all winter and play winter ball."

Back then, in addition to league games, Negro League teams played exhibition games against semipro ball clubs—both black and white—and would go on barnstorming trips in the off-season. One of the most celebrated interracial exhibition games took place on May 31, 1942, in Washington, when Satchel Paige joined the Grays for a day as they took on the Dizzy Dean All-Stars, a major-league team headlined by the former Cardinals pitching star. A crowd of twenty-two thousand fans, more than quadruple the average Senators attendance that season, came out to Griffith Stadium to see the matchup. Dean, who had retired the previous season, pitched just the first inning, surrendering two runs. Paige, meanwhile, gave up one run in five innings, striking out seven, as the Grays won, 8–1. The rush for tickets so overwhelmed the ballpark staff that some fans couldn't get into the stadium until the fourth inning, when Dean was long gone.

The Grays were becoming a hot ticket in Washington, especially when Paige came to town. Three weeks later, Paige returned to Griffith Stadium, but this time in an enemy uniform, as his Kansas City Monarchs took on the Grays. Twenty-eight thousand fans packed the ballpark for the nine o'clock evening game. Paige held the Grays scoreless in his five innings of work, but the Grays' pitcher, Roy Partlow, did him four better, pitching nine scoreless frames. In the top of the tenth, Partlow finally surrendered the game's first run as Kansas City took a 1–0 lead. In the bottom of the inning, the Grays tied the score, and then Partlow won it with an RBI triple. The crowd rushed onto the field to carry him off in celebration.

Around this time, Clark Griffith arranged for a meeting with the Grays' two superstars, Leonard and Gibson. The Senators' owner called them to his office after a Grays game, Leonard recalled in the *Star* article. "You fellows got good size on you and you looked like you were playing to win," Griffith said, before telling the players of pressure from black sportswriters to put them on his team. "Well, let me tell you something: If we get you boys, we're going to get the best ones. It's going to break up your league. Now what do you think of all that?" The players told Griffith that they hadn't given it much thought. They said they'd be happy to play in the major leagues, but that they'd leave it to others to make a case for them. "Well, I just wanted to see how you fellows felt about it," Griffith said.

Publicly, Griffith was singing the praises of the players as well. Two days before the Grays–Monarchs June 1942 showdown, Griffith said of Gibson, "There's a catcher worth $150,000 of anybody's money right now. If I could have had him I'd have gone after him some time ago." Griffith added that Gibson was as good as Hall of Fame catchers Bill Dickey, Mickey Cochrane, and Gabby Hartnett. Of course, Griffith could have had Gibson at any time, if the Senators' owner had been willing to challenge baseball's color barrier.

By all accounts, Griffith was not a racist. He opened the stadium to black community events and was made an honorary deacon by Elder Solomon Lightfoot Michaux of the neighboring Church of God, which held religious services at Griffith Stadium, according to Brad Snyder's detailed history of the Grays, *Beyond the Shadow of the Senators*. "Most black Washingtonians considered Griffith—in contrast to the virulently racist Redskins owner George Preston Marshall—a friend," Snyder writes.

But Griffith had a financial stake in keeping the Grays afloat, receiving rent from the team, which helped him subsidize his own losing ball club. Still, one has to wonder whether Leonard and Gibson could have helped turn the Senators into both a winning team and a profitable one. From 1939 to 1945, the Senators averaged more than eight thousand fans a game only once, and they twice averaged fewer than five thousand fans. The team did pull off two surprise second-place finishes during this period, but otherwise finished sixth twice, seventh twice, and eighth (last) once.

Griffith's meeting with Leonard and Gibson followed years of intense lobbying by black sportswriter Sam Lacy of the *Baltimore Afro-American*, who was joined in his crusade to integrate baseball by fellow African American journalists Wendell Smith of the *Pittsburgh Courier* and Joe Bostic of the *People's Voice* in Harlem. Lacy grew up in Washington, the grandson of the first black detective on the Washington police force, Henry Erskine Lacy. Lacy's father was a passionate fan of the Washington Senators, and the young Lacy worked as a vendor at Griffith Stadium, watching the white stars of the day. Meanwhile, he would play semipro baseball with other black players, including Negro Leaguers.

"I was in a position to make some comparisons, and it seemed to me that those black players were good enough to play in the big leagues," Lacy said in a *Sports Illustrated* interview in 1990, thirteen years before his death at the age of ninety-nine. He continued:

> There was, of course, no talk then of that ever happening. When I was growing up, there was no real opportunity for blacks in any sport. It never crossed our minds as kids to aspire to the big leagues. Even the best players considered it a lost cause. But the idea stuck with me. I felt that not only were blacks being deprived of the opportunity to make some money, but that whites were being deprived of the opportunity to see these fellows perform. I could see that both were being cheated. And so, with a certain amount of ego, I took it upon myself to be the wedge.

In 1935, a full dozen years before Jackie Robinson broke baseball's color barrier, Lacy wrote a column in the *Washington Tribune*, a black weekly newspaper, urging baseball to integrate. "If baseball club-owners are really anxious to come to their own rescue, they should put a little 'color' in the game," he wrote. Two years later, Lacy met with Griffith and quoted the Senators owner as saying, "The time is not far off when colored players will take their places beside those of the other races in the major leagues. However, I am not so sure that time has arrived yet." Griffith also called on Negro teams to organize themselves into a legitimate, professionally run league, and predicted, accurately, that the first black player would be subject to "cruel, filthy epithets."

Lacy's own father had experienced such treatment firsthand by a Washington Senators player. In the *Sports Illustrated* interview, Lacy recalled how his father came out to cheer the Senators during an Opening Day parade in the 1920s. He said:

> And so there he was, age seventy-nine, out there cheering with the rest of them, calling all the players by name, just happy to be there. And then it happened. One of the white players—I won't say which one—just gave him this nasty look and, as he passed by, spat right in his face. Right in that nice old man's face. That hurt my

father terribly. And you know, as big a fan as he had been, he never went to another game as long as he lived, which was seven more years.

Although Clark Griffith had voiced some encouraging words back in 1937, as years went by, he did nothing to integrate the team. According to Griffith's adopted son, Calvin, the Senators owner was talking with the Grays' owner-ship about having black teams take on major league teams. "There were two brothers that owned the Grays. And they were talking to Mr. Griffith about one of these days they wanted to challenge the major leagues for the championship," Calvin Griffith told biographer Jon Kerr years later in *Calvin: Baseball's Last Dinosaur*. "And that's the only reason Mr. Griffith didn't sign some of 'em. But Branch Rickey went out and broke it all up by signing Jackie Robinson. If he hadn't signed Jackie Robinson there could have been in the years to come a challenge of the black to the white."

The idea of integrating baseball while keeping teams segregated was discussed openly back in the 1940s. Satchel Paige endorsed the idea, but Lacy ridiculed it. "Paige's proposal that a colored team be admitted to one or both of the big leagues, as an entity, is foolish," Lacy wrote in a 1942 column. "There can be no compromise with prejudice. Unless Negro players are infiltrated, the same situation will exist. A separate club for Negroes is no more logical than a separate team for Italians, Irishmen, Germans, Poles, Lithuanians, or Jews."

Meanwhile, Leonard and Gibson never heard back from Griffith after their meeting. "I always thought the Senators might be first to take a Negro, because Washington was about half-Negro then," Leonard wrote in 1970. "But Griffith was always looking for Cuban ballplayers."

Griffith's penchant for finding low-cost Cuban ballplayers dated to his days as manager of the Cincinnati Reds. In 1911, he signed two Cubans, Armando Marsans and Rafael Almeida. But it was an opposing Cuban player that really motivated Griffith to start scouting on the Caribbean island.

In the 1933 World Series between the Senators and the New York Giants, the teams were tied, 3–3, in the sixth inning of Game 5, when the Giants sent in their forty-three-year-old reliever, Dolf Luque. The Havana native held the Nats scoreless for four and one-third innings, allowing the Giants to win the game, 4–3, in ten innings, and claim the series, four games to one. Luque struck out five Senators and surrendered just two hits in getting the victory. He retired two years later with a lifetime 3.24 ERA.

Griffith hired Joe Cambria, a former minor-league ballplayer and Baltimore laundry business owner, and suggested he trawl Cuba for prospects. Cambria, who had moved with his parents to the United States from Italy when he was just three months old, helped Griffith open a pipeline to inexpensive Cuban talent. He also owned a Negro League team, the Baltimore Black Sox, as well as a host of minor-league teams. "Papa Joe" Cambria, a familiar figure in his straw hats, became so well known in Cuba that a Havana cigar was named for him. He went on to sign four hundred Cuban players throughout the years, in addition to such Americans as Mickey Vernon and Ed Yost. Among his most notable Cuban finds were pitchers Camilo Pascual, Pedro Ramos, Conrado Marrero, Roberto Estalella, and outfielder Tony Oliva, who signed with the team after it moved to Minnesota.

Even as Griffith resisted integrating baseball with American-born black players, he skirted the color barrier by signing tan-skinned Cubans who could pass as white. "There's no question that some of the ballplayers Mr. Griffith signed had black blood," Calvin Griffith told Kerr. "But nobody said anything about it. Nobody said nothing about it. So why bring up questions about something that nobody asked about?"

The players faced rough treatment on the field and discrimination off it. "The Cuban ballplayers, some of them were as black as your tape recorder," Calvin Griffith told Snyder in an interview. "We had to find places for them to stay across the railroad tracks."

On June 24, 1945, a highly touted rookie with the Kansas City Monarchs came to Washington for a game against the Grays. The *Post* called shortstop Jackie Robinson "amazingly agile" and a "smooth and graceful defensive man" with one of the best arms in baseball. Eighteen thousand fans came out for the doubleheader, more than double the Senators' average crowd that year.

Robinson gave the Monarchs a 1–0 lead in the first inning of the opening game by doubling and scoring, but the Grays stormed back to take the opener, 11–3, over Satchel Paige, and also won the second game, 10–6. Four months later, when Brooklyn Dodgers president Branch Rickey signed Robinson to a contract with the Dodgers, Clark Griffith became one of the deal's harshest critics.

Griffith did not say that blacks did not belong in the game. Instead, the Senators' owner argued that Rickey was wrong to pluck Robinson off the Kansas City Monarchs' roster without compensating the team. "While it is true that we have no agreement with Negro leagues—National and American—we still can't act like outlaws in taking their stars," Griffith said. "If Brooklyn wanted to buy Robinson from Kansas City, that would be all right, but contracts of Negro teams should be recognized by organized baseball."

Griffith, who ironically had traded for a young Rickey forty years earlier as manager of the New York Highlanders, now engaged in a testy public debate with his former player. "There is no Negro league as such as far as I am concerned," Rickey responded. "Negro baseball is in the zone of a racket, and there is not a circuit that could be admitted to organized baseball, Clark Griffith of Washington to the contrary."

Rickey also charged that Griffith had signed Cuban players who were themselves black, a strange charge coming from a man who was integrating baseball. Griffith's response was equally bizarre: "Cuban ballplayers have always been acceptable in organized baseball, and so far as I am concerned no racial problem is involved."

In 1946, as Robinson was making his professional debut with the Dodgers' minor-league team in Montreal, Josh Gibson was playing his final season. Gibson, now thirty-four years of age, was overweight and suffering from high blood pressure and the ill effects of excessive drinking—and possibly drug use. He died the following January of a stroke at the age of thirty-five, just three months before Robinson broke baseball's color barrier.

"Gibson was so good if he was in the major leagues they would have to say that he was the best catcher that ever caught," Calvin Griffith told Kerr. "That's how good he was. He could sit on his ass and throw the ball to second base better than anybody standing up."

The Grays trudged on even after blacks started playing in the major leagues, but the fans' interest, understandably, waned considerably. "We couldn't draw flies," Leonard said. The team played its final game ever at Griffith Stadium in 1950, with old nemesis Satchel Paige fittingly on the mound for the opposing Philadelphia Stars. Paige had made his major-league debut with the Cleveland Indians in 1948, but he returned to the pitch in the Negro leagues in 1950, before rejoining the big leagues in 1951, with the St. Louis Browns. This time, the Grays got the better of Paige, winning, 7–1. They finished the season 100–26, after winning their final game ever, on the road in West Virginia.

But when the 1951 season began, there were still no black players on the Senators. So Washington's African American fans cheered visiting black players, including Larry Doby of the Cleveland Indians. Doby, the first black player in American League history, broke in just three months after Jackie Robinson and faced much of the same abuse as his predecessor. But he had a good experience playing on the road in Washington, one of the southernmost cities in the league.

"When people say, 'You played well in Washington,' well, I had a motivation factor there," Doby recalled in a 1997 interview with the *Post*. He continued:

> I had cheerleaders there at Griffith Stadium. I didn't have to worry about name-calling. You got cheers from those people when you walked out onto the field. They'd let you know they appreciated you were there. Give you a little clap when you go out there, and if you hit a home run, they'd acknowledge the fact, tip their hat.

In 1952, Griffith defensively addressed the issue of why the Senators still had not signed a black player. "My own position with regard to Negro players on a Washington club has come in for criticism and discussion, which has not been fair to me," Griffith, by then eighty-two years old, wrote in a retrospective piece for the *Sporting News*. He continued:

> To those who persist in speaking of me harshly on the Negro player issue, let me say that I would welcome the addition of players like Robinson, (Roy) Campanella, Harry Simpson, Don Newcombe, Larry Doby, and Orestes (Minnie) Minoso to the Washington roster.
>
> I stand ready, and eager, to place Negro players on our Washington club. But they must rate the jobs on the basis of ability, and not merely because they happen to be Negroes. I will not sign a Negro for the Washington club merely to satisfy subversive persons. I would welcome a Negro on the Senators if he rated the distinction, if he belonged among major-league players.
>
> The Washington club has a large Negro clientele. It represents some of the best citizenship of the District of Columbia. I would only be too glad to give that clientele a chance to root for a player of its own race.

Two more years would pass before Washington would finally sign a black player. In 1954, Griffith turned to the island that had been the source of so many players—Cuba—to sign Carlos Paula, a black outfielder. Paula would last only three seasons before he was out of baseball. Washington had been one of the last teams to integrate—only the Yankees, Phillies, Tigers, and Red Sox took longer.

Clark Griffith died in 1955, and his adopted son, Calvin Griffith, took over the team. In 1961, the new owner moved the team to Minneapolis. Seventeen years later, at a Rotary Club speech in Waseca, Minnesota, he said, "Black people don't go to ballgames, but they'll fill up a rassling ring and put up such a chant they'll scare you to death. We came (to Minnesota) because you've got good, hard-working white people here."

The *Minneapolis Star* called for Griffith to sell the team, and civil rights groups called for a boycott of Twins games. Twins star Rod Carew fumed, saying, "I'm not going to be another nigger on his plantation." Carew was traded after the season to the California Angels.

"The words were misunderstood, taken out of context. I had had a couple of drinks and was trying to be funny," said Griffith, adding he did not know a reporter was present. He told Kerr that it was "one of the worst things I ever went through. I went down there to play golf and go to a dinner. But they got a writer there that had to be sensational and intimated things I didn't say. I was shocked as hell."

Griffith recalled his interaction with black fans in Washington, when he oversaw Griffith Stadium during Grays games as Senators vice president. "How could I talk about blacks when our ballpark had 350,000 of 'em every year, and I practically knew half of them," he said. "They've been good to us. They were our bread and butter in Washington. The Homestead Grays brought in money all summer—fourteen games or so. You're not gonna knock anybody that kept you alive."

Carew and Griffith later patched things up. "I can't say there was a racist bone in his body," Carew said when Griffith died. "Look at all the Latin American and African American players he signed and helped. I think some of the things he said came out wrong. I was upset at the time and said some things. Later, I thought it over and apologized to him for what I said."

Hail to the Pitch: Presidents and Senators

HAIL TO THE PITCH: PRESIDENTS AND SENATORS

On April 14, 2005, President George W. Bush achieved something that presidents Bill Clinton, George H. W. Bush, Jimmy Carter, and Gerald Ford couldn't—he threw out the first ball at a Washington baseball game. It had been thirty-six years since Richard Nixon's Opening Day toss in 1969, but Bush's pitch looked far different than those made at old Senators games. In the twentieth century, presidents showed up in a suit and tie, sometimes encumbered by an overcoat, and threw the ball from the stands. Sporting a Nationals jacket, Bush let it rip from the pitcher's mound at RFK.

Presidential tosses at Washington baseball games date back to 1910, with William Howard Taft, and continued with each president throwing out at least one Opening Day pitch in the nation's capital until the city was left without a team in 1972. While most presidents relished the opportunity to get a photo op at the national pastime, not every national leader has been a baseball fan. Taft's predecessor, Teddy Roosevelt, scorned baseball as a "mollycoddle game." (For those not up on their early 1900s lingo, the word "*mollycoddle*" means pampered or overprotected.) In 1907, a delegation from the National Association of Professional Baseball Leagues presented Roosevelt with a season pass, made of solid fourteen-karat gold, to "recognize [his] practical support of a game that nourishes no 'mollycoddles.'" Hey, at least these guys had a sense of humor.

Taft, who at 330 pounds was the size of catcher and infielder combined, took a greater liking to the sport. On April 14, 1910, he started the first-pitch tradition by tossing one to Senators pitcher Walter Johnson, who went on to hurl a one-hit shutout against the Philadelphia Athletics. It was Taft's presence that indirectly cost Johnson a no-hitter. Washington outfielder Doc Gessler later admitted that when a fly ball was hit in his direction, he had been daydreaming of hitting a grand slam and talking to the president about it. Backing up, Gessler tripped over a fan (spectators could stand on the field behind a rope back then), and the ball dropped for a double.

By 1912, the Senators had a new manager and part-owner, Clark Griffith. Taft couldn't make the opening game that year, due to the sinking of the RMS *Titanic* four days earlier. But Griffith wanted to keep a good marketing tradition afloat.

"It occurred to me that this would be a fine annual custom," Griffith wrote in a 1955 *Washington Star* piece titled "Presidents Who Have Pitched for Me." "So I requested a meeting with him (Taft), and he received me very amiably.

'I'd like to establish this as an annual function,' I told him, 'and if you would cooperate it might catch on.'" Taft's reply, according to Griffith, was, "Why sure, Griff. I'll be glad to start the ball rolling."

So began Griffith's long string of relationships with presidents all the way through Dwight Eisenhower. The owner's office was adorned with pictures of presidents throwing out the first ball at Griffith Stadium, and Griffith befriended not just presidents, but Supreme Court justices, cabinet members, and real senators.

Although 1912 was just Griffith's first year in Washington, he already knew something about presidents and baseball. In 1908, as manager of the New York Highlanders (later renamed the Yankees), Griffith had visited the White House in Roosevelt's final year as president. With Opening Day already passed in 1912, Griffith arranged for Taft to throw out the first pitch two months later, on June 18. Taft was "merry with enthusiasm," according to a *Washington Post* story the next day. A crowd of 15,516 fans, the second-largest in Washington history to that point, came out to see the Senators win their seventeenth straight game, a 5–4 victory over the Athletics. It was a great year for the Washington Senators. They finished in second place, with a .599 percentage, their first winning season after eleven straight losing records.

Soon, a new tradition would evolve at Senators games. Sitting in his box, the president would toss the ball over a scrum of photographers into a crowd of players from both teams, who would battle for it like bridesmaids trying to catch a bouquet. Washington would usually start its season a day before the rest of the American League in what became known as the "presidential opener," and Congress would recess for the day so members could watch the president throwing out the first ball.

Taft's successor, Woodrow Wilson, was one of the most enthusiastic baseball fans to occupy the Oval Office. He had a "dugout" at the White House, where he read and talked baseball. Even after he left office, Wilson continued to attend games, perhaps in the sweetest seats in baseball history. Griffith recalled that Wilson, who had suffered a stroke that left him partially paralyzed, asked about coming to games, but Griffith worried about how to accommodate him.

"Finally, I got an idea," the Senators' owner wrote. "I phoned the president of the American League and asked him for permission to have Mr. Wilson's automobile driven onto the field and parked outside the right-field foul line. 'Well,' he said, 'that might interfere with the right fielder, but if the umpires will sanction it, it's all right with me.' Griffith continued, "I got in touch with the umpires, and they gave me permission. Mr. Wilson's car was parked between the foul line and the seats, and I stationed a player out there to sit on the bumper of the car and ward off any foul balls that might be headed for the automobile." Griffith made no mention of any dents to Wilson's car.

At the 1922 opener, President Warren Harding, a former minor-league team owner, called over Walter Johnson's son, who sat in the president's lap in the first inning. "This is a mighty fine boy you have here," Harding told the pitcher. But Griffith saw something else: a person worn down by the presidency.

"The man who threw the ball out in 1922 looked and acted twenty years older than the man who had so confidently and vigorously thrown the ball the year before," Griffith wrote. "It was not a great surprise to me that Harding did not live to finish his one term."

Calvin Coolidge wasn't much of a baseball fan, but he had to fake it. The Senators won their only World Series during his presidency, in 1924, and the team was a national sensation. Coolidge became the first president to attend a World Series opener, where he threw out the first ball. But it was his wife, Grace, who was the real fan in the first family. She kept score during the World Series games and kept her husband in the game.

President Herbert Hoover had the unfortunate distinction of throwing out a first ball during the Great Depression, during Prohibition, and perhaps worst of all, in Philadelphia. Hoover was booed during a World Series game between the St. Louis Cardinals and Philadelphia Athletics, whose fans started chanting, "We want beer!" The Athletics have since moved on, and most of those fans are dead, but Philadelphia fans are still known as the toughest crowd, once even booing Santa Claus. "I left the ball park with the chant of the crowd ringing in my ears: 'We want beer!'" Hoover wrote in his memoirs.

Opening Day at Griffith Stadium was a place to be seen for the Washington elite. Newspaper stories would showcase dozens of members of the city's who's who, from the president to senators, cabinet members, and generals and their family members. A 1935 *Washington Post* Opening Day story put it this way: "It was all very much like a spectacle outside an ancient Roman arena, where senators, statesmen, and military men forgot their dignity in the scuffle to see the famous chariot race between the world's most famous gladiators."

The next year, President Franklin D. Roosevelt made his third Opening Day appearance as the Nationals topped the Yankees, 1–0. The Associated Press captured a series of photos of Roosevelt at the ballpark, clearly enjoying himself as he motions with his fingers, looks up in the sky to track a pop-up or fly ball, and flashes a grin.

But his charisma proved to be dangerous. Senators pitcher Bobo Newsom pitched a four-hit shutout that afternoon, despite suffering a broken jaw when a throw by his own third baseman, Ossie Bluege, nailed him in the face.

Newsom and Bluege had converged on a bunt, and while Bluege fielded it, Newsom took his eye off the ball to glance at FDR in the stands.

Security wasn't as tight as it is today. Still, the presence of Secret Service agents at a baseball game was an unusual sight, and it prompted the following flip description in the *Washington Post* for one of FDR's visits:

> A group of grim-lipped, steel-eyed huskies, all wearing their right hands in their pockets with the nonchalance of long practice, slither past the Washington dugout to the president's box. . . . The Secret Service men are as taut as greyhounds in the starting box. A reporter reaches in his pocket for a cigarette, and his hand is jerked away before he can get it. . . . Finally the presidential heave takes place, and there ensues the maddest scramble you ever saw for the ball. Ball players, news photographers, cameramen, reporters, and a few civilians pile up like sandlot football players.

In 1940, Roosevelt literally threw a wild pitch, as his Opening Day toss slammed into a *Washington Post* photographer's camera. "It was one of the worst that ever left a presidential arm," the *Post* reported, "and that is saying something, for Hoover, Coolidge, Harding, and Wilson also heaved some wild ones."

In all, Roosevelt threw out a record eight Opening Day pitches, but he had a much more important role in helping to preserve baseball during World War II. Shortly after the bombing of Pearl Harbor, the baseball commissioner, Judge Kenesaw Mountain Landis, wrote to FDR to get his views on whether baseball should be played during the war. "If you feel we ought to continue, we would be delighted to do so," Landis wrote. "We await your order."

On January 15, 1942, barely a month after Pearl Harbor, Roosevelt responded in what became known as the "Green Light Letter." In it, the president says it would be best for baseball to continue. "There will be fewer people unemployed and everybody will work longer hours and harder than ever before. And that means that they ought to have a chance for recreation and for taking their minds off their work even more than before," FDR wrote. He also made a pitch for more nighttime baseball, still pretty rare at the time, "because it gives an opportunity to the day shift to see a game occasionally." In addition, FDR made it clear that baseball should not be exempt from the draft when he declares the following:

As to the players themselves, I know you agree with me that the individual players who are active military or naval age should go, without question, into the services. Even if the actual quality to the teams is lowered by the greater use of older players, this will not dampen the popularity of the sport.

Despite the appearance of a cordial correspondence, FDR and Landis disliked one another. It was Clark Griffith, a friend of the president, who laid the groundwork for more nighttime games, according to Bill Gilbert's book *The Seasons: Ten Memorable Years in Baseball and in America*.

FDR would not throw out another ball after the "Green Light Letter." Baseball might have been a good leisure outlet for a country at war, but for a wartime president, there were obviously more pressing responsibilities. By the time World War II ended in 1945, FDR was dead, but his successor, Harry S. Truman, made a point of returning to Griffith Stadium just six days after the Japanese surrender was formalized.

In the midst of a pennant race, Truman arrived at the ballpark on September 8, 1945, to throw out the first ball in a game between the Senators and St. Louis Browns. Washington won the game, 4–1, in front of 20,311 fans, a large crowd for those days. The Senators finished one and a half games out of first that year, in what would be their last serious pennant run. In all, Truman attended sixteen games at Griffith Stadium, more than any other president, according to *Baseball: The President's Game*, by William B. Mead and Paul Dickson.

Truman was the first southpaw to throw out a ball at Griffith Stadium, but he sometimes tried to throw right-handed. At the 1950 opener, Griffith placed a second ball in the president's right hand, and Truman threw both balls. The *Washington Post* assessed the performance, writing, "The first, thrown with his left, was a good one with some loft. It was caught by pitcher Joe Haynes. The right-handed toss was a miserable thing that landed on the turf."

Things were worse for Truman the next year. His appearance at the team's home opener on April 20, 1951, came the day after General Douglas MacArthur spoke before a joint session of Congress, in which he delivered his famous line, "Old soldiers never die, they just fade away." Truman had fired the popular MacArthur as Far East commander earlier that month, and the president was met by a cascade of boos at the ballpark. In an attempt to drown them out, the U.S. Air Force Band played "Ruffles and Flourishes" and "Hail to the Chief."

Truman befriended Griffith, and, in 1959, six years after the president had left the White House, he sent Griffith a telegram on the eve of Opening Day, on which Vice President Richard Nixon was to throw out the first ball: "BEST

OF LUCK TO YOU ON OPENING DAY AND EVERY DAY. WATCH OUT FOR THAT NIXON. DON'T LET HIM THROW YOU A CURVE. YOUR FRIEND, HARRY TRUMAN."

In his first year in office, President Dwight D. Eisenhower decided to blow off the 1953 opener so he could go golfing in Augusta, Georgia, infuriating an important voting group—baseball fans. But the game was rained out, so Ike flew back in time to throw the first pitch at the rescheduled opener against the New York Yankees. He stayed for just one and a half innings before flying back to his golfing trip. The Senators lost, 6–3.

"President Ike gave us a bad scare because Opening Day conflicted with a golfing date he had in Atlanta," Griffith wrote two years later. "We were rescued at the last moment by the weather."

Eisenhower was a fan of the game, despite engaging in what might be called "Golfgate" today. He once said:

> When I was a small boy in Kansas, a friend of mine and I went fishing, and as we sat there in the warmth of the summer afternoon on a river bank, we talked about what we wanted to do when we grew up. I told him that I wanted to be a real Major League Baseball player, a genuine professional like Honus Wagner. My friend said that he'd like to be president of the United States. Neither of us got our wish.

Ike got a chance to redeem himself the following season, in 1954. After Mickey Vernon's tenth-inning home run gave the Nats a 5–3 victory over the Yankees, the president got so excited that he started to make his way onto the field to congratulate Vernon before Secret Service agents intercepted him. Instead, they brought Vernon over to the president's box. "Wonderful, a wonderful home run," Eisenhower told him.

Meanwhile, First Lady Mamie Eisenhower hugged and kissed Griffith. "What an opener!" Griffith told reporters after the game. "We never had one like it—we never had a president practically run out onto the field to salute one of our ballplayers."

Vernon recalled that as he crossed the plate, someone grabbed at him. "I tried to pull away from him; there [were] a bunch of players there, and I thought he was just a guy from the stands," Vernon said. "He says, 'No, come with me, the president wants to talk to you.' So he took me over to his box."

Charlie Brotman, longtime public address announcer for the Senators, recalls irking Eisenhower at the home opener in 1956. In the fifth inning the Senators brought in a relief pitcher, but Brotman couldn't see the pitcher's number as he made his way to the mound. Brotman recounts:

> So one of the guys next to me said, "I think it's Truman Clevenger." So I said, OK, "Ladies and gentleman, now coming in to pitch for Washington, Truman . . ." but now he's motioning me to stop. So I turned off the mike and said, "What's the matter?" And he said, "I don't think it's him." Meanwhile, the word "Truman" is just hanging out. I wish I could grab it, bring it back, put it in my pocket, but it is out there. It's just "Truman." Meanwhile, I'm looking around to see who else I could ask, and there's nobody. And here's the president of the United States, down in the presidential box, and he starts to look over his left shoulder. And I'm imagining him thinking, "What is this, some kind big joke or something? Truman preceded me as president. Is President Truman going to come in and pitch for Washington? Is this a joke?"
>
> Meanwhile, 27,000 people are looking at the president, and the president is looking at me, which made all the spectators look at me. I'm huddling down so that nobody can see me. And I thought, "This is going to be my first and last game. They're going to fire me." Finally, the pitcher reached the pitcher's mound, and he got the rosin bag, and I can see that it was Truman Clevenger. Meanwhile, about twenty seconds had passed. In my mind, it was at least twenty minutes. So I just said "Clevenger." And that was my first game, and probably my most embarrassing moment.

Despite the mishap, Brotman not only kept his job, but must have even impressed one of Ike's men. That fall, someone from the White House called Brotman to see if he would introduce the president at the inaugural parade the next year. Brotman has announced every inaugural parade since, most recently Barack Obama's in 2013. "And it all stemmed from baseball," he says. He continues:

What I discovered is that the president's personality really reflected on the parades and the appearances at the ballpark. Eisenhower couldn't care less about parades, couldn't care less about baseball. It was really no big deal. If anything, it's an intrusion. And so he hoped it would be over within ten minutes. Kennedy was just the opposite. Kennedy's personality came out. He was very gregarious. He'd shake everybody's hand. And same thing with Nixon. But Johnson played it straight and wanted to get it over with.

In 1960, Eisenhower's final year as president, Ike again took off on a golfing trip to Augusta at the beginning of the baseball season, but this time he made a point of interrupting the vacation to fly back to Washington to throw out the season-opening pitch. Washington beat the Boston Red Sox, 10–1, as Camilo Pascual struck out fifteen batters, giving Eisenhower a winning record at Opening Day games.

"Now that makes me four and three," Ike said after the game.

"That's better than .500 and that's okay in baseball," responded Vice President Nixon.

The next year there was a new president and a new team. John F. Kennedy threw out the first pitch at the 1961 opener, inaugurating the expansion Washington Senators. The old team had moved to Minnesota after the 1960 season to become the Twins.

JFK got a rather rude reception for his first pitch as president. White Sox outfielder Jim Rivera, who had snagged the opening toss, was brought over to the box to get the ball signed, in keeping with tradition. According to a story by *Chicago Tribune* writer David Condon years later, "Jungle Jim" looked at the autographed ball and told Kennedy:

What kind of garbage college is that Harvard, where they don't even teach you to write? What kind of garbage writing is this? What is this garbage autograph? Do you think I can go into any tavern on Chicago's South Side and really say the president of the United States signed this baseball for me? I'd be run off. Take this thing back and give me something besides your garbage autograph.

Laughing the entire time, the young president agreed to sign the ball more legibly.

"You know," Rivera replied, "you're all right."

The Senators lost that game, 4–3, but Kennedy proved a good luck charm the next year, as Washington defeated the Detroit Tigers, 4–1, at the first game ever at its new $23 million D.C. Stadium—the ballpark that would be renamed for Kennedy's brother, Robert F. Kennedy, in 1969.

Two players on the Senators had a tough time getting to the ballpark that day. Jim Hannan, then a rookie pitcher, recalls getting a ride from outfielder Jimmy Piersall, whose book about his battle with mental illness, *Fear Strikes Out*, has been turned into a movie.

"He showed up in what looked like a '37 Chevy," says Hannan, now a stockbroker in Washington. "It broke down right in front of the White House. So we had to take a cab to the stadium." Later, Hannan says, the White House placed a call to Piersall, and a secretary told him to hold for the president. "And Kennedy gets on and says, 'What are you doing leaving that piece of junk in front of my house?'" Hannan relates with a laugh.

Piersall and Kennedy knew each other personally, Hannan said. In the 1950s, Kennedy was a real senator, from Massachusetts, while Piersall played for the Boston Red Sox for much of the decade. At the game that day, Piersall playfully slapped Kennedy on the shoulder on his way out to center field.

During a rain delay, Kennedy and his entourage stayed dry in the umpires' room, signing autographs and chatting with the men in blue. Only days before, Kennedy had nominated former NFL star Byron White to the Supreme Court. The president asked umpire Hank Soar, another former NFL player, for a scouting report. Soar told Kennedy he "never saw any better," according to the *Washington Post*.

Kennedy had such a good time at the game that he skipped a 4:30 p.m. appointment at the White House with the Laotian ambassador to stay until the last out. Kennedy didn't get back until 5:30. "The Laotian ambassador, Tiao Klapman, of the patient, understanding East, was waiting for him," the *New York Times* reported. "I'm leaving you in first place," the president told team owner Pete Quesada and general manager Ed Doherty, but the Kennedy magic was short-lived. The Senators finished in last place.

President John Kennedy overlapped with Washington Senators infielder John Kennedy. The two men even shared the same birthday, May 29. The Kennedy who played for Washington from 1962 to 1964 says he never got a chance to meet the president, but the post office once got their mail mixed up. "My girlfriend wrote me a letter, and it went to the White House," he recalls. "The post office saw the name John Kennedy and automatically sent it there. When I went to the ballpark, there was a manila envelope waiting for me from the White House."

Kennedy's vice president, Lyndon Johnson, made a famous quip mixing baseball, religion, and politics. "We cheer for the Senators, we pray for the Senators, and we hope that the Supreme Court does not declare that unconstitutional," LBJ said.

At his first game as president, the 1964 Senators home opener, U.S. senators in attendance were called back to the Capitol via stadium loudspeaker for a quorum call on the Civil Rights Bill. After the team dropped the game, 4–0, to the Los Angeles Angels, some joked that the "wrong senators were asked to leave the ballpark." The next year, LBJ was spotted eating four hot dogs and a bag of popcorn. Washington lost that one, too, 7–2, to the Red Sox, with all nine runs coming on home runs.

For Johnson, baseball was not a high priority. In 1966, when team officials came to the White House for the annual presentation of the season pass, LBJ met with them for about thirty seconds, and then allowed photographers just thirty seconds to take pictures. He then clapped his hands and said, "Let's go, we've got a lot of things to do." Facing the Vietnam War and other pressing issues, Johnson would miss the opener that year, as well as the opener in 1968, his final full year in office.

Richard Nixon was probably the most knowledgeable baseball fan to occupy the Oval Office. He also had some experience at throwing out the first pitch prior to becoming president; in 1959, as vice president, he relieved Eisenhower. Later that year, Nixon traveled to the Soviet Union for the famous "Kitchen Debate" with Soviet premier Nikita Khrushchev. His trip coincided with a horrible Senators losing streak that had reached a dozen games.

According to former Washington slugger Roy Sievers, a Nixon favorite, the vice president called the ballpark from the Soviet Union and said, "I want Lemon, Killebrew, Allison, and Sievers out at the airport when the plane lands," referring to Sievers's teammates Jim Lemon, Harmon Killebrew, and Bob Allison.

"We were all there," Sievers recalls. "The first thing he said was, 'What in the hell is wrong with the Senators?' And I said, 'Mr. Vice President, we're just not hitting good, the pitching's not good.' He said, 'I tell you what, I'll be out the next night.' Usually, when he'd come out, we'd win the ballgame. But we lost." In fact, the Senators' streak hit eighteen before they finally snapped it with a victory over the Cleveland Indians.

Years later, Nixon recalled how taxing it was to be a Senators fan. "You have to have been a real baseball fan to have been a fan of the Senators," Nixon said at a gala luncheon at the Richard Nixon Presidential Library and Birthplace in 1992. "It was no easier to have been a fan of the Senators we had back then than of some of the senators we have in Washington today."

In the mid-1960s, Nixon was out of politics after losing the presidential race in 1960 and the California governor's race in 1962. His career could have taken a different path at that point: He was approached by baseball owners to become commissioner, and by the players' union to become its director, according to *Baseball: The President's Game*. Nixon, of course, went on to become president in 1969. Ironically, George W. Bush tried to gauge interest in becoming baseball commissioner when he was owner of the Texas Rangers, before settling for the White House in 2001.

Nixon made his presidential baseball debut in 1969, along with the team's new manager, Ted Williams, as the Senators lost, 8–4, to the New York Yankees. Sitting next to Nixon was another rookie, Bowie Kuhn, in his first year as baseball commissioner. Kuhn recalled telling Nixon about how Williams was trying to make Senators slugger Frank Howard a more disciplined hitter.

"So here comes Howard to bat, the first pitch bounces six feet in front of home plate, and he swings and misses," Kuhn said with a laugh. "And the president looked at me and didn't say a word. His silence spoke volumes. We both laughed. He was a great baseball fan."

In July of that season, the president received the world champion Detroit Tigers at the White House, who were escorted by Congressman Gerald R. Ford of Michigan—the man who would replace Nixon as president after the Watergate scandal five years later.

"You know I have to be for Washington—do you mind?" Nixon asked the Tigers. Referring to the Senators' 3–0 victory over Detroit the day before, Nixon quipped, "You don't mind passing the wealth around, do you?"

"Yes we do," one of the players laughingly replied.

That night, Nixon was at the ballpark to see the Senators win a second straight game against the Tigers, 7–3. It also marked the team's second consecutive victory with Nixon in attendance.

Nixon was such a huge fan that in 1972, he compiled an all-time All-Star team for the Associated Press. "I like the job I have now," he once said, "but if I had my life to live over again, I'd like to have ended up a sportswriter."

"Of all the presidents, Nixon was the most knowledgeable baseball fan," says Brotman, the former public address announcer. "At first, I told his administrative assistant, 'He must have really boned up, because he's talking to players about batting averages and earned run average.' And the aide said, 'No, no, no, he didn't bone up. He really is a baseball fan. He follows it through the sports pages.'" When the Senators were on the verge of moving to Texas in 1971, Nixon said it would be "heartbreaking," but he declined to get personally involved.

"This may have been practical politics by the president, who can count and is aware of Texas' twenty-eight electoral votes compared to the District of Columbia's mere three," *Washington Post* sports editor Shirley Povich wrote in a requiem for the team. "But it was also pussyfooting, and entirely unlike the pronouncement in 1958 by then-Vice President Nixon that a Washington without Major League Baseball would be 'unthinkable.'"

Still, Nixon was working behind the scenes to get a team back. On October 13, 1971, he met with D.C. mayor Walter E. Washington to discuss the prospects. In a tape-recorded conversation, previously unreported, Nixon mentions several candidates: "The White Sox is [*sic*] a possibility. Chicago really can't support two teams."

At another point, he asks about luring the Cleveland Indians. "Cleveland is not going to support them. They got that lousy lakefront stadium," the president says.

"And they haven't had any attendance," Washington says. The Indians were the only team that year to draw fewer spectators than the Senators, pulling in 591,000 fans, compared to Washington's 655,000.

The president also tees off on the Senators' owner, Bob Short, who had been a chief fundraiser for Nixon's 1968 opponent, Democrat Hubert H. Humphrey. "Short is a jerk," Nixon declares. "I sat behind him at games, and I can tell you—moaning and bitching all the time."

At the end of the meeting, Nixon makes an optimistic—and as history would prove inaccurate—prediction. "I think that with Washington, the (bi)centennial coming up and everything, baseball will be back," he says. In that bicentennial year, 1976, the American League owners voted to expand outside the country, to Toronto, and to another Washington—Seattle.

Although Nixon told Mayor Washington that losing the Senators was "terrible," he was not above trying to capitalize on it politically. On September 22, 1971, the day after the American League voted to allow Short to move the team to Texas, White House press secretary Ron Ziegler told reporters that Nixon would now switch his allegiance to the California Angels, near his home of San Clemente, California. That night, in another previously unreported taped conversation, Nixon called Robert H. Finch, a longtime Nixon loyalist.

"I want you to call (Angels owners) Bob Reynolds and Gene Autry and tell them that the president thinks this is a very significant thing," Nixon tells Finch. "For seventy-one years, presidents, oh, going back to William Howard Taft and all the rest, Theodore Roosevelt, have thrown out balls in Washington." (He was off by about ten years and one president—Teddy Roosevelt never threw a ball out at a Senators game.)

"The president has in effect said, now, that with this change, that each president should throw out the ball in the park of his home team." He continues, "Now what they have to do is change the American League schedule, so that the first game, you see, the way Washington always played the first game, will be in Anaheim Stadium, see? And I'll come out and throw out the ball, and I agree to do it, see?"

Maybe Nixon was cut out for baseball commissioner after all.

"It's really a big deal," Nixon says.

No argument from Finch.

"I think it's great," he says.

But the plan was never put into motion. When the American League schedule came out, the Angels were slated to open on the road in Minnesota, although the game was canceled because of a brief players' strike.

After Washington lost the Senators, presidents would head north to Baltimore to throw out the first ball, but it didn't have the same pomp and circumstance of the capital openers. Kuhn, the former commissioner, remembered President Ronald Reagan's appearance in Baltimore in the 1980s, when Frank Robinson was the Orioles manager.

"After President Reagan threw out the ball, he said to me, 'I'd like to sit in the dugout,'" Kuhn said. "The president selected the home plate end of the dugout, and that's where Robinson sat. So Robinson sat on the other side of the dugout. He did a slow burn and glared at us from the other end of the dugout. It lasted two innings."

Years later, Robinson was in the dugout at RFK when the presidential tradition resumed in Washington with George W. Bush, a one-time owner of the Texas Rangers, which had started out as the expansion Washington Senators.

"I'm excited about the team," Bush told reporters before the Nats' first home game. "I started paying attention to the lineups during spring training. I watch the pitching staff. I know that Livan Hernandez is pitching tonight. I'm watching carefully."

Bush saw Nationals pitcher Joey Eischen in the clubhouse before the game and remembered that the Rangers had traded him for Oil Can Boyd.

"Eischen, right?" the president asked.

"Yes, sir," Eischen responded.

"Oil Can Boyd. Bad trade."

Unfortunately, Bush's appearance kept thousands of fans waiting outside the ballpark as the game began, where they were forced to stand in long lines to go through metal detectors. But the fans went home happy, as the Nationals won their first home game ever, defeating the Arizona Diamondbacks, 5–3, in front of a capacity crowd of 45,596.

Bush, the son of a former Yale first baseman, President George H. W. Bush, made sure he got some practice throws in before the day of the game. The president had the opening pitch on his mind that afternoon, telling the American Society of News Editors, "I've got a decision to make. Do I go with the fastball or a slider?"

He went with the fastball, sending a high, hard one to Nationals catcher Brian Schneider, and bringing a sense of closure to the final Senators game ever played. Thirty-four years earlier, fans swarmed onto the field with two outs in the ninth inning, and the last out of the last game was never recorded. The man on the mound in the middle of that dark anti-celebration, Senators pitcher Joe Grzenda, pocketed the ball and kept it all those years in his home in Pennsylvania. As baseball returned to Washington in 2005, he handed the ball to Bush for the opening toss.

Bush made one more Opening Day toss for the Nationals to mark another historic occasion, the opening of Nationals Park in 2008, and Bush's last full year in office. The president walked out of the Nats dugout onto a red carpet flanked by velvet ropes and then made his way to the pitcher's mound. Sporting a Nationals jacket, he reared back and threw a high pitch to Nationals manager Manny Acta. The Nationals won that game, too, on a walk-off home run by Ryan Zimmerman in the bottom of the ninth inning.

Two years later, President Barack Obama marked the one hundredth anniversary of the tradition by throwing out the first pitch at the Nationals' home opener against the Philadelphia Phillies. Back in 1910, it was the same two cities—Washington and Philadelphia —but different teams in a different league: the American League's old Senators versus the Philadelphia Athletics, who now play in Oakland.

The packed crowd at Nationals Park gave Obama a loud ovation, with a few boos scattered in. The president wore a Nationals jacket and khakis, but when he got to the mound, he put on a cap from his favorite team, the Chicago White Sox. "Bad touch there," said Nationals manager Jim Riggleman.

Obama had tipped off Commissioner Bud Selig that something like that was coming. The commissioner said that when he saw the president in the Nationals jacket, he told Obama, "I don't think I've ever been at a game when you didn't have a Sox jacket."

Obama replied, "I've got something coming."

The president threw a high, wide toss, and he looked awkward in his delivery, double-clutching several times before letting it fly. Nats third baseman Ryan Zimmerman, who received the toss, had to lunge to prevent a wild pitch.

"I said balk right away," quipped Phillies catcher Brian Schneider, a former Nat who had caught Bush's opening toss in 2005.

Obama, who prepped for the game by throwing practice pitches to aides at the White House, had said that he didn't play organized baseball as a kid and that some of the sport's moves don't come naturally to him.

"I was a little disappointed with the pitch," Obama said during a stint in the booth during the Nationals' television broadcast. "It was high and outside." He joked that he was going for an intentional walk, and also suggested he would have gotten better with a little more time on the mound. "If I had a whole inning, I'm telling you, I would have cleaned up," he said. The Nats couldn't have done much worse with Obama on the mound. They lost, 11–1.

By the time of Obama's first pitch in 2010, fans had come to expect a different presidential tradition of sorts—comic-relief races among oversized mascots of the four Mount Rushmore presidents: George Washington, Thomas Jefferson, Abe Lincoln, and Teddy Roosevelt. During the fourth inning, they would tear down the warning track from center field to a finish line along the right-field line. Maybe as payback for Teddy dissing baseball as a "mollycoddle game" more than a century earlier, poor Teddy, his goofy grin unchanging, lost every time for years.

Like a historically bad baseball team, Teddy found countless ways to lose. Sometimes the other presidents played dirty, taking him down in ways that would have earned them unsportsmanlike conduct penalties in the more violent setting of a football game. Other times, a mysterious freelance mascot—including a panther, a leprechaun, a lobster, a pierogi, and even the Kool-Aid man—came out of the stands to tackle Teddy. On other occasions, Teddy was disqualified for cheating, like the time he used a Segueway.

Jayson Werth, who joined the Nats in 2011, after playing for five consecutive division-winning Phillies teams, didn't like the gag. In September of that year, as the Nats were headed for their sixth straight losing season, Werth rushed Jefferson, reached up, grabbed him by the nose, and wrestled the twelve-foot mascot to the ground. Members of the Nats bullpen joined the fracas, too, slamming other presidents to the wall in an effort to pave the way for a Teddy win. But if there was any doubt the fix was in, Teddy took a dive after mixing it up with Abe, and his losing streak continued.

As the Washington Nationals battled for their first playoff appearance in 2012, fans of the twenty-sixth president were mounting a campaign for Teddy's first win at Nationals Park. A Nationals season-ticket holder named Scott Ableman helped galvanize support for the effort with a website called "Let Teddy Win," which became a rallying cry at Nationals Park. Filmmaker Ken Burns and Senator John McCain brought more publicity to Teddy's cause with a mock documentary on his losing streak, which had reached more than five hundred games, dating back to the first race in 2006.

"I've been paying a lot of attention to the fact that one of the truly great presidents in history has never won a race. I am outraged," McCain deadpans in the ESPN E-60 documentary, holding a Teddy Roosevelt bobblehead doll. "That's why I am calling for congressional hearings to right this horrible wrong."

Even the White House jumped on the bandwagon. On Air Force One in late September, President Obama's spokesman, Jay Carney, told reporters about McCain's "important interview," which showed that bipartisanship was still possible:

> Senator McCain pointedly complained about the fact that at Nationals Stadium, Teddy Roosevelt—the mascot for Teddy Roosevelt—has yet to ever win the race among the presidents. This is an outrage. I agree with Senator McCain. I'm comfortable saying that my boss agrees with Senator McCain (Obama's 2008 presidential opponent).

A reporter asked whether Obama aspired to be in the president's race someday. Carney's response: "Let history decide."

Even as the Nationals were poised to make history as the first Washington baseball team to make the postseason in seventy-nine years, they sometimes found themselves portrayed in the national media as the second-most interesting baseball story in the nation's capital. The Teddy quest made national headlines in all sorts of venues, including the front page of the *Wall Street Journal*.

The Nationals fueled the craze, with a little help from McCain. On the third-to-last game of the regular season, the team played a video on the ballpark scoreboard of McCain encountering Teddy lounging in a kiddy pool, next to a beach ball and pool toys.

"Teddy, what are you doing?! What are you doing?!" McCain asks. "You're getting ready for the game like this?"

Teddy pops balloons in defiance. The senator escorts him into another room, telling him they have something to talk about.

"Now first of all Teddy, I am fully aware that you are the victim of a vast left-wing conspiracy, by the commie-pinko libs in this town," the Arizona Republican tells him. "And I got that. And it's tough. But I want to assure you there's going to be a full investigation by the United States Senate. And you're going to be vindicated."

Still, McCain tells his "hero" that he can prevail:

> You can do it, Teddy! I know you can do it! You are the man that inspired generations like mine. And one thing I'm positive of. Aren't you excited about the Nats? We're in the playoffs! First time since I've watched them in 1933, when Joe Cronin was managing. We are now, the Nats are there. They are there. And you're going to lead 'em, Teddy, and you're going to win. Now go out there and do it!

Teddy claps his hands excitedly. He still lost, but the Nats clinched the division title that night despite losing, too, when the Braves dropped a game to the Pirates.

Two days later, in the season finale on a warm weekday afternoon, Teddy raced out of the center field gate to chants of "Teddy! Teddy!" He started out in fourth place, but an emaciated-looking knockoff of the Phillie Phanatic—the fuzzy green mascot of the opposing team—bolted out of the Nationals bullpen by the right-field corner and knocked the other three presidents to the ground. The "Fakenatic" then raced Teddy down the home-stretch before falling off, and Teddy crossed the finish line for his first victory. He did a little victory dance as fans cheered wildly.

"#Teddy won! #Teddy won! #Teddy won!" tweeted McCain. "We've defeated the massive left-wing conspiracy!"

Even the Democrats celebrated the Republican's victory. Senator Chuck Schumer, a New York Democrat, tweeted congratulations, saying, "2 NY's own @Teddy26Nats."

Although Nationals like Werth had been pushing for a Teddy victory, not all of his teammates were as interested. "I am so glad Teddy won, so we can stop talking about Teddy," said third baseman Ryan Zimmerman, whose role as face of the franchise seemed to be temporarily usurped by the twelve-foot version of the Rough Rider. "People get more excited for a mascot race than a game." He added in a sarcastic tone, "Yes, I'm excited Teddy won. I'm ecstatic."

After the season, the Nationals added a fifth president to the race: William Howard Taft, who in real life had some history with his fellow Republican president, Roosevelt. In 1909, Taft succeeded Roosevelt with Teddy's endorsement, but by the end of Taft's term in office, the two men had a falling out, and Roosevelt left the GOP to run on the Progressive Party ticket. That split the Republicans and helped Democrat Woodrow Wilson win the 1912 election.

In selecting Taft, the Nationals created a built-in rivalry between the two allies-turned-enemies. The Taft mascot, who was introduced at the team's NatsFest in January, immediately engaged in some trash-talking, tweeting, "It was lovely meeting all the fans and my only real competition—George, Tom & Abe—at #NatsFest today."

The Nationals gave Taft—or "Billy," as they're calling him—a makeover. The real Taft weighed 330 pounds, but his mascot persona appeared svelte, like a supermodel, as he worked the stage. Or maybe it just looked that way because he was twelve feet tall.

The real Taft would have been no natural in a foot race, but in some ways he's a natural choice for the presidents' mascot race. In 1909, he saw the Senators lose, decided he must have been a "hoodoo" (something that brings bad luck), and didn't attend another game that season. Thankfully, the Senators invited Taft to the home opener the next year, where he made history, becoming the first president to throw out the first pitch, starting a century-long tradition.

SIX

Futility

FUTILITY

The Senators suffered a huge disappointment after winning the 1933 pennant. They finished twenty games under .500 in 1934, ending up in seventh place, thirty-four games behind the American League champion Detroit Tigers. That season signaled a fundamental shift in Washington's fortunes. The team would finish in the top half of the standings just four times from 1934 until it moved to Minnesota in 1961.

Washington began taking apart its championship team even before the 1934 season started, releasing future Hall of Fame outfielder Sam Rice in the off-season. At the age of forty-three, Rice had been a backup on the 1933 team, but he had helped contribute, batting .294 off the bench. It was Rice's nineteenth season in the big leagues, all in a Washington uniform.

"Sam, it is with deep regret that the time has come when your service with the Washington team is ended," owner Clark Griffith wrote to the player nicknamed "Man O'War," "but I hope our personal friendship will carry on for all time."

Rice finished his career in 1934 with the Cleveland Indians, batting .293—a good season for most, but the lowest of Rice's twenty-year career. He retired with a lifetime batting average of .322 and 351 stolen bases and was inducted into the National Baseball Hall of Fame in 1963.

In August 1934, the Senators dumped pitcher Al Crowder, who had helped the 1933 team win the pennant with a staff-high twenty-four wins. Crowder, thirty-five, had slumped badly in 1934, going 4–10, with a 6.79 ERA, before finishing the season with Detroit. The move was widely seen as the beginning of the breakup of the 1933 American League champions. But no one could have anticipated what was next.

The Boston Red Sox had a wealthy new owner, thirty-one-year-old Tom Yawkey. Determined to turn the franchise around, he visited Griffith in his hotel room at the 1934 World Series and offered $250,000 for Washington player-manager Joe Cronin. That was an astonishingly high figure, made in the midst of the Great Depression, and only fourteen years after the Sox had sold Babe Ruth to the Yankees for $125,000.

Griffith had a quick reaction, saying, "Tom, you had better leave."

After the series, Yawkey called the Old Fox at home and asked, "How about that deal?"

"To hell with you!" Griffith yelled, and hung up.

Griffith had good reason to be possessive of his star. The owner had nurtured Cronin from a punchless .242 batter as a twenty-one-year-old to one of the league's most dangerous hitters. In 1934, Cronin had knocked in one hundred runs or more for the fifth straight time. He was the kind of manager Griffith liked, tough and determined. And Griffith could truly look upon his twenty-eight-year-old player-manager as a son: Cronin had recently married Griffith's niece and adopted daughter, Mildred Robertson. Some had muttered that Cronin had married into the manager's job for life, and such talk weighed on Griffith as he began to reconsider Yawkey's offer.

"I said to myself, 'You keep Cronin here and he will continue to be the subject of that son-in-law guff,'" Griffith later wrote. "'Remember, Yawkey is a millionaire, with the sky the limit in his baseball operation. He could do things for Joe and Mildred you could never hope to approach.'"

Perhaps the Nats' owner was just rationalizing, although he conceded that family considerations weren't the only factors. Griffith recalls that the team had lost a "lot of money" in 1934, and that he owed a bank $124,000. "I decided that, for the good of those two kids, and for the financial salvation of the Senators, I just had to let Cronin go to Boston."

But he demanded the Red Sox shortstop, Lyn Lary, and a five-year deal for his son-in-law, at $30,000 a year. Lary lasted just thirty-nine games in a Washington uniform, batting .194 in 1935, before the Senators shunted him off to the St. Louis Browns. Cronin played eleven seasons in Boston, seven as the team's regular shortstop, before finishing his playing career as a utility infielder. In those seven seasons as starting shortstop, Cronin hit .300 or better four times, drove in one hundred runs or more three times, and even developed some power—hitting seventeen or more home runs four times. In thirteen seasons as Boston skipper, Cronin guided the team to nine winning records, including the 1946 pennant, the franchise's first since 1918. He was elected to the Hall of Fame in 1956.

Cronin wasn't the only family member Griffith unloaded. In 1941, he sold pitcher Joe Haynes, whose wife, Thelma Griffith, was another of Griffith's adopted daughters, to the Chicago White Sox. The Senators eventually reacquired Haynes, who became a coach and vice president of the team. Eleven years after trading Haynes, Griffith put his own nephew, utility man Sherry Robertson, on waivers, and he was picked up by the Philadelphia Athletics. Robertson, too, later returned to the flock, running the farm system.

By purchasing Cronin, the Red Sox were starting to make a habit of getting their managers from Washington. Boston's 1933 manager, Bucky Harris, had guided Washington to its first pennant nine years earlier. The Red Sox let him go to make room for Cronin, and, in a bit of managerial musical chairs, Washington rehired its old manager for the 1934 season. Harris had been a success in his only year in Boston, leading the Red Sox to a fourth-place finish, a marked improvement over the team's seventh-place finish the year before.

Still only thirty-eight, Harris was no longer the "boy wonder" who had wowed the baseball world in the Roaring Twenties. There was no magic in 1935, when the team improved by just half a game over the previous season, finishing in sixth place, nineteen games under .500. Attendance slumped to 255,000, the worst since 1919. Second baseman Buddy Myer provided Senators fans with someone to cheer for, leading the league with a .349 batting average and driving in one hundred runs on just five homers.

That year, Griffith purchased pitcher Bobo Newsom from the St. Louis Browns. In a sign of Washington's luck that season, a week later Newsom suffered a broken knee on a line drive in the third inning of a game, yet soldiered on to go the distance. "Tell the fans of Washington I'm sorry my bones ain't together," the colorful Newsom told reporters from the bed of his hotel room. "And tell them I'll be back there sooner than anybody says I will."

In 1936, Washington improbably jumped to fourth place with a record of 82–71. Newsom won seventeen, with twenty-four complete games, while Jimmie DeShong won eighteen. The season would turn out to be but a temporary reprieve for Washington fans, however. It was the Nats' only winning record from 1934 to 1942.

The Senators traded Newsom to the Red Sox in 1937, but he would return to Washington for four more stints. Griffith continued to try to retool the team that year by purchasing future Hall of Fame outfielder Al Simmons from the Detroit Tigers. Simmons, thirty-five, hit a disappointing .279 for the Senators, a drop of forty-eight points from the previous season in Detroit. He stepped it up in 1938, batting .302, with twenty-one home runs and ninety-five RBIs, but Griffith fined him $200 and released him at the end of the season after Simmons cursed out fans at Griffith Stadium. "Simmons still is a good ball player, but he isn't satisfied with Washington nor does he fit in with my plans for a young team," Griffith said of the thirty-six-year-old outfielder.

Despite the cascade of losing teams, Harris stuck around for eight seasons in his second tour with the Senators but the manager didn't have much to work with, as Washington had a thin farm system. Then, as now, there were complaints from "small-market teams" that bigger-market teams were threatening the competitive balance on which the sport depended—with the New York Yankees being the poster boys for buying pennants. Ironically, big-market teams were able to exploit their advantage by building up more expansive farm systems—the very tool that small-market teams use today to offset their financial disadvantage. The era of free agency was still a half century away.

Washington was decidedly a small-market club. Griffith could afford only one farm team, compared to the thirteen clubs owned by or affiliated with the Yankees. He demanded that the Yankees be forced to sell one of their two Double-A teams. "It's not the Yankees I'm agin," he says in a 1940 *Saturday Evening Post* profile. "It's just the idea of preserving a monopoly by means of money. If we let those rich men run things the way that only they can afford to run them, what's going to become of baseball? You want John D. Rockefeller to come into baseball and win the pennant every year?"

Griffith was becoming an anachronism in the world of baseball owners—a former player who had mortgaged his ranch to buy into the team, competing against wealthy businessmen who did not depend on baseball for their livelihoods. The Old Fox did shift his view on one major change to the game. In 1935, the Cincinnati Reds hosted the first major-league night game, prompting Griffith to protest, declaring, "Baseball was meant to be played in God's own good sunshine."

But six years later, on May 28, 1941, the first night game at Griffith Stadium proved to be a real draw. Twenty-five thousand fans came out, one of the largest crowds of the season, to see former star Walter Johnson inaugurate the new era with a ceremonial first pitch. The stadium was dramatically thrust from darkness to light as the engineer flipped a switch to coincide with Johnson's toss. Game time was 8:30, about ninety minutes later than today's starting times.

"Dignity went out the window as the gay and informal crowd shed its coats and rolled up its sleeves," the *Washington Post* reported, adding that the festivities "had all the fanfare of a Hollywood premiere." But the excitement and big crowd couldn't help the home team, which lost its tenth straight game that night.

The Senators continued to draw well under the stars, and Griffith became an enthusiastic supporter, successfully lobbying the league to let him hold more games without the benefit of God's own good sunshine. "When the National League instituted night competition, I hollered plenty," Griffith wrote years later. "I envisioned the ruination of the game in the major leagues. I regarded baseball after dark as strictly minor-league stuff." But after the success of that first night game, he added, "I realized then that I had been wrong about the innovation."

While night baseball may have energized Griffith in 1941, something else weighed heavily on his mind: the prospect of a last-place finish. In August of that year, the team slipped into the American League basement. "You don't understand it," he told reporters before a loss to the Yankees at Griffith Stadium. "But right now I'm a heap more jittery than I'd be if we were fighting for a first-division place. It's been thirty years since I came here, and in all that time we never finished in the cellar. I just don't want to finish last."

But the Senators actually played over .500 the rest of the way, ending in sixth and averting the last-place finish Griffith so dreaded. Shortstop Cecil Travis was the exception to the team's mediocrity, batting .359, but he was overshadowed by two of the best individual seasons in baseball history. Travis finished second in batting to Ted Williams, whose .406 average was the last time a player hit .400 or more. Meanwhile, Joe DiMaggio won the Most Valuable Player Award after setting the single-season record by hitting in fifty-six consecutive games.

The next year, 1942, Washington dropped to seventh place, and Harris quit as manager. The skipper who won two pennants in his first run with Washington had but one winning season in eight years this time around.

Once again, Griffith turned to a former Senators player to manage the team, this time Ossie Bluege, who had been the third baseman on the pennant-winning teams of 1924, 1925, and 1933. Under Bluege's leadership in 1943, the Senators posted their best record since their pennant a decade earlier. Washington jumped to second place, with an 84–69 record, thirteen and a half games behind the first-place Yankees. Starting pitcher Early Wynn went 18–12, with a 2.91 ERA, while rookie Milo Candini won eleven games, with a 2.49 ERA. The Senators drew 575,000 fans, their highest total since 1930.

But the team sank back to the bottom the next year, as Washington lost several key players to the military during World War II. Among those serving in the 1944 season were first baseman Mickey Vernon, second baseman Gerry Priddy, and pitcher Ray Scarborough. Washington finished last, with a .416 winning percentage, twenty-five games behind the St. Louis Browns, who won their only pennant that year. It was the first time a Senators team under Griffith had come in last place, and the first for the franchise in thirty-five years. Griffith was so desperate for players that he signed Eddie Boland, who had been playing for the New York City Sanitation Department team. Boland didn't do too badly, actually, hitting .271 in nineteen games.

In 1945, for the third year in a row, Washington did a complete somersault in the standings. This time they would give their fans a season to remember—the Senators' last real pennant race. Washington competed with a most unusual pitching staff. Four of the five starting pitchers—Roger Wolff, Dutch Leonard, Mickey Haefner, and Johnny Niggeling—were knuckleballers. This quartet had hitters tied up in knots, pitching sixty complete games among them and helping the Senators to a league-best 2.92 ERA. Wolff (20–10, 2.12 ERA) and Leonard (17–7, 2.13 ERA) paced the staff, while the rotation's sole nonknuckleballer, a five-foot, seven-inch native of Lucca, Italy, named Marino Pieretti, won fourteen games.

On offense, Washington made up for a lack of punch with speed on the base paths. The Senators hit just twenty-seven home runs that year, and, incredibly, just one at home—an inside-the-parker by first baseman Joe Kuhel. But Washington hit a league-high sixty-three triples, led by Kuhel's thirteen. Paced by outfielder George Case and second baseman George Myatt, who swiped thirty bases each, the Senators also led the league in stolen bases. Washington got a lift in late June, when outfielder Buddy Lewis returned from the Pacific Theater, where he had been flying cargo planes over the Himalayas. Lewis hit .333, with seven triples in sixty-nine games.

The most colorful player on the team, however, was outfielder Bingo Binks. The twenty-eight-year-old rookie had spent the first two years of the war working as a machinist in a war-materials factory. Although a talented athlete with great defensive skills, he hadn't mastered the game's fundamentals, infuriating his manager, Bluege. Because he was deaf in one ear, Binks had been disqualified from serving in the military. "Bluege would chew him out from time to time, and Binks would say, 'I haven't heard one word you said,'" writes Bill Gilbert, who served as the team's batboy that spring. "He would drive this old-school manager up the wall."

A turning point for the Senators came in mid-summer. Entering August, Washington was just four games over .500, in third place. The Nats then started an insane string of five doubleheaders in five days against the Philadelphia Athletics and Boston Red Sox at Griffith Stadium. Washington won nine of the ten games, catapulting into second place, with a 54–42 record, hot on the heels of the first-place Detroit Tigers.

The city buzzed that year over the pennant race, and the ballpark was often filled with uniformed men from all branches of the military in what would be the final year of World War II. "You would see this sea of colors of military uniforms in the stands: the Army khakis, the Navy white uniforms, the Marine green," says Gilbert. "When a hitter hit a ball into the stands, the fan who caught it always threw it back, because they knew that those balls would go to the military bases for the GIs playing baseball. And if you started to stick it in your pocket, you'd get booed right out of the ballpark."

Washington and Detroit battled it out the rest of the way, but because of a scheduling quirk, the Senators would finish their season a week before the Tigers. Griffith rented out his stadium to the Washington Redskins every year, and the Senators ended their schedule early in 1945 to allow the football team to play its home opener on September 30, one reason the Nats had played so many doubleheaders back in August.

So Washington entered a season-ending three-game series on September 22, against the Athletics in Philadelphia, who were a game and a half behind the Tigers. The Senators won the first game, 2–0, and then suited up for a double-header the next day, knowing they needed a sweep to pull even with the Tigers. But in this improbable season, a sunny break in the afternoon cast a cloud on the Senators' pennant chances.

The first game of the doubleheader went into extra innings, and, in the bottom of the twelfth, with two outs, Philadelphia's Ernie Kish lofted a fly ball to center field. The sun had just come out, and Binks, Washington's center fielder, had forgotten his sunglasses. Losing the ball in the sun, Binks couldn't make the catch, and Kish wound up with a double. Kish scored the winning run on a single, driving a dagger into the Nationals' pennant chances.

The Senators came back to win the second game, 4–3, but found themselves a game out of first—and no games left to play. Now all they could do was hope that the Tigers would lose three of their remaining games. That would result in a tie, and a one-game playoff—or play-off, as it was called back then—to decide the pennant winner.

The Tigers split their first two games, giving Washington fans hope. Now the Senators needed the defending American League champions, the St. Louis Browns, to sweep a season-ending doubleheader against the Tigers on a rainy day in St. Louis. In the first game, the Browns led, 3–2, after eight innings, but in the top of the ninth, the Tigers loaded the bases with one out. Up came their star, Hank Greenberg, who had returned from the army in June. "Hammerin'" Hank parked one in the left-field bleachers, giving Detroit a 6–3 lead. The Tigers held St. Louis scoreless in the bottom of the ninth, clinching the pennant, and ending Washington's season. Detroit would go on to win the World Series against Chicago—and the Cubs haven't been back to the series since. The Senators, meanwhile, finished twenty games over .500, their best record since 1933. It was a mark they would never match again.

The next year was a financial success but disappointing on the field. The Senators drew a franchise record 1,027,000 people to Griffith Stadium in 1946, the only time they broke the 1 million mark, as fans in the first year after the war came out in hopes of another pennant race. But this time, Washington dropped to fourth place, finishing with a 76–78 record, twenty-eight games out of first. Vernon topped the league with a .353 batting average and fifty-one doubles, but the team suffered from substandard pitching and defense. The Senators were the worst fielding team in the league and had the third-worst ERA.

On December 10 of that year, after a nine-month illness, Walter Johnson died from a brain tumor at the age of fifty-nine. Among those keeping vigil at Johnson's bedside was Clark Griffith. Thousands came to Johnson's memorial service at the Washington National Cathedral. Former teammates served as pallbearers, along with former Giants pitcher Jack Bentley, whom Johnson had defeated in the seventh game of the 1924 World Series.

The 1946 season started a long slide for the Senators. In 1947, the team dropped to seventh place, with a .416 winning percentage, thirty-three games behind the first-place Yankees, piloted by former Nats manager Bucky Harris. For the second year in a row, the American League champions were managed by a former Senators skipper; Joe Cronin had guided the Red Sox to the flag in 1946. Vernon, the 1946 batting champion, dropped nearly one hundred points in 1947, finishing with a .265 average. The Senators hit a woeful .241 as a team, with no regular over .280. After the season, Griffith relieved Bluege as manager, making him director of the Senators' farm system.

Of course, Griffith hired a former player to replace Bluege—this time, the team's old first baseman, Joe Kuhel. Although Kuhel belonged to the American Society of Magicians, he could work no magic on this team. The 1948 Nats lost eighteen straight games in September en route to another seventh-place finish and a .366 winning percentage. Vernon, just two years after winning the batting title, bottomed out at .242. After the season, Griffith traded him, along with pitcher Early Wynn, to Cleveland for first baseman Eddie Robinson and two pitchers. In shipping off Wynn, Washington had dealt a future Hall of Famer.

In 1949, the Senators started out 1–7 and then shocked the baseball world by winning nine straight games on a road trip to improve to 12–11. The Senators dropped the last game of the trip to fall to .500, but that was good enough for their overly optimistic fans. Although it was only May, thousands gathered at Union Station to welcome the "Wondrous Nats" back to Washington as heroes. The players were treated to a motorcade down Pennsylvania Avenue, and city commissioners and U.S. senators were predicting a pennant. "We knew all along on the Hill that we had the best team in the American League," said Senator Millard Tydings, a Maryland Democrat. Fans even called the ballpark inquiring about reserving World Series tickets.

By early June, the surprising Nats were 25–20, but as baseball fans relearn every year, it's a long season. The team tanked after its strong start, ending up not at the top of the league, but at the bottom. In fact, Washington's 50–104 record (.325 percentage) was its worst since 1909. Three starters posted ERAs over 5.00—Paul Calvert (6–17, 5.43), Mickey Harris (2–12, 5.16), and Dick Weik (3–12, 5.38).

By the end of the season, it was obvious to everyone—including Kuhel—that the manager would be fired. "I'll probably be canned at the end of the season, and I'm not griping," he was quoted as saying. "That's baseball. But in my defense, I'd like to say this: You can't make chicken salad out of chicken feathers." Turns out he probably said something more colorful than "feathers."

After two seasons, Kuhel was out as manager. For his replacement, Griffith turned to his old standby—Bucky Harris—for his third tour of duty with the team. Harris had led the Yankees to a pennant in 1947, but was fired after the team slipped to third place in 1948. He was managing in the minors when Griffith asked him to return to Washington. The Nats owner gave Harris, fifty-two, a three-year contract, breaking with the team's tradition of hiring managers for just one year at a time.

In the off-season, when Griffith turned eighty, he encountered the only serious challenge to his control of the team. Since purchasing a controlling interest of the Senators after the 1919 season with wealthy Philadelphia exporter William Richardson, Griffith had enjoyed a free rein with the team, so he never felt the need to acquire a controlling interest on his own, knowing that Richardson would always back his decisions. Between the two of them, they held about 80 percent of the team's stock.

Richardson died in 1942, and, after his ownership stake was passed along to a couple of family members, it was sold in 1949 to thirty-one-year-old investor John J. Jachym for $550,000 on behalf of an investment syndicate. Although Jachym stressed that he had no designs on taking over the place, he also made it clear that he was not going to be a passive investor. He had baseball experience as a scout for the St. Louis Cardinals and a Minor League Baseball owner. For his part, Griffith had no interest in sharing ownership responsibilities with the youngster.

The Old Fox owned about 40 percent of the team's stock and couldn't freeze Jachym out on his own, so he enlisted other investors in the team to keep the newcomer at bay—declining the upstart partner a seat on the board of directors, and even refusing to give him an office at the ballpark. Jachym irritated Griffith with such grandiose proposals as a Triple-A team, season-ticket sales, a modern scoreboard, and a public relations director—all elements, of course, of today's teams. "For his $550,000, Johnny got a ten-cent brush off," wrote *Washington Star* columnist Francis Stann.

Within six months, Jachym sold his 40 percent share to H. Gabriel Murphy. "I had the rug pulled out from under me," Jachym said. At least he made an $85,000 profit on the sale.

Murphy was in the mold of William Richardson—a pliant partner. "I bought into the Washington club strictly as an investor," Murphy said. "I have no recommendations to make. Mr. Griffith is the boss, and I'll go along with him in every way. I'm not a baseball man; Mr. Griffith is the best."

Delighted with the switch, Griffith made Gabriel a vice president. "Now we can go ahead without any worries," Griffith said. Murphy made sure of that when he agreed to sell Griffith enough of his own stock to give the Old Fox controlling ownership. Ironically, after Griffith's death five years later, Murphy would become a steely adversary to Clark Griffith's successor, Calvin Griffith, battling the new owner's plans to move the team out of Washington.

Meanwhile, Bucky Harris brought a modicum of baseball success to the Senators in 1950, at least by the team's low standards. Washington jumped to fifth place, but still finished twenty games under .500, and thirty-one games out of first place. The team's young third baseman, Eddie Yost, was starting to come into his own. Just twenty-three years of age, Yost hit .295 and scored 114 runs. Yost, who would become known as "The Walking Man," led the league with 141 walks, and he finished second with an on-base percentage of .440.

On May 31, the Senators traded their first baseman, Eddie Robinson, who had gotten off to a slow start, and two weeks later reacquired Vernon to take his place. Vernon, who was hitting just .189 with the Indians through the first two months of the season, rediscovered his stroke with the Nats, batting .306 the rest of the way.

Although Washington improved by seventeen games in 1950, their fans were not returning. The Senators drew just under 700,000, their fourth straight season of dwindling attendance. That trend continued, for the most part, throughout the 1950s.

The Senators slumped to seventh place in 1951, but Harris managed to squeeze a winning season out of them in 1952—barely. The team finished 78–76, good for fifth place, in what would be its last winning season in Washington. The Nats were even within striking distance of first place most of the year. In late August, they were six and a half games off the pace, but the team finished seventeen games behind the pennant-winning Yankees. Griffith rewarded Harris with a new two-year contract as manager.

Washington made up for an anemic offense that year with outstanding starting pitching. Nats batters hit a league-worst .239, but three starting pitchers posted ERAs under 3.00—Bob Porterfield (2.72), Connie Marrero (2.88), and Spec Shea (2.93). Plagued by poor run support, this trio combined for only thirty-five victories.

Marrero, just five feet, seven inches tall, was one of the colorful Cuban players signed by super scout Joe Cambria. He was coy about his age, although baseball records indicate he was forty-one years old that season. "When baseball writers attempted to wheedle from Marrero his exact age," Shirley Povich writes in his book, *The Washington Senators*, "he merely grinned and pointed awkwardly to the number on his baseball shirt, which read '22.'" Marrero completed sixteen of his twenty-two starts that year and finished with an 11–8 record.

The Senators had an almost identical record the next season, 1953, at 76–76, again good for fifth place. This time, the hitting and pitching were more evenly matched, allowing Porterfield to lead the league with twenty-two wins, despite his ERA increasing by more than a half-run, to 3.35. He also led the league in shutouts (nine) and complete games (twenty-four).

Washington had some hitting stars as well. Vernon led the league with a .337 batting average and forty-three doubles and was second in both RBIs (115) and triples (eleven). A rejuvenated Washington offense hit a respectable .263 that year.

Although the team played some exciting baseball, Washington's attendance went into a free fall that year. The team drew just 596,000 fans, a drop-off of more than 100,000 from the previous year, and its lowest total since World War II.

In 1954, the Senators had new competition in the region. The woeful St. Louis Browns had moved to Baltimore to become the Orioles. After getting some financial concessions, Griffith agreed to waive his territorial rights to the region, a gesture that was not reciprocated by the Orioles years later, when they fought to keep a team out of Washington.

For the Senators, sharing a regional fan base was hardly the only problem the Browns' move posed. Washington also lost a fellow bottom-dweller in the American League. For decades, the Browns had been one of the worst teams in baseball. As recently as 1951, only a last-place finish by St. Louis helped the Senators avoid the cellar; Washington finished seventh that year. The Senators might have won only three pennants, but the Browns had managed just one—and that was in 1944, when major-league teams were stocked with inferior players filling in for regulars fighting in World War II.

The relationship between these two teams changed almost immediately. The Orioles finished behind the Nats in their first year in Baltimore, but drew 1.06 million fans—double Washington's attendance, which had tumbled to 503,000. At one home game, the Senators played in front of just 460 fans. These franchises were going in opposite directions, both at the turnstiles and on the field. The Orioles would never finish lower than the original Senators again.

Washington did pull one fast one on its new neighbor. Before the 1954 season, the Senators traded outfielder Gil Coan to Baltimore for outfielder–first baseman Roy Sievers. Coan was out of baseball a couple of years later, while Sievers emerged as one of the top sluggers in the American League. The Senators also made another shrewd move by purchasing Jim Lemon, who would also develop into a bona fide slugger, from the Cleveland Indians. But the 1954 season was a disappointment for the Senators. After two decent years, Washington dropped into sixth place, twenty-two games under .500.

The Senators fired Harris after the season and replaced him with former Brooklyn Dodgers manager Chuck Dressen. It was Griffith's last managerial move, and it marked the first time he chose someone who hadn't been a Senators player. Harris, who had managed the Nats for eighteen years in three different stints, took the manager's job in Detroit.

Dressen was coming off two straight pennant-winning Dodgers teams in 1952 and 1953, but he could not reverse the Nats' slide. The 1955 Senators finished in last place, with a .344 winning percentage. Attendance tanked to a league-worst 425,000, marking the first time since 1917 that Washington had been outdrawn by every other American League team. The average Nats crowd in 1955 was slightly more than 5,500.

That season also saw the end of an era in Washington. On October 27, 1955, Griffith died at the age of eighty-five. The Old Fox had been with the team, as manager and then owner, for forty-four years. Thousands came to his funeral, including scores of players, managers, and executives from across baseball. Among them were Griffith's two "boy wonder" player-managers, Bucky Harris and Joe Cronin, now middle-aged men of fifty-eight and forty-nine, respectively. Harris and Cronin had accounted for all three of Washington's pennants between them, the last one coming twenty-two years earlier.

"Mr. Griffith was a man of the Old West," recalls Bob Wolff, the team's first television announcer. "He believed in loyalty and trust. At noon, he cleared everyone out of his office except his family. They'd all eat lunch at a big long table. They all worked at the ballpark or played for him." Then, after the game, Griffith would sit in his office by himself, listening to *The Lone Ranger* on the radio, Wolff says, and, in later years, watching it on television after day games.

His widow, Addie Griffith, recalled how her husband had put everything into the team. "He had some hard times, believe me," she told the *Washington Post* in 1956. "It was a struggle. People talk about all the money he had. He never had any money to spend. We never went abroad or took airplane trips. It was always throwing money into the club—every cent we ever had. Clark wasn't rich like the Comiskeys and the Macks."

With his death, Griffith's nephew and adopted son, Calvin Griffith, who had been serving as team president, took control of the team. The Senators were in poor financial straits, Calvin Griffith told biographer Jon Kerr years later, "When I took the club over in 1955 I think we had $25,000 in the treasury."

Within one month, the young Griffith traded away his star first baseman, Mickey Vernon, in a nine-player deal with the Red Sox. Washington didn't receive any impact players in the deal. Calvin Griffith soon entertained more consequential offers—to move the team out of Washington. In October 1956, after another disastrous year in which the Senators finished seventh and drew just 432,000 fans, Griffith told reporters that he was considering moving the team to either Los Angeles or San Francisco. At the time, there was no Major League Baseball on the West Coast.

Gabriel Murphy, Clark Griffith's accommodating partner, now turned on Calvin Griffith. Murphy, who owned 40 percent of the team's stock, threatened to sue Griffith to prevent a move. "I am shocked and saddened to learn that those who succeeded to Mr. Griffith's position would try to erase his efforts within fifty-eight days after the Washington baseball fans erected a monument to his memory," Murphy said. "The Senators must remain in Washington. I feel, as others in baseball, that our club is not merely a local representative. This is a national baseball team. It belongs to the nation as does the city itself."

In the end, the team's board of directors considered bids from four cities—Los Angeles, San Francisco, Minneapolis, and Louisville—before deciding to stay put. "We're happy to remain here, and I hope we stay here the rest of our lives," Griffith said. Addie Griffith called the news wonderful. "Clark loved this city, and I know he never would have left Washington," she said. Clark Griffith had opposed any discussion of moving the team.

But Murphy said the damage had been done. "The attempt to move the franchise to the West Coast seriously impaired the value of the club's most priceless asset—the wholehearted support and confidence of the Washington fans," he commented in announcing that he was quitting his salaried job of board treasurer and director in early 1957, while retaining his stock in the team.

Meanwhile, Griffith was trying to assure Washington fans that the team would stay—for good. In a January 15, 1957, piece in the *Washington Post*, Griffith writes: "This is my home. I intend that it shall remain my home for the rest of my life. As long as I have any say in the matter, and I expect that I shall for a long, long time, the Washington Senators will stay here, too. Next year. The year after. Forever." Griffith later blamed those famous last words on the team's overeager public relations man, who had ghostwritten the piece for him.

The Senators' attendance was truly woeful. Thirteen of the sport's sixteen baseball teams drew more in 1956 than Washington drew in 1955 and 1956 combined. In 1957, the team dropped back into last place, and its attendance remained last in the league—457,000. Griffith fired Dressen after a 4–16 start that season and replaced him with Cookie Lavagetto.

There was a bright spot on that dreadful Washington team—the performance of Roy Sievers. The Senators' slugger hit .301 and led the league in both home runs (forty-two) and RBIs (114). He also tied an American League record by hitting six home runs in six games. His record-tying home run came in the bottom of the seventeenth inning, on his eighth plate appearance of the day, giving Washington a 4–3 victory over the Detroit Tigers. Only 4,601 fans were at Griffith Stadium, and no doubt far fewer were there by the time Sievers hit his walk-off homer. "The next day, the wind's blowing out, and I was hoping to break the record," Sievers recalls. Instead, he had one single in five at bats.

After the season, Sievers went into Calvin Griffith's office and asked for a 100 percent raise. Griffith balked, Sievers recalls, but did wind up giving him a decent salary. Sievers's 1957 paycheck of $36,000 was the highest ever for a Senator. "So I come back the next year, after hitting thirty-nine home runs, driving in 108 runs, and batting .295," Sievers says. "He wanted to cut me $10,000!"

After the 1957 season, the two California cities that had sought out the Senators the year before lured the National League's two New York teams, the Dodgers and Giants, to the West Coast. At a board meeting in January 1958, Griffith said he hoped to keep the Senators in Washington as long as he lived. When asked by a stockholder, "Do you assure the stockholders the club will remain here?" Griffith said, "Yes."

But six months later, Griffith was claiming that he was being pushed to move the team by four owners who served on the American League's relocation committee. "Some clubs are raising hell with us," Griffith said on the eve of a league owners' meeting. "They're sick and tired of playing to small crowds" in Washington. Minneapolis, Houston, and Toronto expressed interest in the Senators.

Griffith's claim was refuted by Yankees owner Del Webb, chairman of the American League relocation committee. "This hits me cold," Webb told the *Post*. "Nobody ever indicated that the Washington club wanted to move or was being forced to move."

At the owners' meeting, Griffith decided not to ask permission to relocate the team after getting resistance from fellow owners, who were concerned about the timing, as Congress was considering legislation to revoke baseball's coveted antitrust exemption. Senator J. Glenn Beall, a Maryland Republican, sent a telegram to American League president Will Harridge, warning that it would be "unthinkable" for baseball to desert the nation's capital.

Just a week later, however, Griffith acknowledged in testimony before a Senate subcommittee that he still might move the team. "We want to stay in Washington as long as humanly possible," Griffith said. "Baseball is a business. If we don't get enough fans, we're going to have to find out if we can carry on. We can't leave the franchise to stay here and rot."

It was doing just that. In 1958, the team once again finished last in both the standings and attendance, drawing just 475,000 fans. The team finished eighth again in 1959, but attendance improved as the team offered fans a couple of new young sluggers. One was twenty-four-year-old Bob Allison, who hit thirty home runs and led the league with nine triples. The other was twenty-two-year-old Harmon Killebrew, who shared the league lead in home runs, with forty-two.

Killebrew became a Washington Senator because of a U.S. senator. Five years earlier, Clark Griffith's friend, Senator Herman Welker of Idaho, told the Nats' owner about a teenager from his hometown of Payette, Idaho, who was worth checking out. Griffith sent Ossie Bluege to scout the seventeen-year-old Killebrew, who went 12-for-12 in a semipro game. Bluege quickly signed the youngster.

Fueled by Killebrew, Allison, and Lemon, who hit thirty-three home runs, as well as seventeen-game winner Camilo Pascual, the suddenly explosive Senators increased their attendance by 130,000 that 1959 season, to 615,000, although they still finished in last place. Still, Calvin Griffith was again entertaining offers to move the team to Minneapolis, saying he needed at least 700,000 fans. "What more does Mr. Griffith expect of fans who have seen the Senators end up in last place for three seasons in a row and in the second division for the past thirteen seasons?" asked the *Washington Star* in an October 6, 1959, editorial.

When it became clear once again that he didn't have the votes among his fellow American League owners to approve a relocation after the season, Griffith announced that the team would not move. Murphy rhetorically—and prophetically—asked what good that statement was. "What happens next year?" he said. "Do we go into orbit again in 1960?" In a word—yes.

In October 1960, Griffith finally won league permission to move the team, coupled with expansion that would put new teams in Washington and Los Angeles. The American League fast-tracked the expansion for the 1961 season

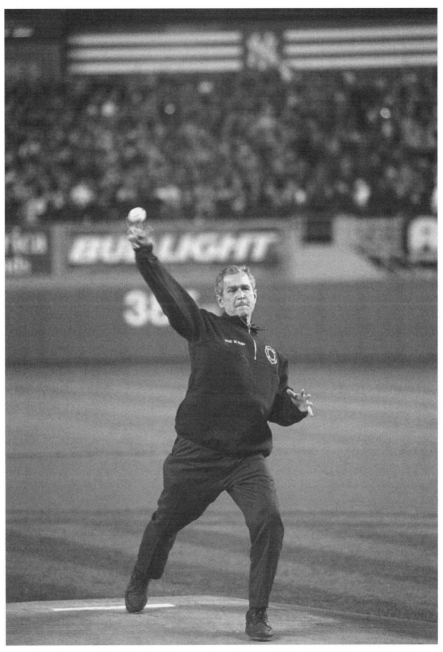

President George W. Bush takes the mound on Opening Day, 2005. Photo by Eric Draper, courtesy of the George W. Bush Presidential Library and Museum.

President Calvin Coolidge learning how to throw a curveball from Walter Johnson (on the right) as player-manager Bucky Harris watches on (left of the president). Courtesy of the Library of Congress.

President William Howard Taft, facing camera, on opening day, April 14, 1910, the day he started a tradition of presidents throwing out the first pitch. Courtesy of the George Grantham Bain Collection, Library of Congress.

President Franklin D. Roosevelt tosses out the first pitch on Opening Day in 1934. Senators owner Clark Griffith is pictured to the right of FDR. Courtesy of the Rucker Archive.

President Harry S. Truman, second from right, on Opening Day 1948 at Griffith Stadium. Photo by Abbie Rowe, courtesy of the Harry S. Truman Presidential Library.

President Richard Nixon prepares for his throw as Ted Williams (left) looks on in the Senators' opening game with New York in 1969. Photo by Robert L. Knudsen, courtesy of the General Services Administration/National Archives.

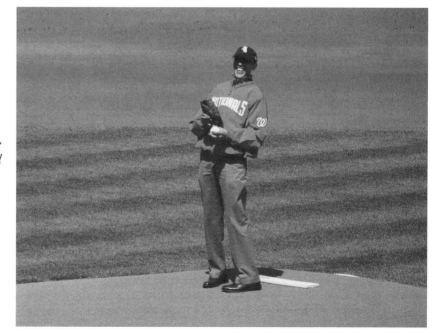

President Barack Obama laughs at the response to his White Sox cap prior to his "high and outside" pitch on Opening Day, April 5, 2010. Courtesy of Michael Myers.

Washington Senator Buddy Lewis with fellow air cadets at Kelly Air Force Field in April 1942. Lewis was one of many Major League Baseball players to have forsaken the game to serve their country during World War II. Courtesy of the Rucker Archive.

Harmon Killebrew (left) being welcomed to the team by Bucky Harris (center) and player Bob Porterfield (right). Killebrew joined the Senators in 1954. Courtesy of the Rucker Archive.

Manager Mickey Vernon (right) greets Cuban great Minnie Minoso in 1963. Courtesy of the Rucker Archive.

Famed slugger Ted Williams (right) as the Senators' manager. Courtesy of the Rucker Archive.

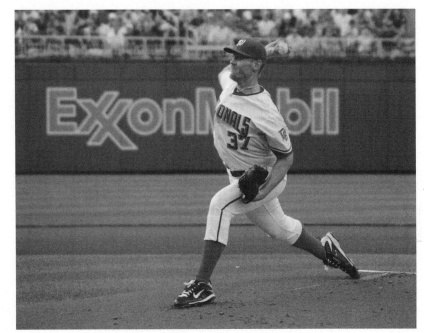

Stephen Strasburg in his major-league debut, 2010. Photo courtesy of Scott Ableman.

Bryce Harper at the plate at the Nationals vs. Orioles game on June 24, 2012. Photo courtesy of Keith Allison.

to beat the National League to the punch. The senior circuit had already announced new teams in Houston and New York for 1962. Ironically, in their last year in Washington, the Senators had their best season in seven years, finishing in fifth place. Attendance increased to 743,000, the highest since 1949.

"I regret leaving Washington, but I just couldn't turn down the Minneapolis deal," Griffith said. "I think we'll draw 1.3 million our first year there, and we'll average more per head than we did at Washington." Griffith wasn't too far off. In their first year in Minneapolis, the newly named Twins drew 1.26 million fans—more than they drew in any year in Washington.

The Twins developed into a successful franchise. They won the pennant in 1965 and back-to-back division titles in 1969 and 1970. In 1987, the Twins won the World Series, the franchise's first in more than sixty years, dating back to the 1924 Senators. But a decade after the Twins' second championship in 1991, Major League Baseball tried to extinguish the team, which had been a charter member of the American League, born in Washington a century earlier. After the 2001 World Series, Major League Baseball targeted the Twins and the Montreal Expos for elimination.

In fighting off the plan, the state of Minnesota, which had lured away Washington's first team, paved the way for baseball's return to the nation's capital. The state-chartered Metropolitan Sports Facilities Commission won an injunction forcing the Twins to play in the Metrodome the following season. Baseball couldn't eliminate just one team, because that would screw up scheduling. So the Expos glommed on to the Twins' lifeline.

As part of a collective bargaining agreement reached a year later, baseball owners pledged not to eliminate any teams through 2006. That meant the only way to get rid of the problem child Expos was to move them. Had the Twins gone under, there would have been no Expos to move to Washington. In a strange way, Washington owes its new team to the state that took its old team away.

SEVEN

A Doomed Rebirth:
The Expansion Senators

A DOOMED REBIRTH: THE EXPANSION SENATORS

There was something unfair about Washington having to start all over again with an expansion team in 1961. After all, the American League wasn't "expanding" to D.C. at all; the nation's capital had been a charter member of the league, dating back to 1901. It was Minneapolis that was the real expansion city, but it was not forced to pay its dues by starting from scratch. Instead, Minnesota received an up-and-coming Senators team from Washington.

The owners of the Cleveland Indians and Detroit Tigers argued that Calvin Griffith should have had to begin with an expansion team in Minnesota and leave his players behind in Washington, but those owners were voted down, 6–2, so Washington got tagged with the new team. This was no semantic point. The old Senators were on the verge of success after seven straight losing seasons, thanks to such rising stars as Harmon Killebrew, Bob Allison, and Camilo Pascual. By 1965, the Twins would be American League pennant winners, something they hadn't achieved in their last twenty-seven years in Washington. "Like the San Francisco earthquake of 1908 [that] leveled a once-booming city, the New Nats must start from the bottom," *Washington Post* sportswriter Bob Addie wrote in a 1961 preview.

The new Senators and the other expansion team, the Los Angeles Angels, would be stocked with rejects from other American League teams during the expansion draft. Still, some Senators fans were glad to be rid of Calvin Griffith and looked forward to a fresh start. "The attitude of the local fans was, the old man, Clark Griffith was cheap—he had to be in order to survive. Calvin is cut from the same cloth. Cheap bastard. Let 'em go, we'll get another team," recalls Phil Hochberg, a lifelong Senators fan who became public address announcer for the new Senators.

But others took the loss harder. "When we heard they were leaving, it was just total devastation," says lifelong Washington sports fan Kevin Dowd. "It's probably like when your mother and father get divorced. The sense of loss was like death."

The American League turned to a Washington bureaucrat to run the Washington Senators—Lieutenant General Elwood R. (Pete) Quesada, the head of the Federal Aviation Administration. Quesada gave up his $20,000-a-year government salary to head up the ownership group. His family went back several generations in Washington, and there was (and still is) a Quesada Street in Northwest Washington, a few blocks west of Rock Creek Park.

Quesada beat out two competing ownership bids—one by New York financier John J. Bergen and the other by Washington lawyer Edward Bennett Williams, who listed Joe DiMaggio as a partner. In the early balloting, the

Quesada and Williams bids each had the votes of three American League owners, with Bergen getting the support of the other two owners. The tie was broken, ironically, by the man who was deserting Washington—Calvin Griffith. He switched his vote from Williams to Quesada. Williams went on to own the Baltimore Orioles and Washington Redskins.

In an editorial, the *Washington Post* applauded the fact that the team would be owned by local investors, adding, "It was of the utmost importance that the Washington franchise be regarded as a long-term investment rather than as a speculative splurge." Unfortunately, the expansion Senators would have neither ownership stability, nor, at the end, a local owner—both factors that led to the team's move a decade later.

There was some uncertainty about whether the American League could actually get the new teams up and running for the next season. Baseball commissioner Ford Frick, calling the American League expansion "hasty and impetuous," told the *Post*, "I believe in expansion. I always have. But I'd hate to see some town ruined by hasty action. There are many, many details to be discussed before a ball club can be put together."

But Congress soon made it clear that any delay in Washington's new team would be unacceptable. "Capitol Hill will not countenance any absence of Major League Baseball in Washington in 1961," said House Judiciary Committee chairman Emanuel Celler, a New York Democrat. "The nation's capital shall not be looted of its franchise even for one season."

Quesada quickly named former Senators star first baseman Mickey Vernon manager. Ed Doherty took the reigns as general manager and made a bold, and, as it turned out, wildly inaccurate prediction: "With good trading and proper selection of players, we'll be a contending team in two or three years."

Dowd says he was excited to see who the new Senators would get. "Well guess what?" he says with a laugh, "These were journeymen and old guys and new guys who couldn't play."

In the first-ever expansion draft on December 14, 1960, the new Senators chose twenty-eight players at $75,000 each. The first player selected, Yankees pitcher Bobby Shantz, never suited up for the Senators. Washington traded him two days later to the Pittsburgh Pirates for pitcher Bennie Daniels and infielders Harry Bright and R. C. Stevens. The trade paid early dividends for the newborn Senators. Daniels became Washington's only winning pitcher that first season, going 12–11, with a 3.44 ERA. Bright wasn't much of a factor that first season, but in 1962, he tied for the team lead in home runs, with seventeen, batting .273.

The Angels and Senators picked players in four categories—pitchers, catchers, infielders, and outfielders. Washington's first infield pick was Detroit shortstop Coot Veal, who played a less-than-stellar season in his only year in D.C., hitting .202, with just eight RBIs in sixty-nine games. He was also thrown out eight times in nine stolen base attempts.

Washington chose as its first outfielder Boston's Willie Tasby, who hit .251, with seventeen home runs and a team-high sixty-three RBIs in his first year with the team, as well as Kansas City's Dutch Dotterer as its first catcher, but Dotterer lost the starting job to Gene Green.

"A lot of things will be by trial and error," Vernon said before the 1961 season. "There have been clubs [that] were new to their managers. But we have a situation here where neither is familiar with the other. . . . This is a completely new experience for everybody."

Spring training is the time of hope for all baseball teams, but it was especially promising for Washington's new team. The Senators had the best record in Florida's Grapefruit League and broke camp with optimism for their first season. Sharing that optimism, hundreds of fans lined up before 7 a.m. the morning Opening Day tickets went on sale. "It was the most remarkable sales in the forty-two years I have been selling tickets for the ball team," tickets director Johnny Morrissey said. "Usually the fans hold off until the day of the game to buy those."

Two weeks later, April 10, 1961, was a day of both firsts and lasts. It was the first game of the new Washington Senators, but the last opener at Griffith Stadium, which was to be replaced the next season by D.C. Stadium (later renamed RFK).

Unfortunately, the enthusiasm of a new beginning, 26,725 fans, and the strong first pitch of the new president, John F. Kennedy, couldn't get the team over the hump, as Washington fell, 4–3, to the Chicago White Sox. Former Senator Roy Sievers drove in the winning run with a sacrifice fly in the eighth inning.

But the team did win an important symbolic game a few weeks later. On May 26, the old Senators, now the Minnesota Twins, returned for the first time to Griffith Stadium to take on their successors. The new Senators beat the old ones, 4–3, behind the pitching of Joe McClain. Washington won the next two games, 14–4 and 6–4, to sweep the three-game series and make the catharsis complete.

It was a proud moment for the new franchise, which was still a tenant of Calvin Griffith in the old ballpark. Nearly 19,000 fans came out for the Sunday finale, a good showing for those days, and the third-best crowd in baseball that day. The sweep catapulted the Senators into fifth place in the ten-team league and dumped the Twins into seventh place.

Washington won its next game against the Angels to climb up to .500 for the first time since the second game of the season. After a slow start, the Senators had gone 17–12 in May, surprising most experts, who had picked them for the bottom of the barrel. The Senators continued to play decent ball for the next couple of weeks, and at the sixty-game mark, their record stood at 30–30, quite respectable for a first-year team.

In mid-June, a trip north to Boston quickly turned the Senators' season south. The Red Sox rallied from a 6–0 deficit to beat the Senators, 14–9, in the opener, and came back from 5–1 the next day for a 6–5 victory. The Sox must have felt they were on to something. In the first game of a Sunday doubleheader the next day, they waited until the ninth inning to make their move, rallying for eight runs with two outs to pull out a 13–12 victory. Thirteen proved an equally unlucky number in the nightcap, as Washington lost, 6–5, in thirteen innings. "You wouldn't believe it if you hadn't seen it, would you?" Vernon said.

Washington came home to play the Tigers in a two-game series, but home cooking didn't help the Senators, who lost both games. Then they dropped four more in Chicago to the White Sox. Washington had now lost ten in a row and dropped like a rock to 30–40.

That spell couldn't begin to prepare D.C. fans for what would come later in the season. On September 1, the team lost its fourteenth straight game, leaving eleven men on base in a 3–2 decision to the White Sox. Washington snapped the streak the same day, winning the second game of a doubleheader, but it was just a temporary reprieve. The Senators lost another ten in a row, culminated by a doubleheader sweep by the Orioles in Baltimore. During a twenty-five-game period, Washington won just once—good for an .040 winning percentage.

When Washington suited up for the final game ever at Griffith Stadium, who better to see off the old ballpark than the Minnesota Twins? A victory over the former Senators would give the new Senators something to cherish from their first season. But the early season Senators magic had vanished. They lost to the Twins, 6–3.

Not many people saw it. Just 1,498 fans showed up, the smallest crowd of the season. In the Washington dugout was eighty-five-year-old Nick Altrock, who had joined the Washington Nationals as a pitcher back in 1912. Evangelist Elder Lightfoot Solomon Michaux of the neighboring Temple of Freedom, who had used the stadium for mass baptisms and sermons, played "Auld Lang Syne" to say good-bye to the old ballpark. "A stadium was laid to rest yesterday,"

Washington Post sports editor Shirley Povich wrote in the next day's paper. "Not many showed up for the services, and the deceased was not much of a draw."

Despite their second-half collapse, the Senators actually had a chance to finish out of the cellar, which would have been a decent accomplishment for an expansion team. Going into the season finale in Kansas City with the last-place Athletics, Washington held a one-game lead over the As. But Kansas City won the game, 3–2, and the two teams finished in a last-place tie—with 61–100 records (.379), forty seven and a half games out of first. After its impressive 30–30 start, Washington went 31–70 in its last 101 games. The team finished eight games behind the other expansion team, the Los Angeles Angels.

The season was a failure by another barometer. The Twins finished eight and a half games ahead of the new Senators and, more importantly, drew 1.26 million fans, more than they had ever drawn in Washington. The Senators drew less than half that, with 597,000—last in the American League. One solace: The Senators took the season series from the Twins, nine games to eight.

After the season, the Senators acquired Jimmy Piersall from the Cleveland Indians for Washington's starting catcher; Gene Green, who had led the team in home runs, with eighteen; pitcher Dick Donovan, who went 10–10, with a league-best 2.40 ERA; and utility infielder Jim Mahoney. Piersall's book about his mental illness, *Fear Strikes Out*, had been turned into a movie in 1957 and had caused quite a stir in baseball.

Piersall was one of the best defensive outfielders in the game and was coming off a career year offensively, in which he hit .322. During a visit to Washington in the off-season, the colorful Piersall said he wasn't disappointed about getting traded to a last-place team. "If you're not traded to the Yankees, what's the difference?" he said. "Anyway, I was glad to get away from Cleveland and those Cleveland writers."

On April 9, 1962, Washington played its first game at its new state-of-the-art D.C. Stadium, with ticket prices the same as the old Griffith Stadium: $3 for box seats, $2.50 for reserved grandstand seats, and $1.50 for unreserved grandstand seats. The ballpark, paid for with federal funds, had a futuristic feel to it, with a sloped top that made it look like a UFO. A crowd of 44,000 people—a then-record for a Washington sporting event—came out to see the Senators get off to a good start, winning 4–1. President John F. Kennedy threw out the first ball in the stadium that would later be named for his slain brother, Bobby Kennedy. At the end of the game, JFK told team president Quesada and general manager Doherty, "I'm leaving you in first place."

But the Senators didn't stay there for long. In fact, seven games into the 1962 season, they were in last place, a position they would hold for the rest of the year. This time, Washington would have the bottom all to itself, finishing 60–101 and thirty-five and a half games out of first—a game off its 1961 pace. The team even finished eleven and a half games behind the next-worst team, the Athletics. Meanwhile, the Angels were showing that an expansion team could have some success, finishing with a winning record, in third place. The Twins rubbed it in some more, catapulting to second place, just five games behind the first-place Yankees, leading Washington fans to wonder what would have been if the old Senators had just stayed put for a couple more seasons.

The new Senators did improve in one important category—drawing 729,000 fans, an increase of nearly 150,000 from 1961, as they enjoyed the benefits of playing in a new ballpark. But that was still just seventh-best in the ten-team league. Another highlight for Washington: playing host to the 1962 All-Star Game. Local fans got to see such legends as Willie Mays, Orlando Cepeda, Roberto Clemente, Mickey Mantle, Roger Maris, Stan Musial, Juan Marichal, and Jim Bunning in one game. The sole Senators representative, pitcher Dave Stenhouse, did not play, reinforcing the team's sense of futility.

But a Washington native literally stole the show that day. Los Angeles Dodgers speedster Maury Wills, who grew up in the projects of Northeast Washington, entered the game as a pinch runner for Musial in the sixth inning of a scoreless game. Wills quickly stole second base and then scored the game's first run on a Dick Groat single.

With the National League up 2–1 in the eighth inning, Wills used his aggressiveness to manufacture an insurance run. After leading off the frame with a single, he took a wide turn around second base on a single by Jim Davenport. Left fielder Rocky Colavito threw to second base, but Wills took off for third and slid under the tag of the relay throw from second. He then scored on a sacrifice fly. The National League won the game, 3–1.

For his exploits, Wills won the game's Most Valuable Player Award, but the day didn't start out that great for him. Because he still had relatives in the city, he stayed with them rather than at the team hotel, and when he arrived at the ballpark, the team was already there.

"When I got there with my Dodger duffle bag, the clubhouse attendant wouldn't let me in," Wills recalls. "He didn't believe I was a baseball player. I showed him my Dodger bag—he still wouldn't let me in—I was too little." (Wills is about five feet, ten inches tall.) He continues:

I said, "I am a Dodger player, and I'll prove it to you. Open the door, and the guys inside will tell you." So he opened the door, and yelled, "Anybody inside know this guy?" And baseball players have a sick sense of humor, and they all looked at me and said, "Never saw him before." And he said, "I knew it, get out of here!"

Wills eventually made his way in to the clubhouse. "After the game, I walked out with the MVP trophy and showed it to him, and he still doesn't believe I'm a baseball player," Wills says with a laugh. Wills had his greatest year in 1962. He set a single-season record with 104 stolen bases, since broken, and hit .299, with ten triples.

From 1959 to 1962, baseball staged two All-Star Games a year, and, in the second one that season, Washington's Stenhouse not only played, but started for the American League. Unfortunately, the game was at Chicago's Wrigley Field, so few Washington fans could see the action in person. Stenhouse pitched two innings, giving up one run on three hits and one walk. He finished the season as the team leader in wins, going 11–12, with a 3.65 ERA.

By September, the Senators were already thirty games under .500, but the team still managed to put together some memorable moments. On September 5, the aptly named Washington Senator John Kennedy slammed a home run in his first major-league at bat—and broke up a no-hitter by Minnesota's Dick Stigman in the process.

"He circled the bases like he was running a hundred-yard dash," recalled manager Mickey Vernon, who died in 2008. "He was white as a ghost."

Kennedy says he ran so hard he could hardly breathe by the time he got back to the dugout. "I went around the bases in a sprint," he says. "I was really excited. That was the biggest home run. I always felt that when you hit a ball, you ran. Nowadays, guys watch the ball, hoping it will sail out of the ballpark. I was taught to run as hard as I can."

One week later, Senators pitcher Tom Cheney set a major-league record for most strikeouts in a major-league game, fanning twenty-one batters in a sixteen-inning, 2–1 victory over the Baltimore Orioles. Cheney threw more than 200 pitches, twice the count that would get him yanked nowadays. After the game, Baltimore third baseman Brooks Robinson said, "You know, there were times I never saw the ball."

There was more excitement in Baltimore the next night, when Senators outfielder Jimmy Piersall jumped into the stands to confront a fan who had taunted him about his history of mental illness. "This guy was on my back while we were in batting practice," Piersall said after the game. "He was calling me things like 'crazy man,' and said I should be in Spring Grove. I didn't know what he was talking about, but later I learned that Spring Grove is a Baltimore mental institution." Piersall continued: "I told him to come down to the field and say those things. He told me: 'You come up here.' So I did. But I never touched him." Both Piersall and the fan were hauled off to the Baltimore police station. Piersall was charged with disorderly conduct but was not convicted.

Shaking things up in the final days of the season, Quesada fired Doherty as general manager and rehired manager Vernon—the opposite of what was expected. Two months later, Quesada hired George Selkirk as general manager. Selkirk had played for the Yankees back in the 1930s and 1940s, taking Babe Ruth's place in the outfield. The new GM came in with an aggressive attitude. "I will trade with anybody," he said. "I don't believe in untouchables. The only 'Untouchables' are in television. We'll make any deal that will help the club."

There were more big changes for the franchise in the off-season. In January 1963, Quesada sold his one-tenth interest in the team and relinquished his presidency, but not before writing a three-part report to the "Greater Washington Baseball Public" slamming sportswriters Shirley Povich of the *Post* and Morris Siegel of the *Washington Star* for alleged distortions. Povich, getting the last word in, wrote, "It was France's Clemenceau who once observed, 'War is too important to be entrusted to generals.' So, perhaps, is baseball."

Bill Gilbert, who was fired by Quesada after serving as the team's marketing director for two years, described him as a micromanaging executive who once invited local disc jockeys to lunch, only to ask them to omit rainy forecasts when the team was home. He also argued that Quesada set the stage for the team's move a decade later by signing only a ten-year lease with the new ballpark, as opposed to the Redskins, who inked a thirty-year deal.

A group headed by former Cleveland Indians co-owners Nate Dolin and Bill Veeck made a $5 million offer for the team—a healthy markup from the $3 million price two years earlier. But instead, five of the original ten stockholders bought out the other five, and investment banker James M. Johnston took over as the new board chairman.

In May 1963, Selkirk fired Vernon, the team's manager since its inception, and replaced him with Gil Hodges, a former star first baseman for the Brooklyn and Los Angeles Dodgers. To get Hodges, who was finishing his playing career with the Mets, the Senators traded Piersall to New York. In his two seasons in Washington, Piersall had hit just .244 and .245.

Selkirk said he was sorry to fire the popular Vernon. "The last thing I wanted to do is what I'm doing," he said. "But I don't want to finish last. This club isn't hustling. The players haven't hustled all year."

Taking over a team with a 14–27 record, Hodges couldn't turn things around. He lost his first four games as manager, and eight of his first nine games. The team solidified its hold on last place, finishing 56–106 (.346), the worst record of the new Senators, and fourteen and a half games out of ninth place—not to mention forty-eight and a half games out of first place. Only 536,604 fans came out that 1963 season, also a low for the expansion Senators, and last in the American League.

Washington hit an anemic league-low .227 that year, with no regular batting over .270. Outfielder Chuck Hinton, who had hit .310 in 1962, slumped to .269, still a team-best. Don Lock, another outfielder, led the team with twenty-seven homers. The team's pitching wasn't much better, compiling a 4.42 ERA, also last in the league, but two starters had stellar years. Tom Cheney led the team with a 2.71 ERA, although poor run support got him just an 8–9 record. Southpaw Claude Osteen won a team-high nine games, losing fourteen despite a 3.35 ERA.

After three straight last-place finishes, the franchise decided not to aim too high for the following season. The cover of its 1964 yearbook had this inspiring rallying cry: "Off the Floor—in '64!" A cartoon showed an oversized, muscle-bound player with "American League" written across his chest, being tugged at by a child-sized player in a Senators uniform, who says, "I'm out to get you this year, fella!"

Washington barely met its modest goal, finishing in ninth place, with its best record—62–100 (.383)—four percentage points ahead of its previous best, in 1961. Claude Osteen, turning into a bona fide ace, won fifteen games, with a 3.33 ERA. But the hitting continued at its awful pace. The Senators batted just .231 as a team, again worst in the league; no regular hit over .275, and six hit under .250. Washington's offense took several days off in early September, failing to score in four consecutive games.

"The first man who scores a run for the Senators," wrote *Washington Post* sportswriter Bob Addie, "should rank among the great trailblazers of history, such as Pere Marquette, Columbus, the Wright Brothers, and the Beatles." The streak matched one by the old Senators, who had lost four straight games by identical scores of 2–0 in 1958.

Still, getting out of last place was an accomplishment. Pitcher Jim Hannan recalls the team celebrating after clinching a ninth-place finish: "We had a little champagne and a party like you won the World Series. It was sort of tongue-in-cheek, I think, but we enjoyed it."

The *Star* asked, "And next year's motto? How about 'Still Alive in Sixty-Five?'"

The Senators made several moves after the 1964 season to improve the club. In a blockbuster deal, they traded Claude Osteen and John Kennedy to the Dodgers for slugger Frank Howard and four other players. Howard, a six-foot, seven-inch behemoth, blossomed in Washington and became a fan favorite. He left behind a team that had won the 1963 World Series and would win the championship again in 1965. In the fourth and final game of the 1963 series, Howard's single and homer were the only hits the Dodgers managed off Yankees pitcher Whitey Ford, but they were enough to propel Los Angeles to a 2–1 win and complete the series sweep.

Howard says it was a worthy tradeoff to get to play every day. In Los Angeles, he usually got between 400 and 500 at-bats a season, and he was coming off his worst year in 1964, batting just .226, with twenty-four home runs. After the trade, "I got a chance to get another 150 at bats, and I had my best years here," says Howard, who still lives in the Washington area.

Howard provided some thump to what had been a listless offense. In his first year in Washington, he led the team in batting (.289), home runs (21), and RBIs (84)—the kind of production the Senators sorely needed. "We have to go for numbers," GM Selkirk said after announcing the deal. "Everybody knows about Howard. He's still young enough (twenty-eight), and Gil Hodges and I think he's one of the most powerful hitters in the game."

Meanwhile, the ownership continued to consolidate. In January 1965, the partners in the investment firm of Johnston, Lemon & Co.—board chairman James M. Johnston and James H. Lemon—bought out the stock of the remaining team owners to take full control of the team. Johnston said that he had received many offers to sell but wanted to retain ownership to ensure that the team would stay in Washington.

For the second straight season, Washington climbed gradually in the standings. The team finished in eighth place, with a 70–92 record—both bests for the new franchise. The trade with the Dodgers paid off for Washington, and not just because of Frank Howard. Southpaw pitcher Pete Richert, also acquired in the deal, stepped into the role of new staff ace, compiling a 15–12 record and 2.60 ERA. Another acquisition in the deal, third baseman Ken McMullen, finished second on the team with eighteen homers.

One low point, at least emotionally, came on the last weekend of September. The city's old team, the Twins, came back home to clinch their first American League pennant, defeating the Senators, 2–1, at D.C. Stadium on September 26. It was the franchise's first pennant since 1933. "Calvin Griffith's band of displaced athletes left here paupers in

1961. They returned as princes of the baseball realm," wrote Addie. The win climaxed a three-game sweep, giving Minnesota a 15–3 margin in head-to-head games that year—and the Twins won the pennant by seven games.

"Few teams did more to give the old Senators, or Twins, an assist toward the championship than did the present denizens of D.C. Stadium," the *Star* wrote in an editorial. The Twins celebrated on the Senators' turf, swimming in champagne, and taking a congratulatory call from Vice President Hubert Humphrey—a transplanted Minnesotan in the nation's capital.

Still, there was reason for optimism in Washington. The team had improved for two straight seasons under manager Gil Hodges, who predicted that the team could finish in the "first division"—or top half of the standings—in 1966. "This will be our goal," he wrote in the *Star*. "I believe we can do it if some of our younger fellows come along as well as we expect them to."

Hodges said he wanted bigger things from his big man. Frank Howard had put up decent numbers in 1965, Hodges wrote, "but Frank is six-foot-seven and weighs 255 pounds, so fans expect more of him. He's capable of doing much more." But Howard would wind up with his lowest home run and RBI totals in a Washington uniform in 1966, hitting just eighteen round-trippers and knocking in a mere seventy-one.

Howard did, however, hit one of the most memorable home runs in Washington baseball history that year. In a 3–2 loss to the White Sox in April, he slammed a ball into the upper deck in center field at D.C. Stadium, a colossal shot some players said would have traveled farther than any ball in history had it not been hit in an enclosed ballpark. "Frank Howard hit that ball like a two-iron right back at the pitcher, who actually fell down on the ground," recalls Senators outfielder Fred Valentine. "And Tommie Agee was playing center field, and he started in, but the ball just kept rising and it wound up in the upper deck. Nobody could believe it."

On July 8, the Senators went to New York to play a five-game weekend series against the Yankees, starting with a doubleheader Friday night. Washington pitcher Jim Hannan was scheduled to pitch the opening game, but Hannan, a New Jersey native, persuaded Hodges to let him pitch the second game so his family could come out and watch him pitch in prime time at Yankee Stadium.

In the third inning, Hannan gave up a home run to Mickey Mantle that rivaled Howard's two months earlier. "Mantle at one point was 19-for-21 off me," Hannan says. He continues:

So I say, "Well, if he hits it, he's gonna have to hit it out in center field. 'Cause I'm pitching it out over the plate." So I throw it out over the plate. He hits it. Center fielder turns around. And I said, "Oh my God, over the monuments. Oh my God, over the backdrop. Oh my God, it's gonna go out of the stadium."

The ball did stay in the ballpark, landing in the bleachers an estimated 461 feet away.

Hannan recalls a testy exchange with Hodges on the mound after that:

He comes out and he says nothing. He put his hand out, and he had huge hands. And I'm thinking, "Son of a bitch, if he's not gonna ask me for the ball, I'm not giving it to him." Gil never wanted to show anyone up and never wanted to be showed up. Well, I'm turned around and I'm showing him up. I don't hand him the ball. I turn around and I just hold the ball.

And he grabs me by the elbow with the other hand and just starts crunching it. And he says, "If you don't give me that damn ball, it's gonna be $500 and . . . and . . ." And, I said to myself, "OK, he talked to me." I turned around and gave him the ball.

Washington wound up losing the game, 7–5, blowing a 4–0 lead. But the Senators took four of five games in the series.

Despite Hodges's preseason optimism, Washington only marginally improved in 1966. The team finished in eighth place again, with a 71–88 record (.447). The Senators' hitting woes continued, as they batted just .234 as a team. Howard's modest .278 average was the best of any regular.

After the season, Washington shipped standout reliever Ron Kline to the Minnesota Twins for an old Senators pitching star, Camilo Pascual, and infielder Bernie Allen. Kline had led the Senators in saves, with twenty-three, and posted a 2.39 ERA. Pascual, a Cuban find by Senators scout Joe Cambria, had twice won twenty games with the Twins, but he was coming off a bad season (8–6, 4.89 ERA). He would bounce back for the Senators in 1967, winning a team-high twelve games, with a 3.28 ERA.

Hodges entered the 1967 season determined to improve the Senators' woeful offense. "Our pitching will be as strong, if not stronger than last year," he said at the beginning of spring training. "And last year our pitching did a fine job." But he noted that the team finished last in runs scored in 1966. "I looked it up because I couldn't quite believe it," he said. "We have to master a better attack, that's all there is to it." Despite Hodges's best efforts, Washington's offense would not improve in 1967, but the Senators would give their fans an exciting season.

In an effort to upgrade their offense, two months into the season, the Senators traded their ace pitcher, Pete Richert, to the Baltimore Orioles for the highly touted slugging prospect Mike Epstein and pitcher Frank Bertaina. Epstein, twenty-four, had been named *Sporting News* Minor League Player of the Year the previous season after hitting .309, with twenty-nine homers and 102 RBIs at Rochester. But when Baltimore tried to send him down again at the end of spring training in 1967, he balked, saying he was returning to college. The Orioles, the defending World Series champions, already had Boog Powell at first base and weren't able to convert Epstein from a first baseman to an outfielder. A week after the trade, the six-foot, three-inch, 230-pound Epstein made his Senators debut in an unexpected way—by hitting an inside-the-park home run at Yankee Stadium. The 200-foot blast came after Epstein visited his grandmother just a few blocks from the ballpark.

In June, the Senators began an unbelievable stretch of extra-inning games, starting with a 7–5, nineteen-inning loss to the Orioles on June 4. Washington scored five runs in the top of the third inning and then put up goose eggs for the next sixteen. Baltimore won the game on a two-run homer by Andy Etchebarren in the bottom of the nineteenth. Hodges tried out a new shift in that game against Orioles slugger and future Nationals manager Frank Robinson. Hodges used his second baseman as a fourth outfielder in the fifteenth and eighteenth innings, and Robinson went 0-for-2 against the softball-style defense.

Just eight days later, the Senators proved they were mastering the art of the filibuster set by their namesakes a couple of miles away on Capitol Hill. They lasted for twenty-two innings against the Chicago White Sox, finally winning, 6–5, on a bases-loaded single by catcher Paul Casanova—his first hit in nine at-bats. More impressive, Casanova caught all twenty-two innings, after catching the full nineteen-inning game the week before. "I could have played thirty innings," he said after the six-hour, thirty-eight-minute game against the White Sox. "I wasn't tired. I could have gone all night."

Or all morning. Sunrise was just a few hours away when Casanova knocked in the winning run at 2:44 a.m., with 2,000 fans still on hand. "The fans were forever yelling and clapping," recalls Fred Valentine, who played the entire game in center field and went 2-for-9. "At that time, you could bring your coolers in, and most of them were boozed up. But they stayed, and that shows how much they supported the team."

The Senators excited their fans with more than extra-inning games that season. In July, they climbed from a virtual tie for tenth place to seventh after winning eight straight games. "The last time they could boast of anything near their current achievement was in 1949, when Harry Truman was living at 1600 Pennsylvania Avenue," wrote *Star* sportswriter Morris Siegel. "All of a sudden Washington has become interested in something besides how many chowhounds the Redskins are assembling at Carlisle, Pa., for the imminent opening of Camp Runamuck."

Washington was still five games under .500 at the end of the streak, but they finally reached the break-even point with a 5–0 victory over the Twins on August 7. After dropping the second game of the series, the Senators climbed back to .500 the next night—and morning. For the third time that year, Washington played a single game that went more than double the length of a normal game, beating the Twins, 9–7, in twenty innings.

Trailing, 7–0, with two outs in the top of the seventh inning, Washington rallied for seven runs to tie the game. The Senators' bats cooled off as quickly as they had heated up, going scoreless for the next twelve innings, before winning the game on a home run by Ken McMullen in the top of the twentieth.

Washington, which had been fourteen and a half games out of first place a month earlier, had now climbed to within six and a half games from the top. Fans started calling the team to ask about World Series tickets. When the Senators came home a week later, they were still at .500, but that was more than enough for their long-suffering fans. Four thousand Senators rooters were waiting at Washington National Airport to welcome the team back from a successful road trip. Now Washington was just six games out of first place. Both fans and players were talking about making a run for the pennant.

More than twenty-seven thousand fans came out to see the Senators open a homestand and crucial three-game series against the Cleveland Indians. For seven innings, a pitching duel between Washington's Barry Moore and Cleveland's Stan Williams kept both teams scoreless, but the Indians rallied for three runs in the top of the seventh inning off the Washington bullpen and held on for a 3–0 victory. Washington bats remained dormant the next night, and the team fell, 1–0.

In the third and final game of the series, Frank Howard ended the team's scoreless streak at twenty-eight innings with a home run in the fourth. The Senators added two more runs in the frame to build a 3–0 lead. But Cleveland eventually tied it, and once again Washington was to play its signature 1967 game—an extra-inning contest. Unfortunately, the offense returned to its comatose condition, failing to score in the game's final twelve innings. Cleveland finally won the game with five runs in the top of the sixteenth. In the demoralizing series, Washington scored just three runs in the series' thirty-four innings and was on its way to a 2–9 tailspin. By the end of August, the team's pennant run was effectively over.

Washington finished 76–85, good for a franchise-best .472 winning percentage. The team also had its highest finish in the standings, a tie for sixth place with the Orioles, the previous year's world champs. And Washington set a franchise record of 771,000 fans.

The team was improving overall, but its offense was not. Washington hit just .223 as a team, last in the American League. Its double-play combination was particularly impotent. Second baseman Bernie Allen hit .193, with three homers and eighteen RBIs in eighty-seven games, while shortstop Ed Brinkman batted just .188, with one homer and eighteen RBIs in 109 games. Slugging first baseman Mike Epstein failed to provide the pop Washington had hoped for, finishing with a .229 average, nine homers, and twenty-nine RBIs in ninety-six games. But Frank Howard was finally emerging as the player many thought he could be. Following Hodges's advice, the big slugger opened his stance and set a new career-high with thirty-six home runs.

The disappointing finish continued into the off-season, when manager Gil Hodges quit to take the manager's job with the New York Mets. Because Hodges had one year left on his contract, the Mets agreed to pay cash and send pitcher Bill Denehy to the Senators as compensation, but Denehy would pitch just two innings for Washington. Hodges had nudged the Senators up in the standings each season after his first year, but the lure of playing for his hometown team and a generous salary proved too much to resist.

"The Mets were desperate, and, besides, they can afford it," wrote Shirley Povich, adding:

> The Senators liked their manager and believed that now he had the Washington team rolling with his sixth-place finish. But the Senators found themselves helpless against baseball's code of the jungle, the honorless system that condones this form of wife-stealing by the Mets or any other team.

Senators pitcher Jim Hannan recalls hearing the news in New York, where he worked as a stockbroker on Wall Street in the off-season. He told his colleagues at the time:

> "Boy you guys have got the greatest coaching staff in the world. You guys, the Mets, will win the World Series in a year or two." And they thought I was crazy. They said, "What? The Mets?" I said, "You wait and see. You got young pitchers by the name of Tom Seaver, Jerry Koosman, Nolan Ryan. They're going to be great pitchers someday. And you're getting a coaching staff that knows how to handle them."

Hodges was taking over a team that had finished in tenth place the previous season. It took him a little time to turn things around—in 1968 New York finished ninth—but the Miracle Mets won the World Series the next year.

Meanwhile, Washington turned to Jim Lemon (no relation to the owner) as its new manager. Lemon had played for the old Senators team for six seasons, hitting thirty-eight home runs in the team's final year in Washington, before moving with the franchise to Minnesota. He had spent the last three seasons as the Twins' first base coach.

In December, the board chairman, James M. Johnston, died of cancer at the age of seventy-two, leaving his investment bank partner, James M. Lemon, in control of the team. Johnston had expressed a philosophical attitude about the lack of profitability in owning the Senators, once remarking, "It's too bad it costs me money, but I suppose you have to pay the piper. I must love the game to put so much money into it—especially since I'm a Scotsman." Within a year, the team would be put up for sale. And, unfortunately for the Senators, their next owner would not have the same attitude as the old Scotsman.

In 1968, riots enveloped the nation's capital following the assassination of Martin Luther King Jr., forcing the postponement of the home opener by two days. Throughout the city, businesses closed out of mourning for the civil rights leader, and officials imposed curfews to stem the rioting. One of the U.S. National Guard soldiers helping to restore order was Senators' shortstop Ed Brinkman, who missed nearly half the 1967 and 1968 seasons for guard duty. "I'd be with the club, traveling, and the phone would ring, and they'd say, 'There's going to be thirty thousand kids rioting against the Vietnam War this weekend, and you've got to come back,'" recalled Brinkman, who died in 2008.

In 1968, Brinkman said he patrolled the city to keep people off the streets during curfew. "I was stationed in a firehouse for a while, because the firemen were going out to all of these fires that people were setting across the city, and the people were ruining the equipment," he recalled. "So they took some of the National Guard guys and put us each in a firehouse so we could protect the hoses and the gear. I hadn't realized when I signed up that Washington, D.C., is probably the worst place to join the National Guard—there's always something going on."

When the Senators finally opened their season on April 10, 1968, Brinkman was at the game—but in the stands in his army uniform, yelling taunts down at his buddy and roommate, Frank Howard, in left field. "The game's going on, and I'm trying to concentrate, and he's hollering at me," Howard recalls with a laugh. "I'm thinking, if we have to depend upon this guy to save us, we're in deep trouble."

The tense situation in the city kept the attendance to just 32,000 people, well short of a sellout. Vice President Hubert Humphrey, filling in for President Lyndon B. Johnson, threw out the first ball, but the Minnesotan was booed when he walked over to the Twins dugout to greet his favorite team. The Twins won, 2–0, wasting a good effort by Senators pitcher Camilo Pascual.

Things didn't get much better for Washington that season. The team slumped to a last-place finish—reversing several years of progress made under Hodges—and drew just 546,661 fans.

Jim Hannan was one of only two pitchers on the staff with a winning record, going 10–6, with a 3.01 ERA (the other was Pascual, who went 13–12, with a 2.69 ERA). But Hannan's most memorable record that year was not his winning percentage, but his strikeout streak—as a hitter. He fanned thirteen straight times but says there's more to the story.

"The coaches thought I was getting tired running the bases, so they didn't want me to get on base," he recalls. "Now four or five of those strikeouts I got on my own, but I went two or three games where I wasn't allowed to swing at a ball. So I was always trying to get a walk—I'd get a 3-and-2 count, and I'd start thinking, 'What's going to happen if I get a walk?'"

Finally, Hannan says, he went to the coaching staff and said, "This is getting embarrassing. It's one thing not getting on base, but just striking out? I'm setting records here. Can I please just swing and hit the ball? I promise you I will not get on base." The edict was lifted. Hannan finished the year with just three hits and an .064 batting average.

Frank Howard offered fans something to cheer for that season. In May, the "Capital Punisher" tied an American League record with home runs in six straight games—walloping an astonishing ten dingers in twenty at bats. He capped it with a 550-foot blast in Detroit, which landed on top of the grandstand and bounced out of the stadium, one of two home runs he hit that day off Tigers hurler Mickey Lolich, the same pitcher Howard had begun his streak off of a week earlier. Howard became only the second player to clear the left-field stands at Tiger Stadium; the first was former Senator Harmon Killebrew, who accomplished the feat as a Minnesota Twin in 1962. Cecil Fielder became the third and final player to do it in 1993, before the Tigers moved to Comerica Park.

"You know when you put a good swing on the baseball—there's no pressure, no white-knuckle effect where there's tension in your swing," Howard recalls:

> It's just a free swing, a smooth swing, a quick swing. I didn't know it went over the roof until I got back to the dugout. You couldn't stand and admire the ball in those days. You're asking to get clipped if you did. That's one thing you couldn't do—you couldn't show the pitcher up out there. He'll put a little part in your hair next time. It's like digging a hole in that batter's box—and Bob Gibson or Don Drysdale would bury you in it.

Howard remembers being ice cold in the two series before the streak, when the Yankees and Red Sox came to Washington. "It's like a water tap," he says. "You can't turn that hot water on and turn it off—you've got to try to keep that water running all the time."

Howard, who had benefited from opening his stance a year earlier under Hodges, further refined his stance under Lemon, by moving in closer to the plate. He led the league that season with forty-four home runs.

But overall, the team's hitting did not improve. True, this was the "Year of the Pitcher," when offense was down so much that the National League won the All-Star Game, 1–0, and Carl Yastrzemski won the American League batting crown with just a .301 average. Even by 1968 standards, however, the Senators were seriously subpar. They hit just .224 as a team, second-to-last in the league (to the Yankees, who hit .214). Howard, who hit .274, was the only Washington regular to bat over .250. The pitching wasn't much better, as the Senators' pitching staff finished with a league-worst 3.64 ERA (the league average was 2.98 that year).

The 1968 season marked the end of an era for the Washington Senators. By the next year, the team would have a new owner and manager, and some enthusiasm for a rejuvenated franchise. But the change in ownership ultimately led to Washington losing yet another baseball team.

EIGHT

A Short Run: The Ted Williams Era

A SHORT RUN: THE TED WILLIAMS ERA

Big changes were in store for the Senators after the disappointing 1968 season. Owner James H. Lemon put the team up for sale, and two men emerged as the leading bidders: comedian Bob Hope and wealthy Minnesota businessman Robert E. Short. Hope talked about including other stars as partners, including Johnny Carson and Steve McQueen. "Maybe we will conduct the whole baseball operation through the Screen Actors Guild," he joked.

But in the end, Hope came up short to the Minnesota hotel and trucking executive, who bought the team for $9.4 million. Short was already deeply immersed in Washington's biggest pastime, politics, having served as treasurer of the Democratic National Committee and chief fundraiser for Hubert Humphrey's 1968 presidential campaign. Back then, there were no campaign finance laws limiting political donations, and Short gave the campaign $125,000. But Humphrey lost to Republican Richard Nixon in the general election. Short had a couple of other political losses on his resume, failing in bids for the U.S. House of Representatives and Minnesota lieutenant governor.

In an editorial, the *Washington Post* suggested that Short and Hope may have been baseball proxies for the presidential candidates that year:

> Robert Short is a Democrat and a friend of Hubert Humphrey—to whose campaign he was a financial contributor. Bob Hope, on the other hand, is a Republican and a friend of Richard Nixon—to whose campaign he was a financial contributor. We all know how that particular contest came out, but lately the two men have been waging a second campaign against each other, not for the presidency this time, but for ownership of the Washington Senators—a sort of baseball team.

Short was no stranger to sports, either. He bought the Minneapolis Lakers in 1957, but moved them to Los Angeles in 1960, right around the time the first Senators had left Washington for Minnesota—an ominous sign for a city trying to hold on to baseball. Short, who had bought the Lakers for $300,000, sold them in 1965 to Jack Kent Cooke for more than $5 million. Cooke, ironically, would later become owner of the Washington Redskins. At the time of the Senators purchase, Short owned a 1 percent share in the Twins but sold it, as required by baseball rules.

Also ominous was a comment Short made to the *Post* after purchasing the Senators, about his negotiations with Webb C. Hayes III, the team's executive vice president and counsel: "I refused to sign any papers that would prevent me from moving the club out of Washington. I told Hayes that I wasn't buying the team to move it. But, legally, I wanted the right to move it if it ever became necessary."

Short had an ambitious master plan for the franchise: out of last place in 1969, in the top half of the standings in 1970, a pennant contender team in 1971, and in the World Series no later than 1972. He would meet only the first goal.

At a press conference at D.C. Stadium, Short said he wanted to see improvements made to the ballpark. "From the outside, it's beautiful. But from the inside, it's dirty. The housekeeping is not as it should be. We should pay enough rent so the place could be clean inside. At least, the concrete could be painted and whitewashed."

He said that his long-range plans for the stadium included "VIP Club seats," which would become standard in baseball years after the Senators had moved away. On a more pressing matter, Short said, "I don't want them running out of hot dogs when they know they're going to have a full stadium." (That's exactly what happened thirty-eight years later, when a full house came out to see the first Nationals home game in 2005.) Finally, Short promised, "We're not going to have any cellar club next year." The team was coming off a last-place finish, thirty-one games under .500.

As one of his first moves, Short vetoed a trade that would have sent catcher Paul Casanova and first baseman Mike Epstein to Atlanta for catcher Joe Torre. That turned out to be a blunder. The Braves instead shipped Torre to the St. Louis Cardinals, where he would knock in more than one hundred runs in each of the next three seasons, including a monster 1971 season, when he won the Most Valuable Player Award with a .363 average and 137 RBIs. Epstein did have a career year in 1969, slamming thirty homers and knocking in eighty-five runs, but he trailed off the following season before being traded in 1971. Casanova would never hit higher than .230 for the rest of his career.

Then Short fired George Selkirk, the team's general manager since 1962, and team manager Jim Lemon, who had been skipper for only one year. And the new owner raised ticket prices—the best seats in the house were jacked up from $4 to $5; the cheapest from $1.50 to $2. But the biggest move was yet to come.

In February 1969, Short announced his new manager—Hall of Fame outfielder Ted Williams, who had been out of baseball since retiring after the 1960 season. The "Splendid Splinter" inked himself a splendid contract—five years at $65,000 a year, plus a deferred option to buy 10 percent of the team. It was the best deal for a manager at the time.

A reporter asked Williams if he would "tolerate a player with a temperament like Ted Williams had as a player." Ted responded, "If he can hit like Ted Williams, yes."

Williams's initial answer to the job offer was "Nooooo," Short recalled in a 1970 *Washingtonian* profile on the new manager. "So then I told him I thought he had a responsibility toward the game, toward the country, toward Nixon, and the whole bunch of bull you throw into a business proposition." Short continued:

> He said, "I'll tell you what I'll do. Goddamn it, I know you're in a hell of a fix. I can't do it, but I'll help you find
> somebody." I knew I had him in the bag then. As long as he's going to draw up lists of who might do the job, it's
> going to come out just like my list. Ted Williams has to come out on top. And that's what happened.

Short's specific appeal to Nixon was no coincidence. Williams was a big admirer of the new president and would even post a grainy photo of Nixon in his office as manager.

Williams's reputation included an adversarial relationship with the press, dating back to his time as an outfielder with the Red Sox. "But by the time he was manager, he was great, he was spellbinding," says former *Washington Post* sports editor George Solomon, who was a columnist for the now-defunct *Washington Daily News* at the time. "You'd sit in lobbies with him, and he would spin tales and talk about Joe DiMaggio and Bob Feller and the great pitchers and great hitters. He was just so interesting. If you were interested enough to ask, he'd be interested enough to talk about it forever."

Short's son, Brian, says that his late father wanted someone with star power to lead the team. "Ted Williams was a star, and my father thought people would buy tickets to the games because of him," Brian Short adds: "My father was a promotional genius. Major-league owners were a stodgy group. Their view was you didn't have to promote, because it was the national pastime."

That season, the American League split into two divisions to accommodate its first expansion since the Senators had entered the league in 1961. Unfortunately for Washington, the two expansion teams, the Seattle Pilots and Kansas City Royals, were put in the Western Division, so the Senators would not have a couple of easy teams to beat out in their Eastern Division. Washington was grouped with the Red Sox, Indians, Tigers, Yankees, and Orioles.

Bill Gildea, who covered the Senators for the *Post* at the time, went down to the Florida Keys to interview Williams at his home there and was struck by how removed the new manager was from the game. "He didn't know who was on the team," Gildea recalls. "He didn't know the league was split into divisions. He was trying to get in his head around how the White Sox could be in the Western Division."

Inheriting a team that had hit just .224 the previous year, the new manager went to work trying to build up the offense. One player who needed a lot of improvement was shortstop Eddie Brinkman, whose consistency in the past two seasons would have been impressive—if it hadn't been so consistently bad. Brinkman had hit .188 in 1967 and .187 in 1968.

When the shortstop arrived at spring training at Pompano Beach, Williams greeted the six-foot, 170-pound shortstop by saying, "Hey, you're even skinnier than I thought you were!"

"I just walked away, thinking, 'Oh my,'" Brinkman recalled.

Later, Williams told Brinkman not to take a glove with him on the field. "If I ever see you with a glove on your hand in the first two or three weeks of spring training, I'm going to hit you over the head with a damn bat," Williams said. "They tell me you can catch the ball, but your weakness is hitting. So carry your bat with you every place you go."

So for two weeks, Brinkman left his glove behind and focused exclusively on hitting. Finally, the day before the first spring training game, Brinkman asked his manager if he would be in the lineup.

"Yeah!" Williams barked.

"You know," Brinkman replied, "I haven't fielded a ground ball yet. I haven't taken my glove out of my locker."

"Oh, geez, you better get it, then, and field some ground balls."

Brinkman said that Williams was adept at getting players to increase their focus at the plate:

> What he helped me with most was the mental part, not so much the physical stuff: "Get a good pitch to hit. Don't swing at the bad balls." He was always by the batting cage, and if you didn't concentrate at all times—if you hit the ball up against the cage or beat one down in the dirt—he'd jump all over you: "Hey!" he'd scream. And his voice carried even when he wasn't screaming. "Wait on the ball! Get on top of the ball! What the hell were you thinking up there?!" It really bothered him when you swung at bad pitches.

So just by him doing that, you would concentrate like crazy, just during batting practice. For me, it would carry over into the game, and I hit a little bit better. I was never going to win a batting title, but I became a better hitter. The concentration level really went up a lot.

But Brinkman had another problem: He had missed about half the games the previous two seasons because of his duties with the U.S. National Guard, making it difficult for him to find a rhythm at the plate. When he told Williams that he had to report for duty when the team returned north, the manager was furious. Military service during World War II and the Korean War service had cut into Williams's own playing career.

Brinkman recalled Williams's reaction: "They ain't going to mess around with my players. They messed around with me for five years; they ain't going to mess around with my players, blah, blah, blah."

So Williams arranged for Brinkman and team representatives to meet with military officials at the D.C. Armory, located across the street from the stadium. They worked out a deal where Brinkman would work at the armory when the team was home, from 6 a.m. to 4 p.m., and then go the ballpark to play at night.

Brinkman recalled:

The team trainer had an old rollaway bed in the clubhouse. So I'd get over there at 4 or 4:30 in the afternoon, and go in the back. I'd lay down on that rollaway bed and sleep for a couple of hours. This was pretty much every day when we were home, with the exception of weekends. So I never missed any games in 1969. When I went on the road, I didn't have to come back for guard duty.

The increased focus that came from Williams's coaching, as well as playing every day, paid off. In 1969, Brinkman raised his batting average by seventy-nine points, to .266.

Williams didn't limit his coaching to the weak hitters. He also jumped on the team's best hitter, Frank Howard, summoning the slugger to the manager's office on the third day of spring training that year. Howard recalls the exchange:

"Skip, you wanted to see me?"

"Yeah, come in, come on in here, Bush." (Williams called everyone "Bush," for "Bush-Leaguer.")

"Can you tell me," Williams asked, "how a guy can hit forty-four home runs but only get fifty-four base on balls?"

"Well, I try to be aggressive when I swing the bat," Howard responded.

"Yeah, yeah, yeah, I've seen you hit. You like that first swifty, that first little fastball you see," Williams said.

"Well, I better like that fastball, because that curveball, slider, and changeup—to me they're UFOs,'" Howard said.

"What do you mean UFOs?" Williams asked.

"To me they're unidentifiable flying objects," Howard explained.

Williams finally managed a laugh.

"Did you ever take two strikes to get a good pitch to hit?" the new manager asked.

"God, Skip, if I took two strikes to get a good pitch to hit, I'd be walking back to the dugout 300 times a year instead of 125."

"Well, can you take a strike? I'm talking about a tough fastball, something other than what you're looking for, a curveball slider or change."

"Well, anybody can hit with a strike," Howard said.

"Well, try it for me," Williams asked.

The experiment was a success. Howard nearly doubled his walk total from fifty-four to 102 that season, without sacrificing any power. He finished with his best season—a .296 average, 48 home runs, and 111 RBIs.

"If it was an identifiable pitch that I could really put a passable swing on, I'd let it fly," Howard says. He continues:

> I started laying off a lot of the breaking balls off the plate in the dirt, and some of those borderline high fastballs that we swing through or foul back or pop up. It took an undisciplined hitter, who had a strike zone from the bill of his cap to his shoelaces, three or four inches in or off the plate, and tightened it up a bit.
>
> I found myself getting more hitter's counts—2–0, 3–1. He [Williams] didn't mess much with guys mechanically if they'd played five or ten years in the big leagues, unless they'd had absolutely no success. But he sure messed with your coconut, your mental processes.

Short, ever the salesman, tried to capitalize on the buzz over the new manager, coining the marketing phrase, "It's a whole new ballgame." A then-Washington record Opening Day crowd of 45,113, including the new president, Nixon, showed up to see Williams in his managerial debut. Ted tipped his hat to the adoring fans during his introduction, something he famously refused to do at Fenway Park after hitting a home run in his final at-bat.

But some traditions die hard, and the Senators lost their seventh straight opener, falling to the New York Yankees, 8–4. Being a manager, Williams told reporters after the game, "felt lousy today," although he was impressed with the fans. "Really and truly, I think they're wonderful," he said. "They certainly got stirred up when we did a little something."

In July, Washington hosted its second All-Star Game in eight years. On the eve of the scheduled game, the Baseball Writers' Association of America named its All-Time Team, voting Babe Ruth the greatest player ever, and former Senator Walter Johnson the greatest right-handed pitcher. Ted Williams was named to the all-time living team, but lost out to rival Joe DiMaggio as the greatest living player. Williams skipped the dinner, held at the Sheraton-Park Hotel.

The next day saw a rainout of the All-Star Game, the first time the game had been washed out in history. When the teams finally played the following afternoon, Howard gave Senators fans a chance to cheer for their hometown hero, smacking a 458-foot home run off Steve Carlton that landed over the clock in right-center field. They also booed the American League's starting shortstop, Boston's Rico Petrocelli, because they believed the rejuvenated Brinkman should have made the team.

Howard hit the longest homer, but the Giants' Willie McCovey hit the most. His two slams paced the National League's 9–3 victory. Howard also dropped a fly ball in the first inning, leading to the National League's first run.

Washington played about .500 ball most of the season, a huge improvement in its own right, but a late surge helped it finish ten games over .500. The team won eight of its last nine games, including the season finale at RFK, which drew more than 17,000 fans, even though the Senators were well out of the pennant race.

"The fans were in a carnival mood, unwilling to let go of the most successful season in memory," wrote George Minot Jr., in the *Post*. "They came to thank the Senators in general, and Ted Williams, in particular, for bringing Washington back into the major leagues."

Williams guided the team to an 86–76 record—a gain of twenty-one wins from the previous year—marking the new Senators' first winning season and the best record for any Washington baseball team since 1945. The Senators had the sixth-best record in the twelve-team league, but came in fourth place in the tough six-team American League East, twenty-three games behind the Orioles, who won 109 games.

Offense was up throughout baseball because of the lowering of the pitching mound that season, but Williams's work with the Senators hitters was phenomenal. The team's batting average jumped twenty-seven points, to .251, fourth-best in the league, and the Senators increased their home runs by twenty-four and walks by 176. In addition to Brinkman and Howard, several other players broke out offensively. Del Unser increased his batting average from .230 to .286; Mike Epstein had career highs in average (.278), home runs (30), and RBIs (85); and Ken McMullen increased his average from .248 to .272.

"Ted gave of himself to that ball club, and it's nice if you have an entire club have a career year for you," recalls Howard. "And that's exactly what happened—we all had career years. As a result, we finished ten games over .500. To be honest with you, we had a fine pitching staff, but if we'd had an ace on that staff, we might have taken them all on. We might have made a run at everybody."

Williams didn't mind taking his share of the credit. "They were all better hitters and not one son of a bitch did I change his style," he said after the season.

"For me, the reason they won eighty-six games that year, when they were so much better, was because Ted taught those guys how to hit," recalls Tim Kurkjian, who was a young Senators fan at the time and is now a baseball analyst for ESPN. "Eddie Brinkman was on my tiny level, he was a great defensive player. But that year, he hit like .270. So we all said that was Ted Williams's work."

Williams's influence on the pitching staff was equally impressive. Despite the game's offensive thrust that year, the Senators' team ERA improved from a league-worst 3.64 in 1968 to a fifth-best 3.49 in 1969. Dick Bosman, who had gone 2–9, with a 3.69 ERA in 1968, improved to 14–5 under Williams, with a league-best 2.19 ERA.

Bosman recalls Williams telling him in spring training of that year, "Boz, you got a chance to be pretty good. You just gotta learn to use what you got."

"When do we start?" Bosman asked.

"We already have," Williams replied.

Bosman said he became a disciple of the new manager.

"Ted and I had a relationship that a lot of guys didn't, and a lot of pitchers didn't," Bosman says. He continues:

> Because, you know, Ted didn't like pitchers very well. And yet, we had a relationship that I would say, 90 to 95 percent of the time, that was very, very good. Ted believed that the slider was the toughest pitch to hit. I always threw a slider, and I made it better. He taught me that cat-and-mouse game about how to go back-and-forth between a breaking ball and a fastball. He taught me how to set up hitters. And basically, I learned how to use my breaking ball to set up my fastball.

Bosman says that Williams's excitement rubbed off on the players. "Ted Williams was enthusiastic," he says. "He was excited to be back in the game. He was big-time excited about being there, and we were, too, because we were scuffling like ducks in the desert. We were bad. So to bring a guy in like that who was so excited about being there, it was infectious man, it really was."

"He was very exuberant," added Brinkman. "He came in with a lot of pep. Chipper, ready for action."

The fans caught the bug, too. The Senators drew 918,000 fans, the best Washington attendance in twenty-three seasons, and the second highest in Senators history—covering both franchises. "Let me say that no one has been more enthusiastic than the 900,000 fucking fans," Williams told reporters after the final game.

Short, the new owner, wasn't satisfied. He told *Washington Post* sports columnist Bob Addie, "With the trade market we have in Washington, we should draw a million people." Back then, that was the gold standard for attendance. Short also complained about having to share the market with the Baltimore Orioles, just thirty-five miles away, a complaint that the Orioles themselves would make many years later in an attempt to keep a team from returning to Washington.

"This is a great baseball area," Williams said after the season. "I can feel the enthusiasm mounting. I walk down the street and everyone tells me that we are doing a great job and that we're going to have a great year next year, too."

Unfortunately, it didn't work out that way. The magic disappeared in 1970, and the Senators dropped to familiar territory—last place. In a foreshadowing of events, the team ended its spring training by playing two exhibition games in Arlington, Texas, on the way up to Washington. Nobody thought anything of it at the time.

One highlight came on August 17, when Jim Hannan came close to throwing a no-hitter at RFK Stadium. With two outs in the fifth inning and the Senators leading the Royals, 7–0, Kansas City's Paul Schaal hit a line drive to left field. Frank Howard lunged for the ball and tried to make a shoestring catch but came up a foot short. The ball raced past him, and Schaal got a triple—the only hit Hannan would surrender that night in front of just 5,700 fans.

"Frank wore glasses, and it was a steamy night in Washington," Hannan recalls. He adds,

> The lights at the time were a little bit low. He got a jump on the ball—he saw where it was coming—and he came in but he didn't really see the ball. He put his mitt in the wrong place, and it went to the fence for a triple, but the guy never scored, and that was the only hit. I understood, because I wore glasses, too, and I knew how they just steamed up and you just couldn't see.

Hannan's 7–0 one-hitter gave the Senators a seven-game winning streak, and the team's second one-hitter in five days (Bosman had one-hit the Twins the previous week). But Washington stumbled after Hannan's game, losing the next three games to drop into last place.

Howard's performance on a September afternoon at Fenway Park seemed to epitomize the team's frustrations. Howard struck out his first four times at bat, and his buddy, Brinkman, sat down next to the slugger in the dugout. "You going to feature a little contact before this game is over?" the feisty shortstop asked.

"And I told him zip it—he hadn't had a base hit in a month," Howard recalls with a laugh. "He's going to get all over me? So I said, 'Don't worry, Wimpy, just get on base in the ninth inning, and I'll pop one up in that net and we'll win a ballgame.' I figured I had this pitcher right in my gun sights to do just that."

In the top of the ninth inning, Howard came up with two outs and two runners on base and the Senators trailing, 7–3. The Washington slugger quickly fell behind with two quick strikes, and Brinkman, who was standing at second base, started taunting him, along with the Fenway fans, who were cheering for another strikeout.

"I'm trying to concentrate on this guy on the mound, and as I concentrate, here's my buddy at second base waving his hands, saying 'Five! You're going down again!'" Howard recalls. "The pitcher throws me another slider, and I strike out for the fifth straight time in a big-league ball game. I wanted to kill Brinkman. He's running off the field laughing."

Boston fans jeered Howard: "I had 34,000 New Englanders all over me—'Go to work for a living, you clown!' I flipped them a bird and said, 'I love you, too, you clam-eaters.'"

Howard's propensity for strikeouts earned him some ribbing from his own manager, too. One of his legacies at RFK is the white-painted seats in the upper deck of the stadium, to mark where his monstrous home runs landed. A friend of Ted Williams saw the seats before one game and asked, "Geez, is that where Howard hit those long home runs?"

Williams responded, "Yeah, and there's 13,980 green seats up there—those are all the times he struck out on me."

When baseball returned to Washington in 2005, some baseball players thought the tale of those painted seats had to be urban legend. Kurkjian, who grew up just outside Washington in Bethesda, Maryland, recalls pointing out the seats to Tom Glavine, then a pitcher for the New York Mets:

> I said, "That's where Frank Howard hit home runs, forty, fifty years ago." And Tom Glavine is a really smart guy, and he said, "No, that's impossible. No one could hit it up there." Because no one was going close to up there—even in batting practice. And I said, "Tom, that's where he hit it. I swear. I grew up here. This is where he hit balls." And he goes, "Well, home plate could not have been where it is now." And I said, "Tom, this is exactly where home plate was."

Kurkjian says he thinks Howard is the "strongest player that's ever lived." Howard had a great year in 1970, despite the five-strikeout game at Fenway Park. He led the league in home runs (44), RBIs (126), and walks (132), and hit a team-best .283. But 1970 was a disaster for the Senators as a whole, especially coming off such a successful season the year before. Washington finished the season with a crushing fourteen straight losses.

Short pulled off a blockbuster trade less than two weeks later, sending his left side of the infield—shortstop Brinkman and third baseman Aurelio Rodriguez—to the Detroit Tigers for talented but troubled pitcher Denny McLain in an eight-player deal. Rodriguez had been acquired by Washington just six months earlier and put up decent numbers in 1970, batting .247, with nineteen home runs and seventy-six RBIs. Brinkman, an excellent defensive shortstop, was coming off his second-straight successful offensive year, batting .262, with a .330 on-base percentage.

Washington also parted with pitchers Jim Hannan and Joe Coleman, and received from Detroit third baseman Don Wert, outfielder–third baseman Elliott Maddox, and pitcher Norm McRae.

McLain, only twenty-six, had been one of the game's most dominant pitchers, winning thirty-one games with a 1.96 ERA in 1968, en route to the Cy Young Award, and going 24–9 in 1969. But he missed much of the 1970 season because of disciplinary problems. Commissioner Bowie Kuhn suspended him for half the year for associating with bookmakers; the team's general manager yanked him for four days after McLain dumped ice water on a couple of sportswriters; and on September 9, the commissioner removed him for the remainder of the season over allegations that the pitcher had carried a gun. Overall, McLain went 3–5 in the shortened year.

Short conceded that Ted Williams was not happy with the deal. "He thinks the price Detroit extracted was too high—although Ted feels he can handle McLain."

Williams told reporters, "This was not my trade. I wasn't 100 percent for it at all. I'm really disappointed to have our best two infielders leave the club."

Short's real motivation was getting more fans into the stadium; Washington's attendance had fallen to 824,000 in 1970, a drop-off of nearly 100,000 from the previous season. He said McLain would "improve the gate" at RFK.

In an early warning about the fate of the team, Short was also beginning to make some noise about improving the lease deal at the stadium. He wanted free rent on the first million fans; parking revenue (of which he received none); and all of the concessions revenue instead of the sliding-scale percentage he was getting. He argued that the increased revenue would allow him to spend money to improve the team.

"If I don't get what I want, I will declare bankruptcy," he said, but added, "If I don't get what I want, the American League will operate the club in Washington. I will not request a move."

Four days after the trade, Short testified at a U.S. House District Committee hearing to make his case for a better lease on the stadium. "I am not trying to get rent free," he said. "I am trying to get someone who runs that building to recognize . . . we don't have the money to police it. We don't have the money to put in the infield and to maintain it. We don't have the money to pay a minimum rental." The lease, which expired at the end of the 1971 season, called for the Senators to pay $65,000, or 7 percent of gross ticket receipts, whichever was greater.

In November 1970, Short acquired outfielder Curt Flood from the Philadelphia Phillies for three minor leaguers. Flood had unsuccessfully challenged baseball's reserve clause—refusing a trade in 1969 from the St. Louis Cardinals to the Philadelphia Phillies—and sat out the entire 1970 season. This deal, too, was made with increasing attendance in mind. Short said he lost $953,000 in 1970.

"We need great players, and these guys are controversial," Short told the *Post*. "With McLain pitching, even if we have a bad team, they'll come to see him because he's a face. Ted Williams is a face. Flood is a face. Frank Howard is a face. Without Frank Howard last season, we wouldn't have drawn flies."

Short's money problems, however, were more tied to his own financing of the team than attendance or lease conditions. More than $700,000 of his operating losses came from interest he paid on loans he took out to buy the team. His poverty cries got a skeptical response from the media, especially because the Senators charged the highest ticket prices in the league.

"If Short needs money so badly, (fans) might ask, why doesn't he sell his jet plane or at least put it in mothballs until his financial crisis is resolved?" Minot wrote. "He uses the Lear jet the way the rest of us use a taxi."

Starting out on a hopeful note, the Senators finally snapped two losing streaks on April 5, 1971. One was the fourteen-game skid that marked the end of the 1970 season. The other was the Opening Day drought dating back to 1963. After eight straight Opening Day losses, the Senators finally gave their hometown fans a win in the American League's traditional opener. Unfortunately, it would be the last Opening Day in Washington Senators history.

Bosman threw a six-hit shutout in the 8–0 victory over the Oakland Athletics, as the Senators beat Vida Blue, who went on to win the Cy Young Award that year. Rookie Toby Harrah, the Senators' new shortstop, got two hits and scored two runs. The team even got off to a 12–8 start and was tied for first place on April 28.

But the famous veterans Short had brought in were not working out. Flood quit the team in late April, after playing thirteen games in Washington. He retired with a lifetime .293 average, but hit just .200 in his one month with the Senators. Similarly, McLain never regained his pitching form, and his problems were compounded by poor run support. He became a twenty-game loser (10–22, 4.28 ERA) three years after becoming baseball's last thirty-game winner.

But the Senators had bigger troubles than their on-the-field performance. In June, the D.C. Armory Board sent letters to Commissioner Bowie Kuhn and American League president Joe Cronin, informing them that Short was $161,000 behind in rent. The board, complaining that Short had not responded to letters and requests for meetings, said it could take several actions against Short, including turning out the stadium lights and locking the gates if rent wasn't received by July 15. Kuhn called a meeting of the twelve American League owners, who authorized Cronin to try to find a solution. After the eight-hour meeting, Short said that he had not sought permission to move the team to Dallas, as had been rumored. "I never wanted to, I never intended to, but that doesn't mean I won't move," he told the *Post*.

Meanwhile, Short denied having polled the other owners to see if he had the required support of nine of the twelve league owners to move the team. "I don't think it will ever come to that," he said. On July 7, Kuhn, Cronin, and Short met with D.C. Armory Board officials, who agreed not to shut off the lights on July 15 and to look into what concessions could be made to alleviate Short's financial woes.

In an effort to keep the team in Washington, the board made an offer to Short for the 1972 season. As the owner had demanded, the team would pay no rent on the first million fans; after that, revenue would be split equally between the Senators and the board. The Senators would also get food and beverage profits during the baseball season, but the board would not agree to give Short the parking revenue he had sought. Overall, the board said, Short would save about $125,000 a year as part of the deal. Short called the offer a step in the right direction, "but kind of late."

As the team began its final weeks in Washington, several groups came forward to try to save the Senators. Bob Hope, who had lost his bid to buy the team in 1968, offered Short $7.45 million, but was rejected. Short, who had paid $9.4 million, wanted $12 million for the team, arguing that he needed the profit to offset $3 million in operating losses.

Joseph B. Danzansky, president of both Giant Food Stores and the Washington Board of Trade, said he would pay $8 million for the team. Bill Veeck and former Tigers slugger Hank Greenberg, who had been partners in the Chicago White Sox ownership, also made a last-ditch effort to buy the team and prevent it from moving.

Short must have been surprised that he wasn't getting better offers. Back in 1969, he told Al Eisele for a *Washingtonian* profile, "The team now probably isn't worth what I paid for it, but nobody ever lost money selling a big-league baseball franchise. Even if I mismanage the team, it will still be worth close to what I paid for it."

Meanwhile, a contingent from Texas was trying to lasso the team. The mayors of Dallas, Fort Worth, and Arlington presented a unified front for a team in Arlington, which was located between the other two cities. Texas banks offered Short a $7.5 million line of credit at low interest.

Just days before a vote by American League owners to settle the fate of the Senators, the major parties were still publicly stating that the team would likely stay in Washington. Commissioner Kuhn said he'd be surprised if Short sought permission to move, and on the eve of the vote, Short told the *Post* that someone would buy the team and keep it in the nation's capital. "I don't think the District of Columbia will allow it to move," he said, adding that he didn't think he would ask permission to relocate the team.

But Short did ask permission to move, and, on September 21, 1971, at a meeting in Boston, the American League owners voted, 10–2, to allow him to do so. Danzansky made a final offer to buy the team, but the owners concluded that the financing was too thin. The only teams to vote against the move were the Chicago White Sox and, ironically, the Baltimore Orioles. Decades later, the Orioles would fight vociferously to keep a team from returning to Washington.

Kuhn said that Baltimore's vote against letting the Senators move was just for show. "They didn't want to make Washington fans unhappy," he said in 2005, two years before his death at the age of eighty. "They knew good and well how the vote was going to go."

Although the Orioles voted against letting the team move, their owner immediately made clear that now that Washington was without a team, the city was Baltimore territory. *Washington Post* sports editor Shirley Povich reported that after the vote, Orioles owner Jerold Hoffberger told his fellow owners, "Gentlemen, this means the Orioles now control all territory within one hundred miles of Baltimore under the American League rules, and I will veto any shift of another league franchise to Washington."

Hours before the vote, the Senators played in front of just 1,300 fans in a home game against Cleveland, reinforcing the funereal atmosphere of the stadium. Only four home games remained after that.

The Senators moved on the watch of a league president and commissioner with strong historical ties to Washington baseball. Cronin had been a popular player for the Senators in the 1920s and 1930s, leading the team to its last pennant as player-manager in 1933. He was even part of owner Clark Griffith's family, marrying Griffith's niece and adopted daughter, Mildred Robertson. "As an old Washington player, this is very sad, indeed, but there was no feasible alternative," Cronin said when making the announcement at 11:30 p.m.

Kuhn grew up in Washington and operated the scoreboard at old Griffith Stadium as a youth. "It is a sad day after the better part of a century in Washington," Kuhn said. "But it's a great day for Dallas–Fort Worth, which everyone agrees is ready for Major League Baseball."

Reflecting on the meeting decades later, Kuhn said, "It was terrible. It was the only time I ever cried as commissioner. I did everything I could to save it. I held it up for months. Finally, we had the American League meeting. I couldn't make an argument against it. I stood there with tears down my face."

ESPN baseball analyst Tim Kurkjian, then a fourteen-year-old "maniacal" Senators fan, had the same emotional reaction. "I literally cried out loud when they left," he says now. "It was really a crushing defeat."

Richard Nixon, the last in a line of twentieth-century presidents to throw out the first ball at the traditional presidential opener, said he was "distressed" by the news and would now switch his allegiance to the California Angels, who were based near his home of San Clemente, California. The Angels, coincidentally, had entered the American League with the Senators in 1961.

Ted Williams said he encouraged Red Sox owner Tom Yawkey to approve the move. "The American League people would have been crazy if they hadn't allowed the shift," he said. He added,

> The way things are set up in this town—bad rent, bad concessions, no television market—hell, nobody could make it. There was a hard core of fans here all right, but there were only six or seven thousand of them. Basically Washington is a city of transient people. Most people don't give a damn.

Unlike the last team move in 1961, this time there was no expansion team waiting in the on-deck circle to take the Senators' place. That meant an end to Major League Baseball in Washington after seventy-one years, three pennants, and one World Series championship.

"I face you all in failure because I was not able to do what I wanted to do," Short told reporters. "I worked with diligence with Mr. Kuhn and Mr. Cronin to find a solution to the problem." He said the Texas deal offered him "more favorable terms than any baseball operator I know of," such as a one-dollar-a-year rent on the first million fans, a share of parking and concession revenue, and a radio-television contract valued at $1 million a year—double what Short had gotten in broadcasting revenue in D.C.

The Senators were moving from RFK Stadium to the inelegantly named Turnpike Stadium, located on a toll road between Dallas and Fort Worth. But it would take some time for the transplanted team, renamed the Rangers, to catch on in Texas. Even with the hoopla of its first year in Texas, the team drew a measly 663,000 fans in 1972, just 8,000 more than the Senators' last lame-duck season in Washington.

"Baseball is a business, as far as Mr. Short is concerned," the *Washington Post* editorialized:

> and his devotion to the idea of keeping baseball alive in the nation's capital was, to be generous about it, wafer-thin. . . . So we say good-bye to Mr. Short with hardly a tear, while wishing the Senators well in their new Texas home. Fans there, inexperienced with the ways of baseball promoters, may be eager for a while to pay big-league prices to see minor-league ball and get free who-knows-what.

A *Washington Star* editorial also criticized Short's reliance on giveaways, for example, Hot Pants Day and Pantyhose Night: "Bob Short was not worthy of us. He spent too much, cared too little, and thought he could buy his way out of his mistakes with high-priced tickets and pantyhose. Let him go. To hell with it."

Fans took the news hard. Bill Gilbert, the team's former marketing director, described in a letter to the editor him telling his seven-year-old son the news: "The blond head immediately buried itself in the pillow on his bed, face down. He was crying. After an eternity, the head struggled its way up from the pillow. . . . He said, 'I'll never see Frank Howard ever again.'" One fan suggested a new name for the team: "The Dallas–Fort Worthless Senators."

Phil Hochberg, a lifelong Senators fan who served as the team's public address announcer from 1962 to 1968, says the move was crushing. "I was 30 years old, and this was as close to a feeling as somebody in my family dying as I have ever had—certainly up to that time," Hochberg recalls. He continues,

> A feeling of total helplessness. You can see it happening, and there's nothing you can do about it. I guess it's all of the emotions that one feels when a loved one dies. Maybe I ought to grow up, but this was an important part of my life, and Bob Short took it away from me. And he didn't have the right to take it away from me. From the time I was seven years old, this was an important part of my life.

The Senators became the fourth team to move in six years. The Milwaukee Braves had moved to Atlanta in 1966; the Kansas City Athletics had relocated to Oakland in 1968; and the Seattle Pilots had left for Milwaukee in 1970, after just one season on the West Coast. With all of the team shifts, Washington baseball boosters were confident they could land a new team. After all, the three cities that had lost teams in the 1960s would land replacement clubs within a few years. But the era of franchise moves ended with the Senators.

Washington officials didn't waste any time trying to get a new team. Mayor Walter Washington named Danzansky to make a pitch to the San Diego Padres, who were struggling to draw fans in only their third year. But nothing came of it. The Padres had entered the National League in 1969, along with the Montreal Expos—the team Washington would finally land thirty-four years later.

On September 30, the Senators suited up for their last game ever, against the New York Yankees. Some 14,460 fans, nearly double the average crowd that season, showed up for the last rites. Four thousand more slipped through unmanned turnstiles as the game went on, writes Jeffrey Stuart in his revealing book, *Twilight Teams*. Like a family trying to unload its unwanted stuff before moving out of a house, the Senators gave away leftover promotional materials, including balls, caps, shirts, and copies of Ted Williams's book, *My Turn at Bat*.

The crowd was festive and sad, trying to celebrate its one last game, while pouring out its acrimony toward Short. "To those among the crowd who had come in sorrow," wrote Povich the next day, "the Star Spangled Banner never before sounded so much like a dirge." To the city's embittered fans, he added, Arlington, Texas, "is some jerk town with the single boast it is equidistant from Dallas and Fort Worth."

Before the game, a couple of fans went on top of the dugout with a sign that read, "How Dare You Sell Us Short." During the game, two long, skinny signs were unfurled from the left-field stands next to one another, with vertical letters spelling out "Short" and "Stinks," prompting a standing ovation. One fan wore a black mourning arm band. At one point, fans started chanting, "We Want Bob Short."

The owner, of course, was nowhere near the place, but he did call the radio station that was airing the game to complain about announcer Ron Menchine, who was criticizing Short throughout the broadcast.

In the sixth inning, Howard gave the fans their final thrill, blasting a home run off the back of the Yankees bullpen, as part of a four-run rally that tied the score. The fan-favorite waved his batting helmet in the air, tossed his cap into the stands, and blew kisses to the fans. He also told Yankees catcher Thurmon Munson as he crossed the plate, "Thanks for the gift." Pitcher Mike Kekich suggested he grooved one to Howard. "It's okay," he said. "Let's just say I tried to throw him a straight pitch."

"This is utopia," Howard said after the game. "This is the greatest thrill of my life. What would top it?" Even now, decades later, Howard says, "It sends chills through your spine, makes your hair stand on edge. You're playing in front of your people, and you want to satisfy them. It was a very emotional highlight in my career."

At the beginning of the eighth inning, some fans started coming onto the field, but order was restored. Williams, sensing pandemonium, lifted Howard from the game. In the top of the ninth inning, fans again raced onto the field, prompting a warning from the public address announcer that the game could be forfeited.

Joe Grzenda took the mound in the bottom of the ninth, with the Senators leading, 7–5. Grzenda had been one of the Senators' few highlights that year, going 5–2, with a 1.92 ERA for a fifth-place team that finished 63–96, its worst record in seven years.

Grzenda recalls how he had instructions to hesitate after getting the second out of the inning, to give the bullpens a chance to empty out. "Because they knew something was going to happen," he says, adding,

> They were rowdy going back to the fourth inning. After I got two outs, Horace Clarke came up. I wasted some time, kicking dirt around, and Horace stood in that batting circle taking those practice swings. And I yelled, "C'mon let's go!" I looked around, and it was over. They came over the fence, and there was actually dust flying. There were hundreds that came over the fence. It looked like a heard of cattle coming in those old movies, when they stampede.

Still, Grzenda says he wasn't scared. "The fans they had in Washington were all good fans. They wouldn't hurt us. I think when Frank Howard went into the dugout, two kids jumped on his back. And when he went down, he just brushed them off with the roof of the dugout."

Tom McCraw, who would become the Washington Nationals' first batting coach in 2005, was on the field as the Senators' first baseman for that final game. He recalls seeing what looked like confetti blowing around RFK in the sixth inning of that final game.

"By the seventh inning, it got worse, then you could recognize what it was—it was part of Ted Williams's book that they were tearing up," he says. He continues,

> I was playing first base, and the umpire said to me, "Mack, they're coming out on this field, and I'm going to get out of here." And I said, "Well if you leave, I will be in your back pocket." And sure enough about the eighth inning, two or three guys came on the field, and it turned into eight, nine, and ten, and then they just kind of swarmed the field in the ninth inning. And hell, he took up, and true to my word, I went right with him. I just went in the clubhouse and waited for a couple of hours.

Play was never restored, and the final game in Washington Senators history was recorded as a forfeit for the Yankees. Fans pulled up bases, numbers from the scoreboard, light bulbs, and chunks of grass. The final score was 9–0, the traditional forfeit score in baseball. But all the records, including Howard's home run, counted.

POSTSCRIPT

The team continued its downward trajectory in its first year in Texas. The Rangers finished 54–100 in 1972, a .351 winning percentage, worst in the major leagues. Ted Williams quit after the season and was replaced the next year by Whitey Herzog. The 1973 Rangers finished with a nearly identical winning percentage of .352, again last in the majors. Billy Martin took over the team at the end of the year and led the team to a second-place finish in 1974. The Rangers didn't win their first division title until 1996, and the team won consecutive American League pennants in 2010 and 2011, but lost the World Series both times.

Meanwhile, a few hardcore Senators fans made it their life's mission to get revenge on Bob Short in the years after the move. Bill Holdforth, who had worked as an usher at RFK, recalls circling a date on the 1972 calendar.

"When we saw the 1972 schedule and saw when Texas would be coming to Baltimore, we said, we would be at that game and we were going to do something," recalls Holdforth, who is known as "Baseball Bill." "We decided we had to take an effigy with us. My brother Bob helped me stuff it with old copies of the *Sporting News*, back when it was a newspaper. We added a shirt and tie. And we put a sign on the front, 'Short Stinks,' got in the car, and went up to Baltimore."

Holdforth and his buddies got tickets in Short's section and laid the effigy under their seats. Then Holdforth approached an usher he knew and said,

I don't know when, but sometime during the game, we're going to take the dummy down and stand right by

Short. We're just going down to taunt him. We don't want to get thrown out, and we don't want to get you in trouble,

so when you want us to leave, we'll make you look good, we'll go right back.

Newspaper photos the next day showed the husky, twenty-one-year-old Holdforth grinning mischievously as he holds the effigy behind Short, who is wearing an exasperated expression. Holdforth's buddy stands behind the effigy holding a sign that reads, "Short stinks."

"I stood over Short for two or three minutes. He looked very uncomfortable," Holdforth recalls, still laughing about it decades later. "And we said, 'What's the matter, Bobby Baby? Is something bothering you?' He turned around and said, 'Why don't you go fuck yourself?' I just busted out laughing. When you get a response like that, then you know you're being effective."

In Washington baseball lore, Holdforth is also the guy credited with dumping beer on Short, but Holdforth insists that part of the story isn't true. An inning later, Holdforth says, he went to the bathroom, and when he came out, fans were in a tizzy over a woman who poured a beer on the Rangers owner. "I wouldn't waste a beer like that," says Holdforth, who worked for several years at the Capitol Hill bar Hawk 'n' Dove.

Holdforth continued his crusade even after Short sold the Rangers and tried to get back into politics. In 1978, Short ran for U.S. Senate as a Democrat from his home state of Minnesota, and Holdforth and his friends formed "Baseball Bill's Committee to Keep Bob Short out of D.C." to try to defeat him. The still-seething Senators fans raised

$3,500 in a backyard fundraiser and used the money to take out a half-page ad in the *Minneapolis Star* the Sunday before the Democratic primary. The ad said:

> Don't Be "SHORT" Changed. Bob Short WAS a Senator. In fact, he was the Washington Senators, the American League baseball club. He purchased the team in December 1968. He moved the team to Arlington, Texas, at the end of September 1971. We in our Nation's Capital were left without a baseball team. We were "short changed." In two days you people of the great state of Minnesota must make a decision. Bob Short held our trust for three years, and we were SHORT CHANGED. So, before you vote Tuesday, please consider these facts about Bob Short as we know him.

The ad then lists several comments Short made, contrasted with his actions that led to the team being moved. "Seventy-one years of baseball tradition meant nothing to him," the ad said. "Minnesotans have a tradition of sending men of national stature like Humphrey, Mondale, and McCarthy to the U.S. Senate. Does Bob Short's record measure up? We think not." And then the kicker: "P.S. You can keep Cal Griffith, too," who had moved the first Senators team to Minnesota in 1961.

Short won the Democratic primary anyway, and the group figured that was that. But a week later, Holdforth says, they got a call from the campaign of the Republican candidate, Dave Durenberger, asking for permission to make copies of the ad and distribute them at Minnesota Vikings football games. "So we said 'sure,'" Holdforth recalls. "We made it clear, we wanted to see Short lose." Durenberger wound up defeating Short, and the senator-elect paid a visit to the group after the election.

"I remember he was just one of those guys that I had to go meet," recalls Durenberger. He continues,

> I wanted to go see my buddy, Baseball Billy! When I met him, I thought wow, how can you miss this guy? He's really a larger-than-life character. I'd never seen a bartender quite that big. He didn't make any bones about

it—was he a big David Durenberger supporter? No. His goal was to keep Short out of Washington, D.C. And he was happy that I was available to do it.

Durenberger thinks the Holdforth effort helped. "The campaign was taking advantage of every anti-Short thing they could take advantage of," he says. "The guy had a lot of negatives, and they wanted to increase it—so Baseball Billy was one way to do it. It was an easy of way of saying, folks in Washington don't want Bob Short any more than people in Minnesota want him."

Holdforth wasn't the only one to hold a grudge. In 2011, after the Rangers lost the World Series to the St. Louis Cardinals in seven games, comedian Lewis Black tweeted a note of congratulation to a St. Louis fan, adding, "Sorry Texas fans. I am from the D.C. area. They should still be the Washington Senators. The pricks."

Washington would continue its quest for a team for more than three decades after the Senators left for Texas. In 1974, the city was so close to landing the Padres that Topps printed baseball cards of Padres players with "Washington" written on them. The deal fell through when McDonald's founder Ray A. Kroc bought the team and kept it in San Diego. In 1977, the National League passed on a chance to expand to Washington, deciding to stay put with twelve teams as the American League expanded to Toronto and Seattle.

Subsequent expansions in 1993 and 1998 also bypassed the nation's capital. In 2001, Major League Baseball tried unsuccessfully to eliminate two teams. One was the Minnesota Twins, the original Washington Senators franchise. The other was the Montreal Expos, the team that would become the new Washington Nationals.

When baseball finally moved the Expos to Washington for the 2005 season, it marked a historical accounting with the city of Montreal. Calvin Griffith, the man who relocated the original Senators to Minnesota, was a Montreal native.

NINE

Fans, Moments, and Memories

FANS, MOMENTS, AND MEMORIES

An old expression about the Senators, "First in war, first in peace, and last in the American League," aptly describes the team's final quarter-century, from the end of World War II through 1971. But a sportswriter named Charles Dryden had actually coined the phrase back in the team's early 1900s infancy, making a play on Henry Lee's eulogy to George Washington: "First in war, first in peace, and first in the hearts of his countrymen."

The Washington Nationals—popularly known as the Senators—started off with eleven straight losing seasons. Clark Griffith reversed the team's fortunes when he took over as manager in 1912, leading them to a strong second-place finish, and Washington actually posted good teams, on and off, through the early 1930s.

But for many Washingtonians, losing was an intrinsic part of being a Senators fan. In 1954, native Washingtonian Douglass Wallop penned *The Year the Yankees Lost the Pennant*, about a middle-aged Senators fan who sells his soul to the Devil in return for being transformed into the young slugger Joe Hardy, who helps the Senators win the pennant. *Damn Yankees*, the musical based on the novel, opened to rave reviews on Broadway in 1955. In real life, the Senators finished in last place that year, thirty-eight games behind the first-place Yankees. It was but small comfort to Senators fans when the hated Yankees lost the World Series that year to the Brooklyn Dodgers.

Kevin Dowd recalls going to his first game in 1955, for the Senators home opener that season, and scheming to get back there as soon as he could. Back then, fans could get into the bleachers at Griffith Stadium for twenty-five cents by cutting out a coupon on the back of a box of cereal. "So I begged my mother to start buying this stuff," he recalls with a laugh. He adds:

> It was inedible. Nobody I knew ate this stuff. My father would eat anything—he was like a machine. Quantity not quality was his motto. Even he couldn't eat this shit. So I'd say, "We need another box," and my mother would say, "I've got a year-and-a-half's supply in the pantry. Nobody likes it."

Dowd's next scam: look for a promotion at the ballpark. He says,

So finally I found one that I knew my mother would be interested in. Every morning of her life, all morning, she'd listen to Arthur Godfrey. So one day I found out that he [was] going to make an appearance at the game. After the game, he and his horse were going to come out. I think he sang a little bit, played the ukulele. So it was like one of the rock shows they have now after the game. So I showed that to my mother, and she said, "I'll go."

But they had to take Kevin's four-year-old sister Maureen, the future *New York Times* columnist, which turned out to complicate matters. Dowd continues,

It was a pretty good crowd for the Senators—I'd say 10,000. So my mother keeps looking at her watch, like, "When's this game going to be over so I can see Arthur and his horse?" The game ends, he finally appears, my mother, of course, is enthralled. Maureen wants a Coke, I'm supposed to go with her. I have to go to the bathroom. So I leave her, come back, I can't find her. The next forty minutes my mother is panicked, she's got it on the PA system. So when we finally found her, wandering around, his act was over—and so was my mother's baseball career.

Kevin Dowd's mother wasn't the only one staying away. The Senators drew just 425,000 in 1955, an average of 5,500 fans a game, dead last in the American League. The team kept that distinction for the following five seasons, before moving to Minneapolis in 1961.

The Senators tried all kinds of promotions to try to entice fans to the ballpark. Dowd remembers a race between pitcher Pedro Ramos and a chicken:

The race was from home plate to first base. Pedro comes out, and he laughs. He gets in a stance. This chicken, I think he thought he was going to escape, 'cause it was like he shot out of a cannon. His trainer was holding him. I guess he saw an opening in right field—he was heading for it, man. Pedro, who was fast, I think he was shocked at the acceleration of the chicken. Pedro lost by about five yards.

In the years before luxury boxes, going to a Senators game was for the hardcore fans only. "There wasn't a lot of passion for the Senators," recalls Phil Hochberg, who was a young Senators fan at the time and went on to become the team's public address announcer in the 1960s. "The fans who were there were passionate, but there were so few. They had been beaten down by so many losing teams for so many years. Between 1946 and 1971—that's twenty-six years—they finished over .500 twice. That's abysmal! So there wasn't any enthusiasm."

Hochberg says that by the 1950s, Griffith Stadium was not a particularly friendly place to watch a game. The park sat at the corner of 7th Street and Florida Avenue, Northwest, near Howard University. "There was no parking to speak of, so you had to park on the street," Hochberg says. He adds,

> So little kids would come by and say, "I'll watch your car, Mister, for twenty-five cents." And if you didn't give them the twenty-five cents, there was no telling what would happen to your car. Griffith Stadium was an old ballpark, it had lots of character, but it was not a particularly good place to watch a ballgame from. You had obstructed seats. You had girders holding up the right-field stands, and you couldn't see the left-field stands. There was nothing wonderful about Griffith Stadium except that it was a baseball stadium.

Dowd says that Griffith Stadium looked like Fenway Park in reverse: "The wall was in right, not in left. But it was the same size, rickety old place. The players were warming up where you could almost touch them."

Joe Dempsey, who went to ballgames in the 1950s, remembers the sounds of the old ballpark: "Get yer' red hots, hare! Get 'em while 'air hot. . . . Col' be-ah, get cher' col' be-ah." One vendor in particular stands out in Dempsey's memory: "In a high-pitched, somewhat raspy voice came a slow drawn-out but very clear 'It is NOW time to EAT, DRINK, and be MERRY! Get yo' hot dawgs, he-ah!'"

"Griffith Stadium was an old rickety, run down stadium," says Dempsey. He continues:

> The girders and beams reminded me of my Erector Set at home. As you entered the seating area, everything was painted dark green, and the emerald lawn of the playing field seemed to jump at you. The sound of the gathering crowds was muffled, and the crack of the ball and bat of batting practice was pronounced.

But some fans thought the old ballpark had charm. Jack Farley, who started going to games in the 1930s, says:

> The right-field wall was a favorite of mine. The scoreboard was attached to it, and someone would go inside
> the wall and hang signs for the runs scored by each team during each inning. Once in a while, the person would
> drop a sign and it would fall on the playing field. Then he would come out of a little door and pick up the sign.
> The crowd loved it.

Manning the scoreboard in the 1940s was Bowie Kuhn, a Washington native who later became baseball commissioner. He held the job as a teenager, before joining the Navy. "It was one of the best jobs I ever had," said Kuhn, who died in 2007. "The scoreboard was in right-center, and it looked out on an alley through a window. There was always a bunch of kids in the alley who I would talk to. I got in the habit of doing play-by-play for the kids, who couldn't see into the ballpark."

"It was a wonderful old stadium," Kuhn adds. "The sightlines were good, as long as you didn't get behind pillars. The pavilion seats were sixty cents, where all the old-time fans would bet on the game. The bleachers were forty cents."

Farley, who is retired in Rehoboth Beach, Delaware, recalls even better specials. "Mom would take me to Ladies Day games, where she got in for twenty-five cents and I got in for free. Once we got there, there would be the wonderful smell of the Wonder Bread Bakery next door baking bread, which would waft into the bleachers."

You also didn't have to pay four bucks for a bottle of water back then—or anything, for that matter. In the summer of 1941, baseball fans were shocked about reports that ushers were charging fans a dime for a glass of ice water. Owner Clark Griffith originally denied this scandalous accusation, which appeared in a New York newspaper called *PM*. But after investigating, Griffith issued this statement:

> I find proof that some concession boys, particularly in the bleachers, took advantage of the big crowd on the
> 29th of June to make themselves a little easy money by selling ice water. The Washington club deeply regrets that
> such a thing could have happened and wants to apologize to the Washington public and assure them that it will

not occur again. In fact, this is the first time in thirty years that anything like this has happened. The boys involved in this circumstance will be discharged.

Griffith made a point of making the place a family friendly environment. He refused to sell beer at the stadium, but he did sell advertising space to beer companies. "The ironic part was the major sponsor, and this big thing on the outfield wall, was National Bohemian Beer," recalls Dowd. "But you couldn't buy it there."

Although there was no Metro and little parking, fans did have another way of getting to the games: the streetcar. "One time, on the way to the game, we saw Buddy Lewis standing in the back of our street car," Farley recalls, referring to the Senators' All-Star third baseman. "Buddy rented an upstairs single room from one of our neighbors during the season."

Farley grew up near Catholic University, and would take the streetcar to North Capital Street. From there, he'd walk five blocks to the 5th Street bleacher entrance. "I went to many games alone at night," he recalls. "I used to leave many of the games early since the team was usually pretty far behind. I used to walk past the small row houses occupied by poor blacks. They would sit on their little step at night trying to cool off."

Some young fans relied on the players themselves for transportation. Henry Fankhauser, who later became a sports-writer for the old *Washington Daily News*, says he and his friends would wait outside the Senators' clubhouse and ask the players for rides home. "We'd follow them out to the parking lot, and ask them for autographs, and say, 'By the way, we live in your neighborhood, can we get a ride?'" Fankhauser recalls.

Bill Gilbert remembers waiting after a game in 1944 for outfielder George Case, who lived in his neighborhood. But when Shirley Povich, who covered the team for the *Washington Post*, came out, he informed the youngster that Case had already left. So Povich, who also lived near Gilbert, not only gave him a ride home, he offered to take him to the ballpark anytime.

"So the next morning, I called and said, 'I'd like a ride to the game,'" Gilbert recalls. "I brought a 110 pennies to pay the $1.10 general admission fee. When we got out of the car, he brought me up to the press gate, and said to the attendant, 'He's with me.' He probably took me to thirty-five games."

The next year, 1945, Gilbert and Fankhauser rode their bikes to spring training at College Park, Maryland (a World War II ban on unnecessary travel prevented teams from going south to train). Gilbert, thirteen, got a job as team batboy. There he met one of the most unusual players in Washington baseball history: Bert Shepard.

Shepard, a fighter pilot who had his left leg amputated under his knee, wound up at Walter Reed Hospital for an artificial limb. While there, he received a visit from the undersecretary of war, Robert Patterson, who asked Shepard what he wanted to do after the war. The former minor-league pitcher said he wanted to pitch again. Patterson called Griffith and asked if he'd give Shepard a tryout. The Senators owner agreed, and after Shepard held his own in the 1945 tryout, the team signed him as a player-coach.

"In the dressing room I would watch as he would strap his artificial leg on before the workout and take it off after and hop on one foot into the shower," Gilbert wrote years later.

Shepard pitched in an exhibition game that season, on July 10, and held the Brooklyn Dodgers to two runs in four innings. On August 4, he finally pitched in an official game. In the midst of a blowout at the hands of the Boston Red Sox, Shepard was summoned from the bullpen at Griffith Stadium to help give the pitching staff a breather; the team was playing its fourth doubleheader in four days, with another one scheduled for the next day.

Shepard came into the game with two outs in the fourth inning and the bases loaded. Striding and landing on his artificial limb, he struck out George "Catfish" Metkovich to end the rally and received a standing ovation. Shepard pitched the rest of way, giving up just one run and three hits in a total of five and one-third innings. That was his first and last performance in a big-league game. His lifetime ERA stands at 1.69.

The Senators' original stadium, known as American League Base Ball Park, was constructed of wood, but after a 1911 fire, the team rebuilt it with steel and concrete. Authorities suspected that the fire had been started by a plumber's blowtorch, prompting the team's former manager, Joe Cantillion, to quip, "They're probably right, and the plumber was probably playing third base." The ballpark was renamed Griffith Stadium in 1920 for its owner.

Griffith Stadium was definitely not a hitter's ballpark. Although the dimensions changed throughout the years, it was usually a monstrous 400 feet or more down the left-field line, longer than any major-league ballpark today. The right-field line, by contrast, was usually around 328 feet, but hitters had to clear a thirty-foot-high fence, a kind of mirror-image Green Monster. The fence in center field cut a sharp turn toward home plate to avoid a large oak tree just outside the ballpark, a popular meeting spot for fans. Both Mickey Mantle and Babe Ruth hit balls into the tree.

No ballpark could hold the Mick. In 1953, his home run shot glanced off the National Bohemian Beer sign on top of the bleachers in left-center field, on its way out of the stadium into someone's backyard. The ball traveled 565 feet, the longest measured home run in major-league history. After the game, a sportswriter suggested that the wind was blowing out, to which Clark Griffith retorted, "Consarn it, that same wind has been blowing for a hundred years, and nobody else ever hit one over that wall."

But the Senators lacked that kind of power, wind or not. The stadium was so unfriendly to the home team's sluggers that in 1945, the Senators went the entire season without hitting a ball over the fence. Washington's sole home run that year came on an inside-the-parker by first baseman Joe Kuhel. And this was one of Washington's best teams, as the Senators finished just one and a half games out of first place.

"I was a dead-pull hitter, and it was 405 feet to left field," recalled Eddie Yost, a Senators third baseman in the 1940s and 1950s. "Once, I hit twelve home runs in back-to-back seasons, and only one of them came at Griffith Stadium." Yost never hit more than a dozen home runs in any of his dozen seasons in Washington. After the Senators traded him to Detroit, he hit twenty-one his first season with the Tigers.

Yost made up for a lack of home-field power with an uncanny ability to draw walks. He led the league in bases on balls six times, including a career-high 151 in 1956, earning him the nickname "The Walking Man." Yost, who died in 2012, was a respected player back in his day, but in today's game, which cherishes on-base percentage, he would be a hot commodity. Although Yost hit only .254 for his career, he finished with a superb .394 on-base percentage.

Griffith Stadium may have been hostile to home runs, but with its vast distances and strange angles, it was friendly to triples. In the fifty-one seasons the team played at the ballpark after it was rebuilt in 1911, the Senators led or tied for the league lead in three-baggers seventeen times—including seven times in the 1930s alone.

When Calvin Griffith took over the team in 1955, after the death of Clark Griffith, the new president moved the fences in about thirty feet all around. He also scrapped the Old Fox's ban on alcohol and opened a beer garden in the left-field seats. "We did it for revenue," Calvin Griffith told biographer Jon Kerr. "We wanted to sell beer out there to stay in baseball. We had to do something different."

Mickey Mantle wrote about the beer garden fondly in his book, *The Mick*, saying, "There were so many good fights in the left field bleachers in the beer garden—or women sunbathing about naked—that several times I was watching that when I'd hear the crack of the bat and I'd have to spin around to see which direction everybody was runnin'."

The ballpark's seating capacity, which also varied through the years, was never more than around 32,000, but the Griffith family supplemented income from the park by renting it out to the Homestead Grays of the Negro League during the baseball season, and to the Washington Redskins during football season. Griffith Stadium hosted the most one-sided game in NFL history, when the Chicago Bears beat the Redskins, 73–0, to win the 1940 championship game.

When the Senators were away, their fans could still follow the action—with a little embellishment from Hall of Fame radio broadcaster Arch McDonald. "Back in those days there was no television, and one had to listen to the games on the radio," recalls Robert G. Hardage of Fairfax, Virginia, who started following the Nationals in the 1940s. "The budget was so tight that the announcers did not travel to away games with the team but had to recreate the contest after receiving a teletype wire about what had transpired.

"For away games, one could hear the teletype in the background as you waited to find out what had occurred," says Hardage, a retired high school football coach and athletic director. "Arch McDonald's trademark was a bell or 'gong' for a base hit. A double was two gongs and, naturally, a home run was four gongs but was generally proceeded by the comment from Arch, 'There she goes, Mrs. Murphy.'"

McDonald would recreate the games from the Peoples Drug Store on G Street, a few blocks from the White House, where he would draw overflow crowds, earning him the nickname the "Rembrandt of Recreation." The Arkansas native coined such popular baseball phrases as "ducks on the pond" and "right down Broadway," and he even came up with the nickname for Joe DiMaggio, "The Yankee Clipper." McDonald announced Senators games for twenty-two years, with a one-year break in 1939 to broadcast Yankee games. "They cut down the old pine tree," he'd say after a Senators victory, quoting from an old country song.

Attendance at Griffith Stadium started to tank in the 1950s, thanks to consistently bad teams. In 1956, Washington hired Charlie Brotman as promotions director, and he tried to generate some excitement at the ballpark. One of his first moves: a simple name change—to what fans had called the team for decades.

Officially, the Washington Senators were the Washington Nationals, and team materials reflected the official name. Brotman recalls asking the team's graphic artist, Zang Auerbach, if there was a way to animate the Nationals on the cover of the yearbook.

Auerbach, brother of legendary basketball coach Red Auerbach, responded, "Nothing. It just lays there."

"How about Nats?" Brotman asked.

"Same thing," Auerbach said. "Nothing."

"Can you do something with Senators? Maybe an old-type senator, with a frock, where he throws the ball and catches it?" Brotman suggested.

"Yeah, I can do that with the Senators," Auerbach said.

Brotman says he ran the idea past Calvin Griffith, and the owner signed off.

When the new Senators moved into D.C. Stadium in 1962 (later renamed RFK), there were more bad teams—and more small crowds. Only once did the expansion Senators finish in the top half of the league in attendance, but that was also the team's only winning season—1969.

ESPN baseball analyst Tim Kurkjian, who grew up in the Washington suburb of Bethesda, Maryland, as a diehard Senators fan, says that more fans turn out now in part because the marketing has improved. "But I think our best fans from the '50s and '60s were probably better than our best fans today, because they didn't have a game on every single night to watch," he says. He adds,

> If they wanted to see the Senators, they had to go to the ballpark. I think our baseball fans today are just a little bit spoiled by the fact that if you don't want to go to the park, you don't have to. The Nationals are on MASN every single day. It's a very comfortable feel. I always thought the fans back then—the ones that did fight the traffic, and did go to RFK in a not very nice section of town to watch a team that wasn't very good—I think those were our best fans.

Ben Walker, longtime baseball writer for the Associated Press, grew up in the Washington area and has a bitter-sweet memory of the 1969 All-Star Game at RFK Stadium. Eleven years old at the time, Walker, his parents, and his best friend, John, arrived at the ballpark early for the game. As Walker recalls:

> Neither John nor I had ever seen a National League player in person. We'd seen color pictures of them, of course, from when my dad brought home the *Street & Smith's* magazine at the start of the season. But we didn't have a color TV and could only imagine how they'd look for real. Funny thing: As much as John and I were eager to see Willie Mays and Hank Aaron and Bob Gibson, we really, really wanted to see Chris Cannizzaro. He was San Diego's lone All-Star representative, and we couldn't wait to look at those mustard-brown Padres uniforms that everyone was talking about.

That year's All-Star Game epitomized the sport's increased offense, thanks to a lowering of the pitcher's mound. In 1968, the National League had won the Midsummer Classic, 1–0. Walker experienced firsthand the harder hits in 1969:

> Now the game starts, and the ball is flying. The NL leads, 9–3, after four innings, and already there have been five home runs. And then comes the hardest hit of the day. To me, anyway. I was eating popcorn when Johnny Bench hooked a hard foul into the third-base seats, a few rows behind us. I turned my head and—whack!—got bonked squarely on the forehead by the carom.
>
> The ball zinged back onto the field, where third-base coach Leo Durocher picked it up and tossed it into the crowd. A few minutes later, a young man brought the ball over to me while several fans poured out their Cokes, grabbed napkins, and put together makeshift ice packs. With a bump forming on my head, my mom is worried and wanted me to see a doctor; my dad figured I was fine and wanted me to see Pete Rose. We stayed, and, to be honest, I don't recall much else about the game. That might be because there wasn't a whole lot of action after that, and it ended up 9–3.

That 1969 season would mark the second Senators franchise's only winning record. The Senators also drew 918,000 fans that year, second-highest in Washington baseball history to that point, and the most ever by the second Senators team. But attendance plummeted the next two years, bottoming out at 655,000 fans in 1971, the team's final year in Washington. Overall, the Senators II finished last in league attendance four times in eleven years. That track record gave Major League Baseball pause before it agreed to bring a team back to Washington for a third time. But Senators players say the fans had a bad rap.

"How many times will you go see a horseshit movie?" asks Tom McCraw, who was the first baseman on the 1971 Senators team and served as the Nats first batting coach. "Now, if you're a horseshit ball club, do you expect people to come out eighty times a season and support you? No, you wouldn't do that. You still need to be entertained. If you're a bad ball club, and if you've been a bad ball club for several years, people aren't going to go see it."

In 2012, the Nationals drew 2.37 million fans—far more than any Washington Senators team ever drew, but still just ninth in the sixteen-team National League.

"I thought more people would show up last year, but maybe now that they've made the playoffs and they've got this bright future, you'll really start to see people latching on to the Nationals—which I have now seen," says Kurkjian. He adds:

> I have people in my neighborhood here, people I meet at the grocery store—men, women, children who are all telling me, "I'm in. I'm hooked. I got it now." And I'm thinking, kind of, "What took you so long?!" There are fifty-five-year-old people, my age, saying, "Hey, I'm interested in baseball." And I'm thinking, "Well, that was me, when I was five. It took you fifty-five years." Whatever. As long as they're here, that's all that matters.

Former Senators slugger and fan favorite Frank Howard says that baseball held onto the old perception of Washington as a small, southern, sleepy town. "I don't care if you're in Battle Creek, Michigan, or Minneapolis-St. Paul, the aura of having Major League Baseball lasts two to three years," he says. "The aura of having a new stadium lasts two to three years. But this is America—we love a winner. And you've got to be competitive. You can't ask the public to buy an inferior product." Howard adds:

I wouldn't trade the seven years I had here in Washington. You talk about courtesy and respect accorded to an individual—it was unparalleled. I appreciate it. The fans were very supportive. Not that they didn't boo me all the time. It's like Don Zimmer used to say, "You're an amazing man. They're either all for you or all against you. You strike out four times, you got everybody in the house coming down on you. You hit a home run, everybody's giving you a standing ovation."

That didn't bother me. It's all part of it. One guy said he'd eat his hat if I hit a home run. I hit a home run, and he started chewing on it. The fans here were great.

Former shortstop Eddie Brinkman said that although few fans came out to see the Senators, he enjoyed the ones that did. "Some came just to scream at us—which was fine," said Brinkman, who died in 2008. "You pay your money, you can yell anything you like. One guy used to always sit by the third base dugout, and he'd get on me all the time. We called him Red Dog because he had red hair. He called me a hamburger—'You hamburger, you bum, you stink!'"

"Red Dog" would bring his cooler of beer and come to every game, Brinkman recalls. "We loved it," he said, adding,

Then in 1969, when I started to do a little bit better, one day I walk out of the dugout and I hear, "Hey Brinkman!" I turn around and it's Red Dog. "You're pretty good." And I said, "Red Dog, you son-of-a-gun, you're always getting on my butt, now you're going to come over here and kiss my rear end? Get out of here. Get back over there and get on me some more. I don't want to talk to you."

TEN

The Washington Nationals: Baseball Returns

THE WASHINGTON NATIONALS: BASEBALL RETURNS

On Sunday, October 3, 2004, the Montreal Expos suited up for their final game as a Canadian team. In an odd bit of historical symmetry, the finale was held at the same place the team had played its first game in back in 1969—Shea Stadium in New York. That location didn't keep Canadian fans from making the trip across the border to see the team off, with some rooters sporting jerseys and caps of such old Expos stars as Gary Carter and even Randy Johnson, who began his career in Montreal in the late 1980s.

Four days earlier, 31,000 fans had come out to watch the Expos' final home game, a 9–1 loss to the Florida Marlins. Had the Expos drawn those kinds of crowds consistently, they would have stayed in Montreal. But the team pulled in just 750,000 fans for the season, dead last in baseball, averaging around 9,400 fans.

In their first game in 1969, the newborn Expos had raced out of the starting gate with an 11–10 victory over the Mets, that year's world championship team. But in 2004, Montreal sputtered to an inglorious end, falling to New York, 8–1, in its final game. Fans behind the visitors' dugout chanted "Let's Go Expos" in the ninth inning, but Montreal failed to rally for any runs. Expos starter John Patterson took the loss, surrendering four runs in four and one-third innings. The team finished with a 67–95 record, barely over .400, last in the National League East.

"I've seen this with some other ball clubs when they were moving, and from a distance it doesn't really hit you," Expos manager Frank Robinson said. "But when you're involved in this thing and it's final—the name Montreal Expos won't be in existence next year, that's a rude awakening, and it's a sad situation because of the people it's going to touch in a negative way."

Washington baseball fans could identify with that sentiment. Twice, they had their team yanked away—in 1961, when the Senators left for Minnesota, and again a decade later, when the second version of the Senators left for Texas. Now, they were finally benefiting from a team move, as the Expos were on their way to Washington. The same day the Expos played their last home game, September 29, Major League Baseball had announced that the team would be relocating to the nation's capital.

Some fans have rooted for the franchise in both its Canadian and Washington incarnations. "I became a Washington Nationals fan in 1991—more than twenty years before they existed," says one of those fans, Devlin Barrett, a reporter for the *Wall Street Journal* in Washington. "Mostly to save money, I had decided to go to college in

Montreal, Quebec. As it happens, I caught the last great years of Montreal Expos baseball. It wasn't a dynasty by any stretch, but it was fantastic." He recalls the "Expos cheer,"

which involved taking the empty seat bottom next to you, and slamming it down again and again to make a satisfying thumping sound echo throughout the giant Olympic Stadium, known as "The Big O." Obviously, the prerequisite of an Expos cheer is that you have a lot of empty seats. That was almost never a problem.

The Expos did have some halcyon days, culminating with a 1994 season when they had the best record in baseball, with a .649 winning percentage, and averaged more than 24,000 fans a game. Unfortunately for Montreal, that season ended in August with a players' strike that wiped out the World Series.

"I remember sitting around a radio pitifully listening to a local radio station's fantasy call of a computer simulation of a Yankees–Expos World Series," Barrett recalls. "The Expos lost in six. Stupid computer."

After 1994, the Expos never averaged more than 20,000 fans a game, and by the time they moved to Washington, the team was on life support. The nation's capital stood out among a field of relatively weak competitors for the Expos: Las Vegas, Portland, Oregon, and Norfolk, Virginia. The stiffest challenge came from the Washington suburb of Northern Virginia.

"Congratulations," Commissioner Bud Selig told Mayor Anthony A. Williams, who had led the effort to bring the team to Washington. "It's been a long time coming." It was baseball's first team move since the Senators became the Texas Rangers after the 1971 season.

In a statement, Selig called Washington one of the world's most important cities. "There has been tremendous growth in the Washington, D.C., area [in] the last thirty-three years," he said, "and we in Major League Baseball believe that baseball will be welcomed there and will be a great success."

That view represented a change of tune for a sport that had kept Washington at arm's length for three decades. Many owners saw the city as a two-time baseball loser that couldn't support a team, and the opposition of Baltimore Orioles owner Peter Angelos resonated with his fellow monopolists in baseball's ownership cabal. Angelos argued that a team in Washington would take fans away from the Orioles, thirty-five miles away. In fact, despite the announcement, Angelos was still not onboard, and it would take several months to come up with a deal to prevent him from suing to block the move.

But former congressman Tom Davis, a Republican who represented a suburban Washington district in Virginia, says that Congress would not have tolerated baseball keeping the Expos out of Washington because of Angelos. "We made it very clear that if baseball bypassed this, and went to some place like Norfolk, that there would be a problem," says Davis, who held highly publicized hearings on steroid use among professional athletes in the 2000s. "Because we were clearly the right marketplace."

"Republicans hate Angelos," Davis adds. "He's given a lot of money to Democratic candidates. There was just no way we were going to let Angelos hold this up. I think at the end of the day there would have been a reaction to that, on top of the steroids hearings."

Washington Post sports columnist Tom Boswell says that by 2004, baseball in Washington had become an inevitability. "This is something that had to be done," he says. "The Washington market is enormous. You can't ignore it. You can't allow the owner of one team to operate as a monopolist and prevent an enormous market from getting a team. You can't have a Ford dealership in Baltimore but not allow them in Washington. So this had to happen."

ESPN baseball analyst Tim Kurkjian, who grew up outside D.C., in Bethesda, in the 1960s, says that after the second Senators team, baseball had written off Washington. "I think people looked and said, 'This is a bad baseball town. They've lost a couple of teams. Why do they deserve another team?'" Kurkjian says. He adds,

> They had a terrible team. And the ballpark was not in a particularly nice place, as we know. It wasn't particularly easy to get to. So I've always thought this was a good baseball town. But I think like most towns, you gotta win. And the Senators just never won.
>
> So I think people nationally, when the Nationals came to Washington, said, "Why do they get another team? Is it just because they're in the nation's capital? Is this like the historic part of it, presidents' first ball and all that stuff?"

RFK, he says, wound up being a big plus for Washington.

Obviously the reason baseball came back was the money that's here, and the population that's here, and mostly, RFK was here. There was a place for the Expos to go. And that really, really helped. Otherwise, if RFK hadn't been here and we didn't have a major-league stadium, who knows where we'd be right now?

Because of the city's commitment to build a new stadium for the Expos, the deal also needed city council approval, which would prove to be far more challenging than initially thought, despite the support of a majority of council members at the time. The baseball owners were blown away by the city's generous offer—a publicly funded $440 million stadium on the Anacostia riverfront, to be paid for by taxes on the city's largest businesses, ballpark concessions, and team rent. (That price tag would swell to around $770 million, according to a *Washington Post* analysis, although some of that was covered by the team, Major League Baseball, and federal government contributions to upgrade the Metro stop and improve the roads near the ballpark.) They also realized that Washington was not the deteriorating, riot-plagued town it had been back in the early 1970s. Instead, with its fast-growing suburbs, the Washington region was one of the most affluent in the nation.

The Expos came to Washington without a single owner—or more to the point, with twenty-nine of them. The owners of the other teams had purchased the Expos in 2002, and had run the franchise on a shoestring budget and barnstorming act's schedule. The Expos played twenty-two "home games" in Puerto Rico in both 2003 and 2004, adding thousands of miles of travel, which took a toll on the players.

The team's name was another uncertainty. "Washington Expos" was never really on the table; the name just didn't fit. Many old-time fans, as well as Selig, favored the name Senators, in tribute to the old Washington teams, but Mayor Williams argued that because the city had no actual voting representation in the Senate (or the House for that matter), the team shouldn't be called the Senators. He favored the Grays, the name of the old Negro League team that was based in Homestead, Pennsylvania, but played many of its home games in Washington in the 1930s and 1940s. A third choice: the Nationals, as bland as the Grays, but with an equally compelling historical justification. Washington's old team was formally known as the Nationals until 1956, although fans often referred to them as the Senators.

A *Washington Post* poll in early November 2004 found that 40 percent of local fans surveyed favored Senators, 14 percent liked Nationals, and 10 percent preferred Grays. The rest had no preference or had some other name in mind (Bureaucrats?). In the end, the Nationals emerged as the consensus choice.

"The Mayor was on Grays," said then-team president Tony Tavares. "Bud was on Senators. I think you see a compromise candidate. But I don't want to sell it as that. I think it's a great name."

On November 9, the D.C. City Council added some suspense to the team's move by delaying a vote on the stadium deal. That stall came after three stadium opponents won elections to the city council, although they would not take office until the following January. Fueled by a backlash against giving hundreds of millions of dollars in public subsidies to millionaire baseball owners to field a team of millionaires, critics argued that the money would be better spent on the city's schools and other pressing needs. Proponents countered that the stadium would help promote economic development in a part of the city that badly needed it, and that much of the money would come from taxes generated by the team.

Meanwhile, Major League Baseball moved ahead with the relocation. On December 3, the owners formally approved the team's move to Washington, 29–1, with only the Orioles' Angelos voting no. But less than two weeks later, the city council threw a high, hard one at the owners, voting to require that at least half the cost of the new ballpark be covered by private money. When Major League Baseball balked at the legislation, it appeared that the Expos' move to Washington could fall through. Baseball owners were furious, believing that the city council had pulled a bait-and-switch.

"The legislation approved by the District of Columbia City Council last night does not reflect the agreement we signed and relied upon after being invited by District leaders to consider Washington as a home for Major League Baseball," said then-Major League Baseball president Bob DuPuy in a statement. "The legislation is inconsistent with our carefully negotiated agreement and is wholly unacceptable to Major League Baseball."

The sport stopped all promotional activities for the team, including a press conference scheduled for that week to show off the new Nationals uniform. Major League Baseball also closed the team store and offered refunds to fans who had put down deposits for season tickets. A sense of doom pervaded the city's baseball fans, who realized that if baseball pulled out of the deal, there surely would not be another chance to get a team.

But a week later, negotiations involving city council chairman Linda Cropp, who had pushed for the private spending provision, Mayor Williams, and baseball officials salvaged the deal. The compromise called for the city to seek private funding for half the cost, but did not require it, and for the city and Major League Baseball to share the cost of insurance to cover overruns on the new stadium. Major League Baseball agreed to reduce the penalty that Washington would pay for failing to open the stadium by 2008, from $19 million to $5.3 million. The city council barely passed the new deal, 7–6. Essentially, one vote preserved baseball in Washington.

"Take me out to the ball game," fans sang in the council chambers after the vote. "Finally and at last, all of us have risen above the fray," Williams said, "and the Washington Nationals are rounding third and heading for home. Isn't that great?"

City councilman Jack Evan, the driving force on the council for the baseball deal, says he never thought the deal was in danger. "I knew we had the votes to get it done," he says. "Going into the baseball process, I knew the activists and the anti-baseball people were going to be against it, because they always are."

With the politics finally resolved, at least for the upcoming season, the Nationals could finally focus on putting players on the field. The team, which had finished fourteenth in the National League in runs scored in 2004, had already made a few off-season moves in an effort to improve its lineup. First, the Nats' aggressive new general manager, Jim Bowden, signed two free agent players to fill out the left side of the infield—third baseman Vinny Castilla and shortstop Cristian Guzman.

Castilla hit thirty-five home runs in 2004 and led the National League with 131 RBIs, although he produced those numbers in Denver's hitting-friendly mile-high atmosphere. Guzman, a good defensive shortstop, hit .274 in Minnesota. But both players became huge disappointments for Washington in 2005. Guzman and Castilla rounded out an infield that featured two productive, but injury-prone, players on the right side, first baseman Nick Johnson and second baseman José Vidro.

Next, Bowden traded for talented but temperamental right fielder José Guillén, sending the team's leading hitter, right fielder Juan Rivera (.307 in 2004), and shortstop prospect Maicer Izturis, to the Anaheim Angels in the deal. Guillén had hit .294, with twenty-seven home runs and 104 RBIs, for the Angels in 2004, but the team suspended him late in the season after he threw his helmet toward manager Mike Scioscia for being lifted for a pinch runner.

And in January, Bowden solidified the starting pitching rotation by signing Esteban Loaiza as a free agent. Loaiza, a twenty-one-game winner with a 2.90 ERA in 2003, had slumped badly in 2004, finishing with a 5.70 ERA, but he would turn things around in 2005.

In February, the Nats finally unveiled their new uniforms, as Guillén, Guzman, starting pitcher Zach Day, and closer Chad Cordero met with fans and the media in the delayed dress rehearsal. Guillén indicated that he would try to keep his infamous temper in check in his new city. "I just have to learn to be a political man," he said. "I think I'm in the right town to start learning that."

On March 2, the Nationals played their first game ever, winning, 5–3, over the New York Mets on a cool, sunny day at Space Coast Stadium in Viera, Florida. Although just a Grapefruit League exhibition, the contest had the trappings of a playoff game. ESPN broadcast it on national television, and the game attracted one hundred members of the media and a sellout crowd.

The ballpark sported the old teal seats from the Expos era, but the team played in brand-new Nationals uniforms—crisp, out-of-the-box white, with red lettering. Guzman got Washington's first hit, a line drive up the middle, and Guillén slammed the first home run, muscling a ball over the right-center field wall.

The Nationals entered spring training enthusiastic about their new home. "It's very exciting for the team to be here," top-flight defensive catcher and clutch hitter Brian Schneider said in a conversation before the team's first spring game against its new regional rivals, the Baltimore Orioles. "To get a chance to play here, to be part of the team that comes back to the nation's capital is very, very special. I'm glad that the city could get a team. I know they've wanted it a long time."

Schneider, whose family is from Annapolis, just thirty miles from D.C., said that Washington was the right fit for the team. "I know toward the end of the Senators, attendance was down, and the team was down a bit, but sometimes it takes someone losing something to really appreciate it." He added, "They lost a team, and they wanted baseball back so much, and the ticket sales obviously show that they're ready for a team."

The starting rotation appeared deep, featuring Livan Hernandez, Tony Armas Jr., Tomo Ohka, John Patterson, Zach Day, and Esteban Loaiza, and the Nationals also had a tough young stopper in Chad Cordero. But the hitting was thin, despite the off-season acquisitions. The team struggled to find the right fit for the top of the lineup, deciding to shunt off its center fielder and leadoff man, Endy Chavez, to the minor leagues after Chavez struggled to get on base during spring training. Two months later, the team traded Chavez to the Philadelphia Phillies for outfielder Marlon Byrd.

Washington went back to left fielder Brad Wilkerson as its leadoff man, a miscast role for a man who had hit thirty-two home runs in 2004. But his excellent .374 on-base percentage made him the default choice.

"I think we have a chance to contend this year," manager Frank Robinson said as he surveyed his team in the spring. "I'm not saying we are contenders. I'm saying we can contend, compete on a daily basis with any team in this league." He added, "There's an eagerness here for this ball club to finally step forward, step up, and for people to stop feeling sorry for ourselves and let's show people that this is a good organization and we have good talent."

Before the Nationals played their first regular-season game, Major League Baseball inked a deal with Orioles owner Peter Angelos that embittered many Washington fans. For years, Angelos had blocked a team from moving to the city, claiming the nation's capital as part of his territory. Now, to placate the litigious Orioles owner, the league announced a new Mid-Atlantic Sports Network that would broadcast Nationals games but give the Orioles the profits. The Orioles owned 90 percent of the network, and Major League Baseball, as owners of the Nationals, owned the rest (with the Nats' percentage set to slowly increase throughout the years). The deal wasn't totally one-sided; the new network would pay the Nationals $21 million a year in broadcast fees.

Still, the arrangement helped reinforce perceptions in Washington that Major League Baseball was willing to sacrifice the new team's profitability and future success to block an Angelos lawsuit. Making things worse, Comcast, a cable company that broadcast the Orioles games, got into a legal battle with Angelos and refused to air Nats games on its system, leaving millions of Washington-area fans without access to the majority of the team's televised games.

A few days later, on April 4, 2005, the Nationals and their fans put aside regional rivalries and politics to mark a momentous occasion: the team's first regular-season game. Although the Nats started their season on the road in Philadelphia, the two-and-a-half-hour drive tempted hundreds of Washingtonians to skip work and head north to see the rebirth of Washington baseball.

The Nats' starting pitcher, workhorse Livan Hernandez, didn't make it past the fifth inning, and Washington fell behind, 7–1. By the seventh, the Nats had pulled to within 7–4, and Terrmel Sledge, who had homered in the previous inning, came up with the bases loaded and a chance to give Washington the lead. But he bounced into a rally-killing double play, and Washington lost, 8–4.

The Nationals rebounded from the loss to win five of their next eight games on the road, and the team came home amid much fanfare with a 5–4 record and a tie for first place in the National League East. The team's home opener on Thursday, April 14, against the Arizona Diamondbacks, was the hottest ticket in town, as lobbyists, lawmakers, celebrity journalists, and lawyers jockeyed for the choicest seats in the sold-out stadium.

Washington's Senators, including Diamondbacks fan John McCain, were on hand to see the old Washington Senators, including Frank Howard, Eddie Brinkman, and Mickey Vernon, take their positions at RFK in a generational passing of the torch. The Nationals' starting players trotted out to their positions to receive their gloves from their baseball ancestors.

President George W. Bush revived an old local and national tradition by throwing out the first ball, but the president's appearance came at a cost. As Bush made his toss, and even as the game started, thousands of fans in the sellout crowd languished outside the stadium, trapped in long lines waiting to go through metal detectors installed for the presidential security. Once inside, fans forked over cold cash for cold dogs after waiting for forty minutes in concession stand lines.

Still, the return of baseball on a beautiful April evening inspired far more celebration than carping. "Ladies and gentlemen," welcomed Charlie Brotman, the former Senators public address announcer, "the moment you've all been waiting for for thirty-four years, let's meet your 2005 Washington Nationals!"

At 7:06 p.m., starting pitcher Livan Hernandez wound up and fired the first pitch in Washington Nationals history. The fastball sailed past Arizona's Craig Counsell for a strike, making a loud pop as it snapped into catcher Brian Schneider's mitt. The ball was sent to the Nats' dugout, a short stop on its way to the National Baseball Hall of Fame in Cooperstown, New York. A few pitches later, Hernandez struck out Counsell looking, and the crowd erupted in thunderous cheers.

Baseball may have undergone an offensive explosion during its absence from the nation's capital, but the hitters offered no evidence of that through the first few innings at RFK. When the Nats came to bat in the bottom of the fourth, it was still a scoreless game. Castilla, the reigning RBI champion, came up with Guillén and Vidro on base, and he crushed the ball the other way, into the right-field corner, for a two-run triple. Fans jumped up and down, and the old stadium rocked. The Nats made it 3–0 when Schneider drove Castilla home with a sacrifice fly.

Two innings later, Castilla widened the lead to 5–0 with a home run into the Washington bullpen and then came out of the dugout for the Nats' first curtain call. Castilla, who had doubled in the second, now needed just a plain old single to hit for the cycle. In the eighth, he came up with a chance to accomplish the feat, but Diamondbacks reliever Lance Cormier drilled him, and Castilla reluctantly walked down to first base, as the virgin Nationals fans booed angrily.

Lest those fans get too spoiled by an easy win, the Nats made things interesting in the ninth inning. Protecting a 5–0 lead, Hernandez walked Luis Gonzalez and surrendered a single to Shawn Green—just the second hit by the Diamondbacks all evening. Chad Tracy followed with a three-run homer to right field, and now it was a ballgame.

Manager Frank Robinson took out Hernandez, who tipped his cap to acknowledge a standing ovation as he walked to the dugout. The team's twenty-three-year-old stopper, Chad Cordero, came in to try to put the game away. He quickly got the second out, bringing cheering fans to their feet. But the next batter, Quinton McCracken, singled to center, and the dangerous pinch hitter Tony Clark came to the plate as the potential tying run. The six-foot, seven-inch slugger sported a .538 batting average in the young season. Clark swung and made good contact with the ball, driving it to center field, but not deep enough at cavernous RFK. Ryan Church corralled the ball for the historic victory, and the aging ballpark lit up with fireworks and photographic flashes.

"Words can't describe it," Church told reporters after the game. "I've never been in a World Series, but I've seen some on TV. And that atmosphere, that crowd noise—it seemed just like a World Series."

The moment provided a cathartic antidote to the last major-league game at RFK, played in 1971, as the Washington Senators were about to move to Texas. With two outs in the ninth inning and the Senators leading the New York Yankees, 7–5, fans swarmed onto the field. Play could not resume, so the Senators were forced to forfeit the game—their ninety-sixth loss in yet another abysmal season.

Washington fans had no rational reason to expect anything better from their new team. After all, the Expos had finished with nearly as many losses in 2004 (ninety-five), and despite some off-season upgrades, most experts picked them for last in the National League East in 2005. True, it was only April, but Washington's home opener victory put the team into sole possession of first place, with a fat .600 winning percentage. And the Nationals would prove they had contending power well beyond April.

On May 19, the Nationals climbed five games over .500, with a 3–2 victory over the Milwaukee Brewers, as Livan Hernandez improved to 7–2. The team then left for a ten-day road trip that almost knocked them out of the race. Washington went just 2–7 against Toronto, Cincinnati, and St. Louis, and the squad returned home on May 30 a .500 team.

Worse, Washington faced the two best teams in the division upon its return—the Atlanta Braves and Florida Marlins. The Braves had a chance to bury the upstarts in a crucial four-game series. Instead, the Nationals won three of four, including two games by one run each. In the finale, the Washington bullpen blew a 3–2 lead in the eighth inning, surrendering four runs. Trailing, 6–3, the Nats rallied for five runs in the bottom of the frame to pull off an improbable 8–6 victory, thanks to backup catcher Gary Bennett's three-run double. With the victory, Washington pulled to within one and a half games of the Braves and Marlins, who were tied for first place.

Next up were the Marlins. No problem. Washington won the first two games of the series to leapfrog over Florida, but the team still trailed the Braves by half a game. The next day, Sunday, June 5, the Nationals accomplished something that hadn't been done in seventy-two years—a Washington team in first place this late in the season. The last time it happened, the Washington Senators were on their way to the 1933 pennant. The 2005 Nationals did so by coming from behind for the fourth straight time, overcoming a 2–0, seventh-inning deficit against tough Florida pitcher A. J. Burnett on their way to a 6–3 victory. Washington took over sole possession of first place with Atlanta's 5–2 loss to Pittsburgh.

"You couldn't ask for any more than we've done in the first seven games against these two ball clubs," Robinson told reporters after the game. "These were tough ball clubs. They were leading this division. For us to come up and stand up and pull down the wins against them, it's a good feeling."

Incredibly, the Nationals won their next six straight, to extend their winning streak to ten games and wrap up a 12–1 home stand. In eleven of the victories, the Nats came from behind to win. As they exchanged high fives on the field following their tenth straight victory, a 3–2 win over Seattle, fans gave them a standing ovation—and some players applauded back. The 37,000 fans on hand that day deserved it just as much. They had catapulted the Nats' attendance to 1,056,642, breaking the single-season Washington attendance record set in 1946. And it was only June 12.

With the victory, Washington improved to 37–26 and a baseball-best 24–9 at home. They left home with a game-and-a-half lead over the second-place Philadelphia Phillies. They then won five of nine in a road swing through Anaheim, Texas, and Pittsburgh, maintaining their hold on first place. When they came home, the Nationals won five of six games in the final week of June to cap an unbelievable month of baseball. Washington went 20–6 in June—a .769 winning percentage.

"That's a tremendous year, or month, I'm sorry," Robinson said after the Nats defeated the Pirates, 7–5, on June 30, completing a three-game sweep. "After the last three years, it seems like a year. That's a tremendous month, and the players deserve an awful lot of credit for the way they have performed and the way they have handled things. They just keep going out and doing the job."

Washington's victory over the Pirates, the team's fifteenth win in its last sixteen games at RFK, improved the Nats' home record to 29–10. Chad Cordero saved his fifteenth game of the month, tying a major-league record. The

Nationals' performance transfixed a city that had been without baseball of any kind for three decades, and without a legitimate pennant contender for far longer. Crowds of 30,000 or 35,000 routinely came out each night, tripling the typical attendance for the old Senators teams.

The Nats continued to confound the baseball world by going to Chicago and sweeping a three-game series against the Cubs. In the finale, Washington blew a 2–0 lead in the ninth and a 4–2 lead in the eleventh, but the team won the game on Brian Schneider's twelfth-inning home run. Cordero snapped a string of twenty-six straight saves by blowing the ninth-inning lead.

The victory gave the Nats a 50–31 record at the midpoint of the season, a .617 winning percentage, and a five-and-a-half-game lead in the National League East. The team was on pace to win one hundred games. If this seemed way too good to be true for a team that had lost nearly one hundred games the year before, well, it was.

Things went south just as the second half of the season began, and on a day that should have been a natural for a Washington team—the Fourth of July. The Nats looked like they were on their way to another low-scoring victory, taking a 2–0 lead against the New York Mets into the seventh inning behind the pitching of John Patterson. But Patterson tired in the seventh, giving up a single and double, and reliever Louis Ayala surrendered two more hits, allowing both runners to score and the Mets to tie the game. Then New York rallied for three runs in the ninth against Sun-Woo Kim to pull out a 5–2 victory.

Although Washington beat Pedro Martinez the next night to even the series, the Mets took the final two games. Then the Nationals went to Philadelphia and lost two of three as they headed into the All-Star break. Despite the rough week, the Nats were still in good shape at the break. They owned a 52–36 record, and a two-and-a-half-game lead in the division.

The question was, how were they doing it? All year long, injuries had decimated Washington's lineup, taking chunks of the seasons of José Vidro, José Guillén, Nick Johnson, Brad Wilkerson, and Ryan Church. Washington scored fewer runs than any team in baseball, was tied for last in homers, and had actually been outscored overall. But the Nats, dubbed "one-run wonders," were a staggering 24–10 in one-run games. Fans who subscribed to the law of averages—now more commonly called the regression to the mean—knew that the team couldn't sustain that pace.

During the All-Star break, Bowden picked up veteran left-hander Mike Stanton, two weeks after the Yankees had cut him, to help solidify the bullpen. More importantly, Bowden made an effort to upgrade Washington's listless offense by trading for Rockies slugger Preston Wilson, dealing starting pitcher Zach Day and minor-league outfielder J. J. Davis.

Prior to the trade, Wilson had batted .258, with fifteen home runs and forty-seven RBIs, putting him on pace for nearly thirty homers and 100 RBIs for the season. But like Castilla the year before, Wilson had benefited from the inflationary effects of Denver's thin air. RFK offered hitters no such advantage. In fact, prompted by a *Washington Post* aborted surveying expedition, team officials remeasured the distances to the outfield wall and found that the power alleys were 395 feet from home plate, not the 380 feet posted on the wall. That helped explain why RFK had been the stingiest home run park in the major leagues in the first half of the year.

But the midseason acquisitions didn't help, and the All-Star break couldn't stem Washington's recent slide. The Nats won just three of their first eleven games after the break, and Robinson decided to bench shortstop Cristian Guzman, whose .189 batting average sat like an albatross on the weak Washington lineup. The team headed to Atlanta for a crucial three-game series on July 26. Washington's five-and-a-half-game lead had vanished; the Nationals and Braves were now tied for first place atop the division.

Washington got a psychological boost when its injury-plagued Opening Day infield started a game together for the first time since May 4. But the one-run magic that had carried the team through the first half of the season had evaporated. They lost the first game, 3–2, after Cordero blew a 2–1 lead in the bottom of the ninth inning. Atlanta won the game in the tenth, when Andruw Jones walked with the bases loaded, and Washington was out of first place for the first time in more than a month.

Atlanta took the next two games of the series, 4–3 and 5–4, to complete a devastating sweep and drop the Nats three games out of first place. The baseball karma had turned on the team; Washington's losing streak in one-run games would reach an unlucky thirteen.

Still, the Nationals stayed in the hunt. They didn't play great baseball, but they rebounded from a terrible July to play around .500 in August. By the end of the month, they had fallen to last place in the hypercompetitive Eastern Division, despite having a winning record. But more importantly, even if the division title was looking like a long shot, Washington was in the midst of the wild card race.

As late as mid-September, the Nationals looked like they were going to make a strong run for the playoffs. They went to New York and swept a three-game series against the Mets and then extended the winning streak to four on September 16, by taking the opening game of a series in San Diego. With just two weeks left in the season, the Nationals had somehow remained contenders—only two and a half games out of the wild card lead.

The next night, the Nats had a 5–0 lead in the bottom of the ninth and appeared to be on their way to their fifth straight win. The Padres put a run across to make it 5–1, and then Khalil Greene stunned the Nationals with a game-tying grand slam off Cordero, Washington's fourth pitcher of the inning.

Three innings later, Ramon Hernandez tagged Washington pitcher Jon Rauch for a three-run home run and an 8–5 Padres victory. The crushing loss dropped the Nationals three and a half games behind the Houston Astros in the wild card race.

The next afternoon, the final game of their six-game road trip, must have felt like a screening of *Groundhog Day* to the Nationals. Washington led, 1–0, in the eighth inning, but Greene once again came through, this time in less dramatic fashion, with a game-tying sacrifice fly in the bottom of the inning. San Diego won the game in the ninth, when Washington reliever Joey Eischen threw errantly to first base after fielding a sacrifice bunt attempt, allowing Miguel Olivo to score the winning run. The second straight bullpen meltdown wasted a great performance by starter Esteban Loaiza, who had pitched seven scoreless innings. Now the Nats were four and a half games out and effectively out of the playoff hunt.

The Nationals returned home after those dispiriting losses to face the San Francisco Giants. Clinging to a 2–1 lead in the top of the ninth inning, Washington faced Barry Bonds with two outs and a runner on first base. Bonds had just returned the week before after missing most of the season recovering from knee surgeries, but he had smashed an upper-deck home run earlier in the game. So Robinson told pitcher Livan Hernandez to pitch Bonds carefully, and Hernandez walked the Giants slugger on four pitches. The strategy backfired when Moises Alou followed with a three-run homer, and the Giants staved off a Nats rally in the bottom of the ninth to hold on for a 4–3 victory.

Those three late-inning collapses marked the final turning point of the Nationals' inaugural season. What could have been a seven-game winning streak heading into the final stretch turned into a three-game losing streak. Washington was officially eliminated from the race a few days later, losing to the Mets, 6–5, at RFK, as New York completed a three-game sweep. The Nationals fell to an even .500 for the first time since May, and back into last place. "In the second half, we collapsed," said catcher Gary Bennett. "Plain and simple. We didn't get it done."

With six games remaining, the Nats still had a couple of goals left: to finish over .500 and out of last place. After sweeping the Florida Marlins in a three-game series, that looked like a pretty good possibility. Not only were the Nats three games over .500 with three games to go, but they had pulled into third place, barely above the Marlins and Mets.

But the hungry Philadelphia Phillies, still alive in the wild card race, came to RFK and swept a season-ending three-game series. That dropped the Nats to a final record of 81–81, and dumped them to the bottom of the division. A .500 record would have been good enough for second place in the Western Division and a share of third in the Central, but that was small consolation to a team that had ruled the East for a good chunk of the summer.

"It would have been really a fairy tale if we could have pulled this thing off," Robinson said after the final game, a 9–3 loss to the Phillies. "They wouldn't have even touched this in Hollywood."

At the finale, the 36,000-plus fans gave the Nationals a standing ovation as the players took their positions and then applauded for more than five minutes after the final out. The players and coaches returned the favor by throwing hats, balls, and other souvenirs to the fans. Robinson made a "No. 1" gesture to the fans.

"It was very special," the manager said. "Very special. The fans have been special all year long. They had a lot of feelings for this ballclub, and this ballclub had a lot of feelings for them. And without them, we wouldn't have had the season that we did have."

He might have said seasons, because the Nats really played two different mirror-image seasons in 2005. At the midway point, the Nationals played an over-their-head 50–31; from then onward, they posted an underachieving 31–50 record. The team that at one point was 23–7 in one-run games finished 30–31 in such contests.

For fans of the old Washington Senators, the 2005 Nats offered some interesting historical parallels. The last time Washington got a new team, in 1961, it, too, had shocked experts early on, although not to the degree the Nats did. The 1961 team started out 30–30 and then collapsed in the last one hundred games to finish in a tie for last place.

Guzman, who hit .219 only after a strong finish, was an echo of weak-hitting Senators shortstops. Eddie Brinkman hit .188 and .187 in back-to-back seasons in the late 1960s, and the 1961 starting shortstop, Coot Veal, hit .202, with just eight RBIs in 218 at bats that year.

While the rest of the Nats didn't struggle as badly as Guzman, the offense failed to offer much of a threat. The lineup had no .300 hitter, no slugger with 25 home runs, no 100-RBI man, not even one player with as many as 10 stolen bases. Nick Johnson led the team with a modest .289 batting average, and José Guillén paced the team with twenty-four home runs and seventy-six RBIs. Brad Wilkerson walloped an impressive forty-two doubles, but he hit just .248, and his eleven home runs at cavernous RFK marked a huge drop-off from 2004, when he had hit thirty-two.

The Nationals finished last in the league in hitting (.252), home runs (117), runs (639), and slugging percentage (.386). But that wasn't nearly as awful as the 1960s Senators teams, which hit .227, .231, .228, .234, .223, and .224 in a six-year period from 1963 to 1968. And the 1945 Senators would have killed for 117 home runs. That team hit just twenty-seven round-trippers all season, and just one all year at home, but still managed to finish in second place.

The 2005 Nats also continued a tradition of former Hall of Fame players running the team as manager. Ted Williams, like Frank Robinson, exceeded expectations in his first year in Washington, guiding the 1969 Senators to a winning record before the team tanked in subsequent seasons. Although the 2005 Nats had a poor finish, they still improved by fourteen games over the 2004 Expos.

"I wonder what team came back after the All-Star break, because it wasn't the team that left," Robinson would reflect in 2012, before throwing out the first ball at the Nats' first home playoff game.

The Nationals had other accomplishments to point to in 2005. Stopper Chad Cordero led the National League with forty-seven saves, and his 1.82 ERA paced a Nats pitching staff that posted the fourth-best ERA in the league (3.87). Relievers Hector Carrasco, Luis Ayala, and Gary Majewski all had ERAs under 3.00. Several starters had good years, too, including John Patterson (9–7, 3.13), Esteban Loaiza (12–10, 3.77), and Livan Hernandez (15–10, 3.98).

But the most impressive statistic was the Nat's attendance: 2.7 million. Only ten teams drew more than the Nationals, despite a television deal that shut out many fans and a late start in marketing the team. The Nationals averaged 33,728 fans per game in an outdated ballpark, easily shattering the Washington attendance record of 13,516 fans per game set nearly sixty years earlier.

ELEVEN

Political Baseball: The Nationals Fan Base

POLITICAL BASEBALL: THE NATIONALS FAN BASE

On August 12, 2012, *Wall Street Journal* Washington bureau chief Gerald F. Seib tweeted a warning to his followers who tracked both the Nationals and national politics: "OK, Nats fans, time to start considering: Possible conflicts between NL postseason games and VP debate Oct. 11, and Prez debate Oct 22."

Seib's heads-up showed how the political class in Washington had grown attached to the hometown team. And while the Nationals didn't make it far enough to conflict with the presidential debate, their Game 4 walk-off win in the National League Division Series did take place on the same day as the vice presidential debate. Many of Washington's insiders were in Danville, Kentucky, for the debate—but had an eye on the action back home.

One of them was Fox News analyst Juan Williams, a Nats season-ticket holder. He says that big monitors in the dining area before the debate were tuned to the Nationals–Cardinals game, which was tied 1–1 from the third inning until Jayson Werth's game-winning home run in the bottom of the ninth.

"People were at tables, and then as the excitement grew, you just saw chairs shift from facing each other to facing the monitors," Williams recalls. "And then Werth hit the home run, it was a like a huge shout-out."

The Nats fan base includes politicians and policymakers, columnists and consultants. It isn't quite like the old days, when Congress would recess early for the day so that members could watch the Senators' traditional "presidential opener." But with virtually every game now available on television, even outside D.C., today's political and media elite have a much easier time watching the Washington team play from wherever they are. Many of the politicos, commentators, and journalists who root for the Nationals aren't Washington natives, and they have different stories of how they came to embrace the local nine.

For Senate Minority Leader Mitch McConnell, a Republican from Kentucky, it was a gradual process, starting with the Nats' first season in 2005. McConnell was born in Alabama in 1942 and naturally rooted for—the Brooklyn Dodgers?

"I grew up in the Deep South, and when I started my life, there was no team in the Deep South," he explains. He elaborates:

So my dad and I had a playful rivalry—he liked the Yankees, and I pulled for the Dodgers. We moved to Kentucky, and in the eastern part of the state, and in Louisville, they tend to follow the Cincinnati Reds, and in the western part, the St. Louis Cardinals. For whatever reason, I never warmed up to either one of them and continued to follow the Dodgers out on the West Coast—although it's pretty hard with the three-hour time differential. And then over a period of years, I lost interest altogether.

McConnell says he started paying attention to baseball again a bit during the Nats' first season. Given the Senate schedule, he'd get home around 8:30 or 9 p.m., flip on the television, and catch the end of the Nats game. He'd even stay up to watch Nats Extra, the postgame show.

"So by the time the 2012 season started, I had a growing sense of fanaticism," he says with a laugh, adding,

> My definition of fanaticism is I got the baseball package (of out-of-town games) down here in Louisville. In 2012, I saw all or of most of the games, either in Washington or in Louisville. So I got thoroughly addicted. It has kind of renewed my interest in my childhood sport. I'm definitely a Nats fanatic now.

"Mitch and I watch virtually every Nationals game," says McConnell's Democratic counterpart, Senate Majority Leader Harry Reid of Nevada. "We don't watch them together, but we talk about it quite often."

Reid grew up in Nevada, another place without Major League Baseball, and rooted for the Cleveland Indians, including the 1948 World Series championship team. But he long ago lost interest in the Indians, picking up other teams along the way. In 2012, he gravitated to the Nationals because of fellow Nevadan Bryce Harper, who won the Rookie of the Year Award in a breakout season. Reid, a Democrat, met Harper on the field prior to a game that year.

"Baseball season is my favorite time of the year," says Reid, "because I can go home, grab a bite to eat, and even if I only watch an inning or two, it's like meditation for me."

Has baseball helped the relationship between the Senate leaders?

"*Anything* helps our relationship," Reid says with a laugh. "A little baseball doesn't hurt." He says it's also helped the two parties get along a little better. "It's obvious it hasn't helped very much, but it's helped. Any time you have something that creates conversation, that's good. And that's created a lot of conversation."

Bob Stevenson, a Washington lobbyist and former Senate GOP leadership spokesman, says all political stripes and creatures are represented at Nationals Park: "Liberals, conservatives, Tea Party activists, socialists, progressives, independents, Democrats, Republicans, lobbyists, lawyers, reformers, New Dealers, Reaganites, Clintonistas, etc.—and it's one of the few places you can witness them all pulling for the same team."

Stevenson says he's been surrounded at games by NBC's David Gregory, columnist George Will, PBS analyst Mark Shields, and Bloomberg's Al Hunt, among others. "You never know who you will see, but you are bound to see someone," he says.

Juan Williams, the Fox News commentator, thinks that the Nats have helped bring liberals and conservatives together in Washington. "I come across it every day because I work with Charles Krauthammer, and Krauthammer is a big conservative," he says. "I think they might have dubbed him critic-in-chief for President Obama. But Charles and I are both Nationals fans, both season-ticket holders. And so for us, the common ground, when we see each other, is always to start with the Nationals."

But Democratic political consultant James Carville is skeptical. "I think we can ascribe too much to baseball. Freud once said a cigar is just a cigar," he says with a laugh. "Maybe sometimes a baseball game is just a baseball game. A lot of members of Congress have their own teams. If you come from Chicago, and you're a congressman in Washington, you're not a Nats fan. You're a Cubs fan or a White Sox fan."

Or if you're the president, like Barack Obama, you can stick with your hometown Chicago White Sox, but pull for the Nats as your National League team.

Krauthammer is in Carville's camp—on this question, if nothing else. "I don't believe that there's one comma of any bill that's been changed because of the comity between the two parties sitting at games," he says. He adds:

> But I do think it's just something that people kind of rally around and it develops camaraderie. I think it's a bit of a conceit. I mean, it is true if I run into a liberal and he runs into me and we don't particularly want to have a presidential debate between us right there on the street, we'll talk about the Nats. And that's a nice, safe, happy place.

Krauthammer was born in the United States, grew up in Montreal, and rooted for the Yankees as a child, but lost interest in the sport in 1965, when he was fifteen. "I think I discovered girls," he quips. Ten years later, while attending Harvard Medical School, about a mile from Fenway Park, he recalls,

The smell of the Crackerjacks reached me. And then there was Game 6 of the 1975 World Series. I was sort of a casual fan and I watched that game, and it was like a light turned on in me. A lot of people say it was the greatest game ever. So I became a Red Sox fan. I just couldn't help liking these guys.

"Then came 1986"—the year the Red Sox were one out away from winning their first World Series since 1918, only to see the New York Mets rally for three runs to win Game 6 and force a seventh game, which the Mets also won. "So I began to wean myself off the Sox, 'cause I figured life is hard enough," says Krauthammer. "What do I need, extra tragedy? I mean, do I need this?"

By 1986, Krauthammer was living in Washington, so he became a fan of the Baltimore Orioles and then switched to the Nats when the franchise moved to town from Montreal. Others initially remained fans of their hometown teams even after baseball returned to Washington but found it impossible to resist the Nats. Stevenson was a Red Sox fan when Washington got a team in 2005.

"After several years of divided loyalties, the Nationals have won me over," he says. "I now consider myself a Nats fan first and foremost. And I am not alone. In a transient city like D.C., you can find hard-core fans of every MLB team. But the Nats have overcome that hurdle and captured the loyalties of many locals who once supported other MLB franchises."

Carl Hulse, deputy Washington bureau chief of the *New York Times*, wrote a column announcing that he had been "unfaithful"—to his Chicago Cubs. "Although I am a die-hard, long-suffering Cubs fan, I have been sneaking around a corner of southeast D.C. with the younger, sexier, more exciting Washington Nationals and loving every minute of it," Hulse writes. "I'm not the only guilty party. There are thousands like me."

Carville didn't have a team to root for growing up in New Orleans, which has never had Major League Baseball. Now, he's a Nationals season-ticket holder and jokes that he's such a big fan, "my kids won't go to college before I give those seats up."

"I am deep, deep, deep, deep, deep way into the Nats," says Carville. "I like the cut of their jib. I'm a real homer. I'm a pro-Nats guy."

So much so that he got to throw out the first pitch at a Nationals game.

"How much goddamn heat can you take?" Carville says with a laugh. He elaborates:

They call your name out. And you know you're in Washington, and you know a good 90 percent of the people there are just dying for you to throw the goddamn thing in the dirt. I literally—my throat is closing up, I'm so goddamn scared. So I just turned around and said, "You know what? We're just going to let it rip." I let it go, and it was a strike. Ross Detwiler caught it, and he comes out and says: "That was a strike!"

Presidents make the biggest splash when they're at Nationals Park, throwing out the first pitch on Opening Day in a tradition that dates back more than a century. But other high-ranking government officials from all three branches of government often come out as well. In 2012, Vice President Joe Biden saw a Nationals game, as did senators, House members, military leaders, and members of the cabinet, including Attorney General Eric Holder and Director of Homeland Security Janet Napolitano. More than half of the nine Supreme Court justices have taken in a home game as well, including Chief Justice John Roberts, Stephen Breyer, Anthony Kennedy, Elena Kagan, and Sonia Sotomayor.

Sotomayor's appearance at the ballpark isn't a surprise. She's a noted baseball fan whose 1995 ruling as a federal judge in New York ended the baseball strike, which had canceled the previous year's World Series. Sotomayor, a Bronx native, warmly greeted Yankees shortstop Derek Jeter on the field at Nationals Park before a Nats–Yanks game in 2012.

Gregory McCarthy, the Nationals' vice president for government and municipal affairs, helps to coordinate the logistics of such visits. He says that the team offers discounts of 20 to 40 percent off to federal employees, including those who work on Capitol Hill, about a mile up the road from the ballpark.

"It makes sense for us because they are our hometown industry. So you want to cater to them," McCarthy says. He says that while some teams will show famous fans on the stadium Jumbotron, the Nationals have decided not to do that with their celebrity boosters. "A lot of people just want a night out, and we don't want to risk somebody getting booed in a very, very partisan nature," he says. "And most people wouldn't recognize Senator X anyway."

McCarthy recalls preparing Bryce Harper for his meeting with Senator Reid. "I began to explain to him, 'Now, Senator Reid is the Senate majority leader,' and he said to me in a very nice way, 'I know who Senator Reid is.'"

Federal Reserve chairman Ben Bernanke is sometimes spotted at the ballpark, eschewing his suit for jeans, a short-sleeve shirt, and a worn-out red Nats cap. Before 2012, he was one of the few experts—albeit not a baseball one—to accurately predict the team's success. "This is the year. We're very optimistic," he told ABC News.

Then, on the eve of the playoffs, Bernanke wrote an op-ed column for the *Wall Street Journal* holding the Nationals out as an example for Washington to follow. "People decry the absence of leadership in Washington these days. My response: Look no further than the home-team dugout at Nationals Park," Bernanke writes.

Stevenson says that while the new ballpark and a fan-friendly environment have helped the popularity of the Nationals, "on Capitol Hill and Pennsylvania Avenue it's results that matter. Washington's political professionals admire two things—success and a well-executed plan—and they have found both manifested in the Nationals."

Baseball stadiums are full of critics, but at Nationals Park, the players and managers aren't the only ones on the hot seat. "The beer men—God are they sophisticated," says Krauthammer. "What other park do you get a guy come over to you and give you a critique of the penultimate paragraph of your column? You know, with a great big smile and a bellowing laugh."

Krauthammer's interest in the sport is so keen that on a regular basis, he and columnist George Will meet for lunch with ESPN baseball analyst Tim Kurkjian. The talk is exclusively baseball.

"I'm happy to go, because these are two tremendous baseball fans," says Kurkjian, who grew up a fan of the Washington Senators in the 1960s. He adds,

> In fact, I remember one lunch several years ago, and Charles says, "You know, I read the front page for thirty seconds every day and then I go straight to the box scores." And George looks at Charles and says, "Why do you waste the thirty seconds?" And to me, that's who those guys are—they love box scores.

Kurkjian *really* loves box scores. In 2010, he wrote a piece for *ESPN The Magazine* about the end of a twenty-year streak, from 1990 to 2009, of clipping every box score of every baseball game and taping them into a spiral notebook. He writes,

> On one memorable night in 2002, I went to bed at 11 o'clock, realized in horror I had forgotten to do my box score book, got dressed, clipped and taped my box scores, then lay down for a restful six hours of sleep as my wife looked at me and wondered how she could have married such an unfathomable geek.

Kurkjian says with a laugh that if the talk at his lunches with Will and Krauthammer were to ever turn to politics, "I would be out of the conversation, because I'd have no idea what they're talking about."

Kurkjian once mentioned work he was doing to select the best players for each uniform number. The conversation turned to number 21: Robert Clemente or Warren Spahn? "When lunch is over," Kurkjian recalls, "George looks at me and goes, 'We want to be you. We're going back to write about President Obama and gay marriage, and you're going to pick the greatest 21 of all time.'"

Kurkjian concludes, "And that's where it dawned on me, again, how lucky I am for what I do. Because I'm still in the toys-and-games department; those guys are doing real serious stuff."

McConnell, the Senate minority leader, recalls being invited to a lunch in 2012 with Will and Krauthammer, along with Supreme Court Justice Samuel Alito and Baltimore Orioles manager Buck Showalter. Again, baseball dominated the conversation, even with two of the most powerful people in Washington in attendance. McConnell continues:

> Alito must be in my category—a fan but not nearly as knowledgeable as the rest of them. So we sat there at lunch and listened to this extraordinary conversation between George Will, Charles Krauthammer, and Buck Showalter about baseball. Have you ever been in one of those conversations where you're afraid to say something, because you might look stupid? So I just didn't say much because I didn't want to sound stupid, but it was a smorgasbord of interesting and unusual baseball tidbits.

Of course, the Nationals are a point of pride for local politicians, too. Mayor Vincent Gray, who served on the D.C. City Council when it approved the baseball stadium lease in 2006, appeared on the field for a ceremony prior to a game in 2012. The mayor was there to honor ballpark usher Andre Hawthorne, who had saved kids from a dog attack in Northeast D.C., and was himself mauled by the dogs.

"And somebody yelled to the mayor from the stands, 'You have a lot of nerve since you voted against baseball for being down there,'" recalls Nats vice president McCarthy. "And the mayor, instinctively, without a moment's thought, turned around, and very angrily pointed at the man and said, 'Get your facts straight. I voted *for* baseball, unlike my predecessor'"—Adrian Fenty, who voted no on the lease as city council member.

McCarthy adds:

And that said to me, that politically, baseball had come of age, at least locally here. That the mayor felt that it was in his interest to correct the facts, to stand up, to kind of take credit for what was going on—and then to make the contrast to, hey, the guy before me who opened the ballpark, who voted against it.

From Last to First: A National Resurgence

FROM LAST TO FIRST: A NATIONAL RESURGENCE

The Nationals started the 2006 season still owned by the sport's other twenty-nine teams, prolonging the team's vagabond status. Finally, a month into the season, Major League Baseball announced it had selected a buyer: a local ownership group led by eighty-year-old real estate developer Ted Lerner and his family. The baseball franchise had turned out to be a good investment for Major League Baseball, which had purchased the then-Montreal Expos for $120 million in 2002 and was now selling the team for $450 million.

"Our long Nationals nightmare is over," writes ESPN's Tim Kurkjian, a play on President Gerald Ford's nearly identical line after succeeding Richard Nixon in the wake of the Watergate scandal (minus the "s" in Nationals).

"Wow, it's been some kind of day," Lerner said at a news conference announcing the deal. "It's something I've been thinking about all my life, from the time I used to pay twenty-five cents to sit in the bleachers at Griffith Stadium."

The ownership group included team president Stan Kasten, a veteran sports executive who helped turn the Atlanta Braves into an elite franchise. Kasten said the team would focus on developing the farm system—in tatters after years of neglect. "We are going to become the next big sports phenomenon," Kasten predicted. "And when we succeed, because every country in the world [that] plays baseball has a media presence here, we will be a phenomenon, not just nationally, but internationally."

Lerner brought two qualities that had been lacking for much of Washington's previous baseball ownership: local roots and deep pockets. Those missing qualities played a big role in the city losing two earlier franchises, both called the Senators, and Washington was without Major League Baseball for more than three decades.

In 2005, the city's new franchise, the Washington Nationals, started off with a surprising and encouraging .500 record. But after that, the Nationals had to take four or five steps back before taking another step forward. In 2006, the team slipped to 71–91 under the new ownership. Frank Robinson was out as manager, replaced by Manny Acta, who improved the team by only two wins in 2007.

The following season, the team moved into its new stadium, Nationals Park. After starting out in fully encircled, multipurpose RFK Stadium, the team now had a baseball-only ballpark near the Anacostia River with views of the Capitol and Washington Monument from some seats. The outside of the ballpark featured glass, steel, and concrete. The stadium included a corner in right-center field, a tribute to a similar idiosyncrasy at old Griffith Stadium.

The Nationals recreated another old Washington baseball tradition for their first regular-season game at the new ballpark. The Washington Senators used to play the "presidential opener" a day before the rest of the American League, with the president throwing out the first pitch. The 2008 Nationals christened their new ballpark a day early, with President George W. Bush throwing out the first pitch on a cold March evening, televised nationally on ESPN. Ryan Zimmerman took care of the last pitch, smacking it over the left-center field wall in the bottom of the ninth inning for a walk-off home run and a 3–2 Nats victory.

But the momentum didn't last. The Nationals finished the season 59–102 in 2008, and followed that with a 59–103 record the next season—worst in baseball both years. In March 2009, General Manager Jim Bowden resigned, and the Nats named his assistant, Mike Rizzo, acting GM. Rizzo, a career scout, brought a more steady leadership to the post, and he soon began putting his scouting and player-development stamp on the franchise. By August of that year, Rizzo became permanent general manager.

"We came in here and we made a lot of changes in our scouting staff, our player development staff, and got people who are great talent evaluators, that understand not only what the tools of the player are, but makeup of the player, character of the player," Rizzo recalls. "We would forego some ability level for guys who are tremendous makeup players and character-building guys and leaders on the club."

Rizzo says he had to change the culture in the front office, in the clubhouse, and on the field, because the Nationals had lost so many games that losing had become ingrained in the team. "We wanted to attack it with scouting and player development," he says, adding,

We went very, very aggressively into the amateur draft, and felt that was an avenue that we could really find some value in players, and develop our own, and in several years we could possibly contend. Once you build your own real starting rotation, anything is possible, and until you build a rotation, nothing's possible.

More changes came in 2009. The Nationals fired Acta halfway through the season and replaced him with Jim Riggleman. On their way to 103 losses—the most from a Washington team since the 1963 Senators lost 106 games—the Nats and one of their die-hard fans experienced one of the weirdest unlucky streaks in sports history.

Stephen Krupin, a Nationals season-ticket holder since the team moved to D.C., went to nineteen games at Nationals Park in 2009, and, amazingly, the Nats lost all nineteen. That was more than double the Nats' longest losing streak of eight games in 2009. At the end of the season, he posted the dubious streak on his Facebook page, and his cousin, Matt Swartz, who writes for *Baseball Prospectus*, saw the post and crunched the numbers. Swartz calculated the odds: 1 in 131,204.

Krupin says he had started to notice the streak when he kept hearing the same song on the way out of the stadium: "Three Little Birds" by Bob Marley, which the Nats played after a loss. The song includes the lines, "Don't worry about a thing, cause every little thing gonna be all right."

"And I realized I had no idea what song we played when we won," says Krupin, a political speechwriter and D.C. native. "And then I went back to my calendar and checked how many games, and realized the number." After nineteen games, he had plans to go to a twentieth at the end of the season, but he decided to see a U2 concert that night, where he heard "Beautiful Day"—the song the Nats played after a victory. Of course, the Nats won that night. As bad as the Nats were that year, they actually had a winning home record in games he didn't attend (33–29).

The streak hit twenty the next year with an Opening Day 11–1 thumping by the Phillies. Finally, Krupin and his father, who have been to all thirty ballparks, saw the Nats win in May against the Atlanta Braves.

Krupin's father yelled, "Yeah, the streak is over!"

"And everybody was like, 'Why is this guy so excited?'" Krupin recalls.

Krupin takes the whole thing in stride: "I'm kind of used to it as a D.C. sports fan. I didn't take it personally. This is my experience of being a sports fan—you lose more than you win."

The Nationals finished thirty-four games behind the first-place Phillies in 2009, and three and a half games behind the second-worst team in the National League, the Pittsburgh Pirates. The old expression about Washington baseball— "First in war, first in peace, and last in the American League"—seemed to still apply, except now you could throw in the National League, too. But those 205 losses in 2008 and 2009 earned the Nats the top draft choices when two of the biggest phenoms in years were available—Stephen Strasburg and Bryce Harper.

The hype surrounding Strasburg was almost as overwhelming as his fastball, which topped one hundred miles per hour. ESPN seemed to catch the mood of the baseball world when it posed the question, "Is Strasburg the Best

Prospect Ever?" In his final season at San Diego State, Strasburg struck out nearly two batters per inning, won thirteen of fourteen decisions, and posted a 1.35 ERA.

But after the Nats drafted Strasburg with the top pick in the 2009 draft, signing him was no sure thing. The strapping right-hander was represented by Scott Boras, known for his tough negotiating. With less than two minutes left before the signing deadline, the Nationals agreed to pay Strasburg a record-breaking $15.1 million deal for four years.

The team didn't complain about the price tag. Rizzo called Strasburg the "most coveted amateur player in the history of the draft." It was a particularly fruitful draft for the Nats, who also selected pitcher Drew Storen later in the first round.

The next year, in spring training, Strasburg picked up the nickname "Jesus." "That's what everybody says the first time they see Strasburg throw—Jeeee-sus," said Nationals outfielder Nyjer Morgan.

After a brief stint in the farm system, where he dominated minor leaguers as easily as he did college players, Strasburg was called up to the majors. On June 8, 2010, he made his debut in a playoff atmosphere between two teams that were certainly not playoff-bound: the Nats and visiting Pittsburgh Pirates. Both would finish last in their respective divisions that year, but for this night, at least, it was a showcase matchup, dubbed "Strasmus." A sold-out crowd of more than 40,000 jammed Nationals Park, providing a light show of camera flashes as the twenty-one-year-old threw his first pitch—a ninety-seven-mile-per-hour ball to Andrew McCutchen. The pitcher was just getting started, sparking oohs and ahs when the scoreboard showed his fastball hitting one hundred miles per hour. He would fan fourteen batters in seven spectacular innings, giving up just two runs on four hits and no walks in the Nationals' 5–2 win.

Syndicated columnist and Fox News political analyst Charles Krauthammer, a Nationals season-ticket holder, says that Strasburg's debut was the most exciting Washington game he's been to. "Now, you know there was nothing at stake in the standings," he recalls. "But he mowed down the last seven Pirates. The place was electric—every single pitch they were standing, everyone. The Strasburg game was just—am I really seeing this? This is his first game ever, he's striking out fourteen in seven innings."

Krupin, the unlucky fan, recalls that Strasburg retired the first two batters on balls in play, which amped up the excitement for his first strikeout. Then Lastings Milledge came up. "And with two strikes, in the top of the first in a Tuesday in June, the place was standing, cheering like it was the end of a playoff game," Krupin says. Strasburg struck him out looking for his first career K.

Strasburg's debut was reminiscent of another Washington legend's a century earlier. In 1907, nineteen-year-old Walter Johnson gave up two runs in eight innings against the Detroit Tigers at an old Washington field called American League Park. Although no radar guns were around to measure Johnson's fastball, Detroit Hall of Famer Ty Cobb's firsthand account provided a rough barometer: "I hardly saw the pitch, but I heard it. The thing just hissed with danger."

Like Strasburg, Johnson was heralded as the next big thing, and his first game was hyped in similar fashion—minus television and the Internet, of course. The predictions proved true. Johnson would become one of the greatest pitchers in baseball history.

"No youngster that has broken into fast company in recent years is attracting as much attention as Walter Johnson . . . the baseball world will watch his debut into fast company with a great deal of interest," the *Washington Post* reported in July 1907. And the paper wasn't disappointed, raving after the game of Johnson's "wonderful speed, perfect control, and deceptive curve, not to speak of his spitball."

More than a century later, Johnson's grandson attended Strasburg's debut at Nationals Park and was similarly impressed. "Fantastic," said Henry W. Thomas, who wrote a biography of his grandfather. "What a performance."

Tim Kurkjian, who covered the game for ESPN, calls it one of his five favorite nights he's ever spent in a major-league stadium—partly because he grew up in the area, and partly because Washington fans were so starved for baseball.

"The Strasburg game had to be the biggest game played in this town in maybe almost seventy-five years or so," he says. He continues,

> And for that kid to do what he did was unbelievable. No one in history had ever walked none and struck out fourteen in their major-league debut, ever. And with all the hype, and I can't remember any one player being hyped quite like this kid, to exceed the expectations, to go beyond the hype, was remarkable.

Kurkjian interviewed Strasburg on the field after the game. "And I'm telling you, I looked right in his eyes, and he had no idea what I was talking about, the first question I asked," Kurkjian recalls. "He was completely still in the moment of the hype and the hysteria and everything."

Strasburg continued to excite fans, both in Washington and across the country, as national television networks often featured the Nats when he pitched. Meanwhile, the next big thing was coming for Washington, courtesy of their baseball-worst record in 2009, which "earned" them the top pick in the 2010 draft. A day before Strasburg's debut, Washington selected the second half of its phenom bonanza: seventeen-year-old Bryce Harper, who had been anointed "Baseball's Chosen One" on the cover of *Sports Illustrated* when he was just sixteen.

"You don't know him, but every big-league scouting director does," the magazine extolls. "He hits the ball a desert mile, clocks ninety-six on the gun, and he's only sixteen, more advanced than A-Rod and Junior were at the same age. And his ambition is as great as his talent."

According to the *Sports Illustrated* story, when a sports announcer had dubbed Strasburg the "Lebron James of Baseball," Harper responded with playful exasperation: "What? Hey they stole that from me!" He told the magazine that his goals were to make the Hall of Fame, play in pinstripes, and "be considered the greatest baseball player who ever lived. I can't wait."

Harper didn't have to wait long. He accelerated his path to the big leagues by skipping his final two years of high school. The hitting prodigy earned his G.E.D. and played just one season at junior college. The Nats picked him with the first overall pick almost exactly one year after he appeared on the cover of *Sports Illustrated*. The Nationals said they would convert Harper from catcher to outfielder.

Like Strasburg before him, Harper chose Scott Boras as his adviser, and this time getting a deal proved even more nerve-wracking. With just seconds to spare on the August 16, 2010, midnight deadline, the Nationals signed Harper to a deal worth $9.9 million over five years. Team president Stan Kasten celebrated by smashing a whipped-cream pie in Mike Rizzo's face. "With a full minute to go, Mike and I both thought we were not going to have a deal," Kasten said.

Ten days later, during a visit to Nationals Park, Harper put on a show during batting practice, hitting a dozen home runs, including one to the third deck. The seventeen-year-old was instantly at ease at a news conference that followed.

"It felt like home," he said. "It was a blast going out there and hitting with a couple of the guys, and being able to hit on a pro field. That's always fun. That's a kid's dream. I'm like a little kid in a candy store right now."

Harper sported a pink tie and black suit, which was quickly covered by a Nats jersey with the number 34—which he had chosen as a kid in tribute to his hero, Mickey Mantle, after another child had taken Mantle's number, 7. "Three plus four equals seven. So it just stuck with me."

While he said he had no idea how long it would take to make the majors, he added, "I set high standards for myself. I think I should be perfect in every aspect of the game."

He seemed unfazed by the attention. "I've had a lot of people on me my whole life," he said. "I'm really used to it now. I've had a lot of media, a lot of little kids looking up to me. That's the biggest thing, I'm trying to teach the little guys how to go out there and just have fun. Just go out there and play ball."

Nats fans' excitement over Harper was tempered the very next day, when the team announced that Strasburg had a torn elbow ligament and would miss the rest of the season—as well as most of 2011. The rookie finished with an impressive ninety-two strikeouts in sixty-eight innings and a 2.91 ERA.

Between Strasburg's debut and Harper's signing, the 2010 season had offered Nationals fans hope for the future. Unfortunately, the present continued to look like the past. The Nationals finished in last place in the National League East for the fifth time in their six years since moving from Montreal in 2005, going 69–93. One small sign of progress: For the first time in three years, the Nats didn't have the worst record in baseball.

There was much change in the off-season. The team's best hitter, Adam Dunn, who had slugged thirty-eight homers in each of his two seasons with the Nats, signed as a free agent with the Chicago White Sox, and the Nats traded outfielder Josh Willingham to the Oakland A's. But both moves were overshadowed by the signing of free-agent outfielder Jayson Werth to a seven-year, $126 million contract, which left other teams questioning the huge payout.

Under Manager Jim Riggleman, the 2011 Nats started to show some spark, winning eleven of twelve games in June to sneak over the .500 mark. Then, Riggleman abruptly quit, complaining that the team refused to pick up his option for the 2012 season. "I'm fifty-eight. I'm too old to be disrespected," he told the *Washington Post.*

Davey Johnson, who had served as senior adviser to Rizzo since 2009, took over as skipper. Johnson, who was sixty-eight at the time, had managed the New York Mets, Los Angeles Dodgers, Cincinnati Reds, and Baltimore Orioles.

"I got his input on a lot of different aspects, and a lot of different fronts, when he wasn't even in uniform," Rizzo recalls. "He knew all the minor-league players coming up, so I thought he was the perfect fit when we needed a manager midseason."

The Nats went 40–43 with Johnson at the helm and finished the season 80–81, good for third place in the National League East, and Washington's best record since 2005. The team's pitching was vastly improved, posting a 3.58 ERA—more than a half-run improvement from 2010. Young starter Jordan Zimmermann led the starters with a 3.18 ERA and 124 strikeouts, and closer Drew Storen saved forty-three games. The team got a psychological boost when Strasburg came back at the end of the season, fanning twenty-four batters in twenty-four innings, while giving up only four earned runs.

Unfortunately, the Nats offense did little to support the pitching, as Washington hit a meek .242 as a team—second-to-last in the league—and struck out a league-high 1,323 times. Werth was a bust in the first year of his gigantic contract, hitting .232, with just fifty-eight RBIs, although he did slug twenty home runs. Injuries slowed Ryan Zimmerman, who hit only a dozen homers in 101 games, and new first baseman Adam LaRoche, who hit .172 in forty-three games.

But there were encouraging signs, too. Michael Morse, who played first base and outfield, had a breakout season, leading the team in home runs (31), RBIs (95), and batting average (.303). Second baseman Danny Espinosa, in his first full season, hit twenty-one home runs.

More promising was the complete turnaround of the farm system. When *Baseball America* released its rankings of minor-league systems after the season, the Nationals were ranked first—up from last in 2007.

"Their scouting department has done an outstanding job of signing quality athletes, and their farm system's done a great job of developing them," observes former Washington Senator slugger Frank Howard, who worked as a scout for the Yankees until a few years ago. "When they moved here from Montreal, their farm system was very thin."

The team continued to be aggressive in the off-season. Although many thought the Nats would try to upgrade their offense by making a run at free-agent slugger Prince Fielder, they focused instead on pitching. In December, the Nats acquired All-Star lefty pitcher Gio Gonzalez from the Oakland A's in exchange for three pitching prospects and a minor-league catcher. Gonzalez had won sixteen games for the A's in 2011, with 197 strikeouts in 202 innings. The next month, the Nats locked him up to a long-term contract extension that could keep him in Washington through 2018.

Soon afterward, the team signed free-agent pitcher Edwin Jackson to a one-year deal. In 2011, Jackson had won five of seven decisions for the St. Louis Cardinals after being acquired in a midseason trade, helping the team on its march to the World Series title. So with a couple of moves, the Nats had vaulted their already good pitching rotation to premium status for 2012. Few teams could match the team's projected top four starting pitchers of Strasburg, Zimmermann, Gonzalez, and Jackson.

While the Nats didn't make major improvements to their hitting, they did make a major investment to their lineup by signing third baseman Ryan Zimmerman, the "face of the franchise," to a six-year, $100 million contract extension. The Nationals had drafted Zimmerman in 2005, their first year in Washington, and he made the big leagues that September at the age of twenty. Zimmerman had won both a Gold Glove for defense and a pair of Silver Slugger Awards for his hitting.

Most baseball experts didn't see Washington as a serious contender for the National League East division title in 2012. The *Sporting News* predicted a fourth-place finish in the five-team division, behind the Philadelphia Phillies, Miami Marlins, and Atlanta Braves. *USA Today* and ESPN's Kurkjian also picked the Nationals fourth, while Fox Sports' Ken Rosenthal predicted a third-place finish for the Nationals.

Washington Post baseball writer David Sheinin predicted that the Phillies would repeat as division winners, and that the Marlins would grab one of the wild card spots, along with the Arizona Diamondbacks of the National League West. Sheinin writes, "The ETA for the Nationals as a true contender remains 2013, but they have the pieces to make 2012 very interesting."

But some saw the team arriving in 2012: Yahoo!'s Jeff Passan predicted that the Nats would make the World Series after winning a wild card spot. At *Sports Illustrated*, two of eight "resident experts" said that the Nats would win a wild card spot, but the other six predicted the team wouldn't make the playoffs. ESPN's Buster Olney picked the Nationals as a wild card team.

Nationals manager Davey Johnson was in the latter camp. During spring training, Comcast Sports Net's Kelli Johnson asked him if the season would be a failure if the team didn't make the playoffs.

"No question in my mind. You know, and they can fire me," Johnson replied.

"Strong words," the reporter said.

"Yeah," Johnson said. "I mean, we should make the playoffs. There's no doubt in my mind."

Several Nationals players say they didn't buy into the "one year away" consensus. "We felt like we were kind of getting the eye rolls from the reporters when we said we really had a shot," recalls reliever Drew Storen. "We knew what a good core we had and with the veteran guys that we had come in, and those guys are saying, 'Hey, this is a really good team.' And those were guys who had been on winning teams. So we knew we were going to do what we were going to do."

"We had too much talent to think, 'Oh, we're another year away,'" says second baseman Danny Espinosa. He continues:

> That was kind of a joke in our minds. When you have Ian Desmond, Jayson Werth, Zimmermann, LaRoche, we had Harper come up, we had Mike Morse. I mean, that kind of offense, with our pitching—we had the best all-around staff last year—to think that we needed another year was kind of mind-boggling.

Washington's starting rotation was so deep that the team sent John Lannan, who was making $5 million, to the minors before the season. The lefty was a victim of a pitching surplus, with Ross Detwiler taking his slot in the rotation alongside Strasburg, Zimmermann, Gonzalez, and Jackson. Lannan, the team's Opening Day pitcher in 2009 and 2010, responded by demanding a trade.

"I know what my rights and the team's rights are, and while I am still a member of the Washington Nationals organization, I let Mike know that I believe a trade would be the best solution for everyone in both the short and long term," he told reporters in an e-mail, referring to GM Mike Rizzo.

But Rizzo declined. "I've known John Lannan a long time," Rizzo told the *Post*. "He's an ultracompetitive person. And he's frustrated and upset and mad. If he was any other way, I would wonder about him."

While the Nationals pitching rotation was enough to inspire confidence, their lineup hadn't improved much from the 2011 team, which had hit just .242. The Nats were hoping that increased offense would come through Jayson Werth and Adam LaRoche returning to form. But the team started the season with its best hitter from 2011, Michael Morse, on the disabled list. He would miss the first fifty games of the season. In addition, the bullpen was unsettled, with closer Drew Storen also on the shelf until midseason.

On Opening Day in Chicago, Werth and LaRoche went a combined 0-for-6, but the Nats beat the Cubs, 2–1, behind Stephen Strasburg's seven-inning, one-run start. Newcomer Brad Lidge, who was sharing the closer role with Henry Rodriguez in Storen's absence, pitched the ninth inning to pick up the save.

A week later, the Nationals returned to Washington for their home opener 4–2 and tied for first place with the New York Mets. A sellout crowd of 40,907 fans greeted the Nationals on a cloudy, cool weekday afternoon game against the Reds. Washington's major winter pitching acquisition, Gio Gonzalez, faced off against Cincinnati's big off-season pickup, Matt Latos.

Gio did not disappoint the fans, striking out seven in seven scoreless innings, walking none, and surrendering just two hits. LaRoche staked the Nats to a 2–0 lead with a two-run single in the fifth, and Washington held the lead into the bottom of the ninth, when Lidge came on seeking another save. But the Reds rallied for two runs, sending the game into extra innings. Nats reliever Craig Stammen struck out the side in the top of the tenth, and in the bottom of the frame, Ryan Zimmerman scooted home on a wild pitch, giving the home team a 3–2 victory.

The next night, Washington again pulled out an extra-inning game, defeating the Reds, 2–1, in thirteen innings. Jayson Werth knocked in the winning run with a single, and Stammen picked up his second consecutive victory, again striking out three hitters in one inning.

The Nationals continued their hot start, and, by April 25, they were 14–4, good for a National League-best .778 winning percentage. But they lost their next five games, scoring just seven runs, which underscored the team's anemic offense to start the season. Washington hit just .226 in April, third-worst in the major leagues. The Nationals' pitching staff carried the team, posting a baseball-best 2.33 ERA.

Washington's lineup was lacking some of its major pop with Morse on the disabled list and Ryan Zimmerman sidelined with a shoulder injury. At the beginning of their losing streak, the Nationals decided to try to inject some instant offense by calling up nineteen-year-old phenom Bryce Harper ahead of schedule, even though he had been hitting only .250 at Triple-A, with one home run and three RBIs in seventy-two at bats. He joined the team in Los Angeles.

Rizzo admitted to reporters at the time it wasn't the "coming-out party for Bryce that we had in mind." He added,

> This isn't the optimal situation developmentally. . . . We still have a very good and committed developmental plan for Bryce in place. I still believe very passionately in the plan, and am committed to it. But it was expedited by the circumstances. We felt that we needed to bring in an impactful, left-handed bat that could play the corner outfield.

Some were skeptical of the move. "Forgive me if I'm picturing Washington Nationals GM Mike Rizzo making the call to Syracuse to recall Bryce Harper while sitting in his chair and staring down the barrel of a gun held by the team's VP of sales," wrote ESPN's Keith Law.

Nats owner Mark Lerner admitted that when Rizzo told him the team was bringing up Harper, "I was taken aback. Like most, I did not see this happening so quickly." Lerner added that there was a good chance the prospect would return to Triple-A for more seasoning. Lerner wrote on his blog on the eve of Harper's debut in Los Angeles:

> As "Hollywood" as this script seems, this was not how it was supposed to happen. Sure, the scenic backdrop, the 50,000-plus fans and the A-list celebs will be fantastic for the history books, but Bryce is here tonight on someone else's terms. Unfortunately, Ryan Zimmerman's shoulder soreness has prompted a DL stint. Thankfully, this won't be a prolonged absence for Ryan, but it does leave an immediate void in Davey's lineup.

Lerner, who was in Los Angeles for the rookie's first game, cautioned that Harper "should not be seen as a panacea. He's not our run-production savior. That would be unfair. But Mike does think—and I agree—that Bryce can provide our roster a healthy jolt."

Greeted by a throng of reporters at Dodger Stadium on April 28, Harper said that once the fans showed up and the lights went on, "I think that's when my energy level's going to go through the roof. So I'm trying to be as mellow as I can right now. My dad told me 'Just to go out and have fun. It's the same game you've been playing your whole life.'"

Batting seventh in the lineup, Harper went hitless in his first two at bats, but in the top of the seventh, he sent a screamer over the center fielder's head and the ball short-hopped the wall for a double. As Harper raced toward second base, he threw his helmet off. Then in the bottom of the inning, he uncorked a laser from left field that would have choked off the tying run had catcher Wilson Ramos not dropped the throw.

In the ninth, with the score tied, one out, and a man on third, Harper stung a ball to left field for a go-ahead sacrifice fly. In the dugout, he emphatically high-fived teammates who came over to congratulate him for his first career RBI. The Nats would lose the game in extra innings, but Harper had showed he belonged.

"I really didn't have butterflies at all. I think that's one of the first times I've never gotten butterflies," Harper said after the game. "I was sitting in the dugout before the game and I was thinking to myself: 'Wow, I'm in the big leagues.'"

Eight days later, on May 6, the Nats faced off at home against their division rival, the Philadelphia Phillies, in a nationally televised Sunday night game on ESPN. Harper was now batting third in the lineup, and in the bottom of the first, Phillies pitcher Cole Hamels nailed the rookie in the lower back with a fastball. Harper bent over, stretched his fingers down to his toes, and trotted down to first base.

The next batter, Jayson Werth, singled to third, and Harper raced to third base. He soon had an answer for Hamels's provocation. The lefty pitcher, with his back to third, made a pickoff throw to first base. Harper, channeling Pete Rose, immediately took off for home. First baseman Laynce Nix turned and fired home, but Harper beat the throw to steal home, giving the Nats a 1–0 lead.

"I was trying to hit him. I'm not going to deny it," Hamels said after the game. "That's something I grew up watching, that's kind of what happened, so I'm just trying to continue the old baseball because I think some people are kind of getting away from it." Major League Baseball suspended the pitcher for five games.

When told of Hamels's admission, Harper responded, saying, "He's a great guy, great pitcher, knows how to pitch. He's an all-star. It's all good."

Harper went 2-for-3 in the game, including his fifth double in just eight games, to raise his batting average to .308. But not much else went right for Washington, as the Phillies crushed the home team, 9–3. Worse, Werth broke his left wrist trying to make a catch in the outfield, sidelining the right fielder until August. Visiting Phillies fans in right field, still angry that Werth had left the team as a free agent after the 2010 season, jeered him as he left the field.

Despite the loss, the Nats sensed that the Phillies—who had won 102 games the year before, en route to their fifth consecutive division title—were now taking them seriously. "Usually it seems the Phillies aren't that hyped up to come play us," shortstop Ian Desmond later told the *Post*. "I think that they realize that they needed to step up a little bit, and that's nice. . . . I think that they realized that we've got a good ball club and they needed to kind of take it up a notch."

Indeed, even with the loss, the Nats had taken two of three from the Phillies, and the standings were reversed from previous years. It was still early, but the Nationals sat in first place; the Phillies were parked in last, four and a half games out. The series had started with a "Take Back the Park" night, in which the franchise encouraged Washington fans to come out in large numbers to outnumber Phillies fans, who often invaded the stadium in such high numbers that the place felt like a road game for the Nats.

The bad blood continued after the series. Werth told the *Post* in an e-mail: "After walking off the field feeling nauseous knowing my wrist was broke and hearing Philly fans yelling 'You deserve it,' and, 'That's what you get,' I am motivated to get back quickly and see to it personally those people never walk down Broad Street in celebration again."

Meanwhile, Rizzo was furious with Hamels, telling the *Post* he'd never seen a "more classless, gutless chicken [bleep] act in my thirty years in baseball." He continued, "Cole Hamels says he's old school? He's the polar opposite of old school. He's fake tough. He thinks he's going to intimidate us after hitting our nineteen-year-old rookie who's eight games into the big leagues? He doesn't know who he's dealing with." Major League Baseball fined Rizzo for his comments.

Democratic political consultant James Carville, a Nationals season-ticket holder, says he'd like to see a good rivalry develop with the Phillies. "In New York, they can start a depression. In New Orleans, we can start a party. In Los Angeles, they can start a movie. In Washington, they can start a war. In Philly, the only thing they can start is a fistfight," he taunts.

Less than a week after Werth landed on the disabled list, the team suffered another potentially season-wrecking injury, when catcher Wilson Ramos tore his ACL after chasing a passed ball. The injury ended Ramos's season and seemed to confirm the Nats as a jinxed team: Their slugging left fielder, $126 million right fielder, bullpen closer, and now catcher were all on the shelf.

"We're going to have to start eating bananas or something to change our luck," Davey Johnson said. "We've had more than our fair share of key players go down." For Ramos, a young player on the rise, it was another challenge in a trying spell of several months. The previous fall, he had been abducted at gunpoint in Venezuela, freed two days later by police commandos.

Now down three regulars, the Nationals were forced to turn to reserves to keep their strong start going. Jesus Flores, the team's former starting catcher, took over for Ramos. To pick up the slack for Washington's two downed outfielders, the team deployed a consortium that included Rick Ankiel, Steve Lombardozzi, Roger Bernadina, Xavier Nady, and Tyler Moore.

The Nats soon went to a similar approach in their bullpen. On May 22, the Nationals demoted Henry Rodriguez, who threw one hundred miles per hour but struggled with control, from the closer role. Brad Lidge, who had started the season as co-closer, was on the disabled list, so Davey Johnson said he'd turn to a bullpen by committee until Storen's return. But Tyler Clippard would soon seize the job.

After owning first place for most of the first two months of the season, in June the Nats went on an interleague road trip to Boston and Toronto, and the team swept all six games against the Red Sox and Blue Jays. The Nationals returned home with a five-game lead over the Braves.

During the trip to Toronto, Harper catapulted a skyscraping home run off a BlackBerry sign in center field, which, appropriately enough, featured the words, "Be Bold." But the nineteen-year-old would make an even bigger mark with a snappy postgame comment. A Canadian reporter asked Harper if he would celebrate the home run with a beer, noting that in Canada—unlike the United States—the player was of drinking age.

"I'm not answering that," Harper replied. "That's a clown question, bro."

Harper's quick retort quickly became part of pop culture, going viral on the Web—especially Twitter—adorning T-shirts, and earning a place in Urbandictionary.com: "A stupid and/or irrelevant question. Made famous by the Washington Nationals' Bryce Harper." (Harper would even dress up as clown for Halloween after the season, wearing a T-shirt that read, "Don't be a clown, bro," along with an oversized bowtie, big red nose, and rainbow wig.)

Fox News' Chris Wallace used the line in an exchange with befuddled anchor Shep Smith, who didn't get the reference. Senate Majority Leader Harry Reid, a Democrat from Harper's home state of Nevada, jokingly used the line at his news conference with reporters, who did get it. And at a meeting of the Commodity Futures Trading Commission, Commissioner Bart Chilton rhetorically asked, "Do we need Dodd-Frank?"—referring to the financial regulatory law. "That's a clown question, bro."

Another clown question: Were the Nationals the real deal this time around? Now a full sixty-one games into the season, they sported a .623 winning percentage, just three points short of the best record in baseball. And Washington had reinforcements coming later in the season, the likes of Morse, Werth, and Storen.

By the All-Star break in early July, roughly midway through the season, the Nationals were fifteen games over .500, and had the best record in the National League. Several Nats were selected to play in the All-Star Game in Kansas City: Bryce Harper, who was hitting .282 with a .472 slugging percentage; shortstop Ian Desmond, who was among the league leaders with seventeen home runs and twenty-four doubles; pitcher Stephen Strasburg, who topped the National League with 128 strikeouts; and pitcher Gio Gonzalez, who had the second-best record and was fourth in the league in strikeouts. Desmond was a late scratch to rest his sore left oblique, and Harper was a late addition, replacing another injured player.

National League manager Tony La Russa, who had guided the St. Louis Cardinals to a World Series title the year before, said he was excited about matching Harper up against the American League's twenty-year-old rising star, out-fielder Mike Trout of the Los Angeles Angels. "It would be nice to put our National League young phenom against an American League phenom, because they've been exciting our baseball world," said La Russa, who was coming out of retirement to manage in the All-Star Game. "It's been really good for our game to see Trout and Harper come into it."

President Barack Obama also gave Harper a plug before the All-Star Game, telling KSNV-TV in Las Vegas, "one of the biggest stars right now in Washington is Bryce Harper, who comes out of Nevada, and I know folks are really proud of him, he's doing great. It's my second-favorite team now—after the Chicago White Sox."

In the National League clubhouse prior to the game, Braves third baseman Chipper Jones, making his final All-Star Game appearance, gave a little shout-out to Harper in a televised pep talk to his teammates. "Look, you guys belong here. It doesn't matter whether you're nineteen," he said, pointing and smiling at Harper, "or you're forty, like me. We are all equals here." He also encouraged the players to enjoy the experience.

"I got a good chance to bring my four boys out here, watch you guys hit home runs. Bryce almost killed my seven-year-old yesterday with a line drive—but he loved it," Jones said. "That's what it's all about, bringing your kids out here, have a good time with it, soak it up."

Washington's two pitchers got to see action quickly. Gonzalez and Strasburg pitched back-to-back scoreless innings in the third and fourth frames, and by the time they were done, so was the American League, down 8–0. Harper led off the fifth inning as a pinch hitter, walked, and then tagged up on a fly ball to left field to take second base. But his signature aggressiveness cost him on the next play, when he took off for third on a ball up the middle that pitcher Jered Weaver snagged, and Harper was tagged out in a rundown.

Things got even worse for the Nationals rookie in the bottom of the inning. Harper, playing left field, lost a fly ball in the lights, and it landed behind him for a double. But given the score, the mishap hardly mattered. The National League went on to an 8–0 victory.

A low point for the Nationals came a couple of weeks later, on July 20, when they blew a 9–0 lead to the Atlanta Braves. Even more excruciating, after the Braves took a 10–9 lead in the top of the ninth, the Nats rallied to tie the score, only to lose when Atlanta scored an unearned run in the eleventh. Strasburg, who started off with five scoreless innings, retired only one batter in the sixth and surrendered four runs. Reliever Drew Storen, in just his second appearance since coming off the disabled list, gave up two runs, as did Sean Burnett and Tyler Clippard.

The loss marred what turned out to be the Nationals' best month of the season, when the team won seventeen of twenty-six games for a .654 clip. Especially impressive was the offense, which had been so icy cold in early spring. The Nats hit .280 in July—just a percentage point behind the St. Louis Cardinals for tops in the league.

Second baseman Danny Espinosa, who failed to hit higher than .236 in any of the first three months, found his groove in July, batting .300, with eight doubles in one hundred at bats. "Hitting's contagious. Some guys get hot, and it tends to get the whole team going," says Espinosa. He continues,

> Some guys are slow starters, some guys are fast starters. We just turned it around; we continued to work hard. We all knew that we had the talent and the capability to do what we could do, so we kept going. For me, it was just to work on staying on top of the ball and getting a pitch that I could drive.

And offensive reinforcements would soon arrive. On August 2, Werth came off the disabled list after missing seventy-five games with a broken wrist. Fittingly, he made his return against the Phillies and went 1-for-3 with an RBI to help the Nats to a 3–0 victory over Cole Hamels. Ross Detwiler pitched seven innings of three-hit ball for the win.

The next day, Washington upgraded its lineup at another position, by acquiring twenty-nine-year-old catcher Kurt Suzuki from the Oakland A's in exchange for a minor-league prospect. Suzuki replaced Jesus Flores, who had hit just .221. Suzuki had been hitting even worse for Oakland (.218), but he would turn his season around for Washington and become one of the league's most dangerous eighth-place hitters.

In Suzuki's debut, the Nats beat the Marlins, 10–7, paced by home runs from Harper, LaRoche, and Espinosa. The victory served as a launching pad for the Nationals on their way to their hottest stretch of the season. Four games later, reserve outfielder Roger Bernadina leaped into the angular nook in left-center field at Houston's Minute Maid Park, making a game-saving catch just before crashing into the wall. The catch iced the Nationals' 3–2 extra-inning win over the Astros, Washington's fifth straight win. Some commentators immediately hailed it as the best catch of the year. The Nationals extended their winning streak to a season-best eight, opening up a four-and-a-half-game lead over the Braves.

By the middle of August, Davey Johnson had made Werth the leadoff man—an unusual spot for a six-foot, five-inch hitter with power, but one that Werth relished. The Nationals lineup was taking its final form, with Werth and Harper forming a one-two punch, followed by a power trio of Zimmerman, LaRoche, and Morse, and then Desmond, Espinosa, and Suzuki.

But there was drama as the Nats approached the stretch drive—or maybe you could call it "Strama." General Manager Mike Rizzo had announced at the beginning of the season that his prized pitcher, Stephen Strasburg, would be shut down after pitching around 160 innings, to minimize Strasburg's workload in his first full season following Tommy John surgery. *Everyone*, it seemed, had an opinion on Rizzo's decision, from Chipper Jones to the *Washington Post* editorial page.

"If I was sitting over in that clubhouse, I would hate to squander this opportunity," Jones said during a Braves' visit to Washington in late August.

The *Post* had a more long-term outlook on the situation. "By shutting down Mr. Strasburg in September and reducing his risk of future injury, Mr. Rizzo—who calls the decision 'mine and mine alone'—is making both the admirable choice for Mr. Strasburg and the prudent, if painful, choice for the Nationals," the newspaper wrote in an editorial, adding, "We hope they won't need him to push deep into the playoffs this year. They do need him to be healthy for the next ten."

The paper's veteran sports columnist, Thomas Boswell, was more pointed in his defense of the team's decision. "There is no debate here, no 'two sides,' about the Nationals' intention to shut down Strasburg's season at 160 to 170 innings, probably about September 10," he writes. "There is only the Nats' side, which is correct, and the nincompoop side, even if it is endorsed by former players or 'experts.'"

Even the city's mayor, Vincent Gray, weighed in. "I think it's very wise," he said, adding that "the young man has his entire career ahead of him."

Commentators based outside the beltway were not as sympathetic. Ken Rosenthal of Fox Sports wrote a sarcastic column begging the Nats to shut Strasburg down early. "Strasburg surely will jeopardize his future if he pitches beyond 180 innings this season, or whatever righteous number the Washington Nationals choose," he writes.

Sports Illustrated columnist Phil Taylor imagined Bud Abbott and Lou Costello as present-day Nats fans discussing the Nationals' plans for Strasburg in a *Who's on First* spoof:

> **LOU:** Let me get this straight. The Nationals are afraid of losing Strasburg to a career-ending injury in the future?
>
> **BUD:** Right.
>
> **LOU:** So, they're going to pretend that Strasburg has a career-ending injury right here in the present?
>
> **BUD:** Now you're getting it.
>
> **LOU:** I don't know what I'm getting!

Strasburg himself opposed the move, but his agent, Scott Boras, had pushed for the innings limit.

In an "open letter" to Strasburg, former pitcher Jim Kaat, a MLB Network analyst, encouraged the young pitcher to make the decision for himself. Kaat wrote:

> If you can imagine what it would feel like to ride down Pennsylvania Avenue in a victory parade with your teammates and wave to the White House and hundreds of thousands of Nationals fans and feel that feeling, you would give a lot of thought to whether it was right or wrong not to pitch anymore this season.

But Pennsylvania Avenue in front of the White House isn't open to traffic, as it was when Kaat pitched in Washington in 1959 and 1960.

Kaat said that back in his day, pitchers who got to play in the World Series didn't think about what the condition of their arms would be the next year: "This was the World Series—the ultimate stage. Who knows if we'd ever get back there again? Give this some thought." It's not Rizzo's career or Davey Johnson's or Scott Boras's, he counseled. "It's yours."

On September 2, Strasburg capped a Nats impressive four-game series against the defending champion Cardinals at Nationals Park, pitching six scoreless innings, giving up just two hits and striking out nine. The Nationals held on for a 4–3 victory, taking the series three games to one. But after the win, Davey Johnson announced that Strasburg would pitch just two more games before the Nats would shut him down for the year.

There was a brief hiatus in the Strasburg drama when the Cubs came to town for a four-game series to face off against the Nats' other four starting pitchers. Washington won the first game, 2–1, behind seven shutout innings from Detwiler for the team's eighty-second victory, ensuring the Nationals their first winning season since coming to Washington in 2005. The Nats obliterated the visitors after that. Washington hit a combined dozen home runs in the second and third games, after which Chicago manager Dale Sveum pretty much waved the white flag, saying, "That's just men playing against boys right now." The "men" capped off the four-game sweep with a 9–2 throttling that was marred by a bench-clearing brawl, when the Cubs took exception to the Nationals stealing a base and swinging on a 3–0 count with a five-run lead. The sweep left Washington seven and a half games ahead of the second-place Braves.

It was right back to Strasburg after that for a Friday night matchup against the Marlins. In the end, Johnson's leash proved shorter than even the two games he had projected. The Marlins pounded Strasburg for five runs in three innings, and the Nats decided to end his season the next day.

"The media hype on this thing has been unbelievable," Johnson said in announcing the news. "I feel it's as hard for him as it would be anybody to get mentally, totally committed in the ballgame. And he's reached his innings limit. So we can get past this and talk about other things for a change."

Strasburg's final line was outstanding: a 15–6 record, 3.16 ERA, and 197 strikeouts in 159⅓ innings. At the time, he was among the league leaders in strikeouts, ERA, winning percentage, and wins.

Johnson said:

> My job is to do what's best for the player. And this is what's best. If you're not there 100 percent mentally—he's a gifted athlete, his velocity can still be there—but I don't see the crispness. I don't see the ball jumping out of his hand. I'm a firm believer that this game is 90 to 95 percent mental. He's only human. I don't know how · anybody can be totally mentally concentrating on the job at hand with the media hype to this thing, and I think we'd be risking more by sending him out.

Strasburg didn't take the news well. "I don't know if I'm ever gonna accept it to be honest," he said. He added:

> It's something that I'm not happy about at all. That's not why I play the game. I play the game to be a good teammate and win. You don't grow up dreaming of playing in the big leagues to get shut down when the games start to matter. It's gonna be a tough one to swallow . . . all I can do is be the best teammate possible for these guys.

The right-hander said he thought he had another start coming. "It was pretty shocking, and honestly, I'm not too happy about it."

When a reporter asked about Kaat's letter, Strasburg snapped, "Who cares about that? Everybody's got something to say."

Rizzo recalls that his own father, a longtime scout, initially thought his son was making a mistake by putting Strasburg on an innings limit. Rizzo recounts:

> It was scout-to-scout. My dad's one of my senior advisers. He's been in baseball a long time, and knows players. The knee-jerk reaction was, "Let him decide, let him pitch." And when I shared with him the information that I had, and the entire dossier of the Strasburg situation, he then very easily agreed with what I was doing and the decision that I made.

The GM notes that he treated Strasburg the same way he did other young pitchers coming off Tommy John surgery, like Jordan Zimmermann the year before. He says that it was part of the vision he had for the team, dating back to when he became general manager in 2009. "It wasn't the first pitching limit decision that we've made in this franchise; it won't be the last," he says. "We haven't wavered one bit from our developmental philosophy, and we won't."

Meanwhile, while one ultra-phenom was done, another was on the rise following a two-month nosedive. Bryce Harper, who hit well enough in the spring to win an All-Star selection, had hit just .203, with a sickly .288 slugging percentage from June 16 to August 15, according to MLB.com. Lefties were especially hard on the rookie, limiting him to a .132 batting average during that period. But in the twenty-five games that followed, Harper hit .330, with a .681 slugging percentage. Harper maintained that pace through all of September, hitting .330 for the month, with seven home runs, seven doubles, three triples, and eleven walks for an off-the-charts 1.049 OPS (on-base percentage plus slugging).

Former Senators slugger Frank Howard, who hit at least forty-four home runs for three consecutive seasons (1968–1970), says Harper reminds him of Mickey Mantle and Reggie Jackson: "The same type of determination to excel, great baseball acumen. Those types of players operate a level or two above us mere mortals." Howard notes that Hall of Famer Mike Schmidt hit just .196 in his first full season in the majors, at the age of twenty-three.

"Well, the rest is history," he says, adding:

> You aren't going to suppress that kind of talent, because it comes along once every twenty-five, thirty, thirty-five years in baseball. So this young man Harper, as he grows and develops and continues to improve—which he will, 'cause he's got a great mindset for baseball—he's going to be a bona fide superstar.

Harper helped fuel a lineup that had become dangerous from top to bottom, nearly unrecognizable from the feeble early season offense that hit only .226 in April. Cleanup man Adam LaRoche hit .327 in September, with nine home runs and a 1.045 OPS; Ian Desmond cranked at a .314 average, with six home runs; Ryan Zimmerman hit .290, with seven homers and a team-high twenty-five RBIs; and even eighth-place hitter Suzuki hit .300, with four home runs. Overall, the Nats led the majors with forty-nine home runs in September and were also tops in team slugging percentage and OPS.

Davey Johnson had emphasized trying to pull the ball, rather than what he considered too much of an emphasis on going the other way during Riggleman's tenure. Nationals radio announcer Dave Jageler says that by midseason, Johnson had put his stamp on the lineup. "You see a first-pitch fastball, he wants you to hit it where it's pitched, and drive the ball," Jageler says. He adds,

> And if you get a 2–0 count and you get a fastball, swing at it, and try to hit a double or a home run. Don't take the 2–0 fastball and then swing at the 2–1 slider off the outside corner and try to flare it to right. Desmond

bought into that philosophy, and now you see him driving the ball. Whereas Davey felt that the year before, he was trying to basically hit singles to the opposite field. So Davey and hitting coach Rick Eckstein changed the hitting philosophy.

The ascendant offense was merely catching up with the team's pitching, which had been outstanding all year. Washington would finish first in the National League in both the traditional barometer of pitching—ERA—and the modern Society for American Baseball Research–driven standard—WHIP (walks plus hits per innings pitched).

Even without Strasburg, the Nats continued their march to the playoffs. On September 12, in what would have been Strasburg's next scheduled start, the team turned to John Lannan, who just a few months earlier had demanded a trade after being shipped to the minors. The southpaw, a Long Island native, pitched five and two-thirds innings of shutout ball in front of his friends and relatives at Citi Field in New York, leading the Nats to a 2–0 victory. The win widened Washington's lead in the National League East to a season-high eight and a half games.

For almost all Washington baseball fans, a pennant race in the nation's capital was a first-time experience. The last D.C. major-league team to make the postseason was the 1933 Washington Senators, back when Franklin D. Roosevelt was president, the country was in the midst of the Great Depression, and the hometown team was led by a twenty-seven-year-old player-manager, Joe Cronin. After that team clinched the pennant, Cronin was "besieged in the clubhouse by a hero-worshiping throng of thousands of fans of both sexes gone mildly mad," according to a September 22, 1933, *Washington Post* story. Cronin slipped out of the clubhouse onto the field, where "shrieking women" ran after him, and he had to sprint to escape them, the *Post* reported.

Seventy-nine years later, Nats fans might not have matched that level of stalking fanaticism, but they were clearly in love with their young, hustling team. Fans serenaded Michael Morse when he came to the plate with his signature song, the 1980s hit "Take on Me" by the Norwegian group A-ha. The stadium sound system would blare the chorus, "Take on Me," and the fans would answer in a collective high-pitched "I'll be gone . . . in a day or two!" The song became an unofficial rallying cry for the team, and A-ha even posted an item about it on their official site that sounded like a Ph.D. dissertation: "The Washington Nationals 'Take on Me' Phenomenon."

Jageler, the radio announcer, says he and fellow announcer Charlie Slowes incorporated the fans into their home broadcasts in 2012 to a greater extent than previous seasons. "We kind of made the crowd a character in our broadcast," he says. "When Morse came to the plate and they played "Take on Me," we'd stop what we're doing, and Charlie and I wouldn't talk, and they'd pick up the sound of the crowd singing the chorus of the song."

Longtime fans were joined by swelling crowds, drawn by the team's success. Syndicated columnist Charles Krauthammer, who suffered through the one-hundred-loss seasons in the late 2000s, didn't feel any resentment toward the bandwagon fans. "These are the healthier people," he says. "I've been sitting there when they were losing. I'm a grown man, and I care about these kids who never heard of me, and don't care. The idea of fandom has always been a mystery to me. It makes no sense. Why should my day be wrecked by them losing?"

On September 20, more than 30,000 came out for a historic night at Nationals Park. Fans knew that a win over the Los Angeles Dodgers would clinch a playoff berth for the Nats, and they displayed such signs as "World Series Bound" and "Let's Make History Tonight Boys!!!" Even the super-expensive President's Club seats behind home plate, often dotted with empty seats, were packed.

Washington took a 1–0 lead in the bottom of the third on an RBI double by Zimmerman, who made it 2–0 when he scored on a wild pitch. The Dodgers pulled within 2–1 in the fourth, but the Nats answered with two more runs in the bottom of the inning on Danny Espinosa's RBI double and Kurt Suzuki's sacrifice fly. With a strong start from Detwiler, who gave up just one run in six innings, the score remained that way as the game moved into the late innings, and the excitement began to build.

"They're starting to feel it," said Nats play-by-play man Bob Carpenter.

"They're starting to feel it, we're starting to feel it," replied color commentator F. P. Santangelo.

In the bottom of the ninth inning, Drew Storen came out of the bullpen with a chance to save the game. He struck out Matt Kemp looking and then fanned Adrian Gonzales swinging. With fans standing and screaming from their seats, Storen finished the perfect inning by striking out Hanley Ramirez swinging.

Red and white fireworks exploded in the night sky, and the scoreboard exalted, "NATS CLINCH." The players celebrated in an understated way, exchanging high fives on the infield and on the way into the dugout, but not jumping into a scrum. Players slipped on red "Natitude Postseason" T-shirts over their jerseys and gray-and-white baseball caps that read, "Playoffs 2012."

"We've got a few more games to win before we can really celebrate," said Ryan Zimmerman, speaking in a television interview from the field.

Added Ian Desmond, who was celebrating his twenty-seventh birthday along with the clinching victory, "We got a bigger picture in mind."

Jayson Werth said that there had been some talk about not celebrating the playoff clincher at all, but he talked his teammates out of that. "The next one would not be as subdued, I would imagine," he predicted.

Harper said he didn't know until the game was over that the team had been on the verge of clinching a playoff berth. "Everyone's going crazy," he said. "I looked at the fireworks and I go: 'I guess we just did something.' Then somebody handed me the playoff shirt and playoff hat and I said, 'Well, I guess we're going to the playoffs.'"

The players did a champagne toast in the clubhouse and asked Johnson to say a few words. "And I said, that 'We ain't done yet,'" the manager recalled. "They all had the same feeling, that this was just a baby step, to get to the playoffs."

Johnson mistakenly suggested that the postseason berth was "probably a first for D.C." When a reporter corrected him that it was the first since the 1933 pennant, Johnson quipped, "1933? I can't remember that year."

Johnson said he was glad to see Storen, who had saved forty-three games the year before but missed more than half of the 2012 season with an injury, get the clinching save: "I know it meant a lot to him. 'Cause it's been a rough year for him, not closing. So that was kind of a fairytale ending."

Storen still savors the moment. "That experience was unbelievable," he says. "It was just an electric atmosphere, and the fans were all about it. And it doesn't get any better than that."

He adds that the players developed an appreciation for what the team's success meant to some of the old-time Senators fans, who had waited decades for that moment. "I think that's one of the things that's been a really pleasant surprise—just hearing the outpour of support through the older baseball fans," Storen says. "People who had been around, the people who were the Senators fans. I got a letter at the end of the year from a lady saying she was seventy-three, she used to go to games with her dad, and how much it meant to her for us to do what we did."

"We definitely knew that it was something special," adds Danny Espinosa. "Having not been back to the playoffs in so long and the team basically finishing under .500 every single year since they've been back in Washington. We were excited for the city; we were excited for the fans."

The day after the clincher, President Obama gave the Nationals a shout-out at a campaign event, held at the ballpark of the Potomac Nationals, the Class-A minor-league affiliate of the Nats. "I want to congratulate the Washington Nationals for bringing playoff baseball to D.C.," the president said to applause. "You guys are looking good. I am looking forward to a White Sox–Nationals World Series. It's going to happen. White Sox are still in first place. But I got to admit, you guys are looking a little better right now. You guys are looking very good."

Washington mayor Vincent Gray said that the city's John A. Wilson building on Pennsylvania Avenue, home to his office, would turn red at night in honor of the team's accomplishment. Even the Washington Redskins' new star quarterback, Robert Griffin III, praised his new hometown baseball team. "Congrats to the Nats on their playoff clinchinization," he tweeted. "Yes I know that's not a word. But real words cannot describe how big it is."

On NBC, *Meet the Press* host David Gregory shifted from politics to baseball at the end of the broadcast and brandished a Nationals playoffs baseball cap. "We've got to tip a cap, quite literally, to the playoff-bound Nationals, the Washington Nationals," Gregory said, as panelist Joe Scarborough could be heard off camera yelling, "Oh yeah! Oh yeah!"

"First time that Washington's had a playoff team since 1933, when I was just a boy," quipped the youthful Gregory. "A little painful that they clinched this against my Los Angeles Dodgers, but they have been so great to follow. FDR was president when they were playing the Giants in the World Series that year. He said, 'I'll just sit on both sides to keep it even.' Washington—going all the way."

Just two days after clinching a playoff berth, the Nats celebrated another accomplishment when Gio Gonzalez won his twentieth game of the season. In a dominant performance against the Milwaukee Brewers, he allowed just three hits and two runs (none earned) in seven innings, lowering his ERA to 2.84. He became the first Washington southpaw pitcher to win twenty games since Earl Whitehill in 1933.

Gonzalez also fanned his 201st batter of the season, becoming the first Washington pitcher to top 200 strikeouts in one year since Walter Johnson nearly a century earlier (1916). "This is like a dream," Gonzalez said. "I feel like I'm still sleeping in it."

But if Gonzalez was getting too heady at the historic accomplishments, a pitch in the seventh inning literally brought him back to earth. He lost his balance during delivery, sending him and the pitch in opposite directions. The ball went flying over the catcher's head and bounced off the net behind home plate. Gonzalez, meanwhile, landed face-first on the grass in front of the mound.

"I caught my spike on the side of the mound, and I couldn't keep my balance after that," he recalls now with a laugh. "If I'd had a third leg I would have definitely kept my balance. But I landed face-first, and I guess the team had a nice kick out of it. And they were all laughing about it."

Even as the Nationals were ensured a playoff spot, their hold on first place was getting more tenuous. At stake was more than just bragging rights. If the Nats were to blow their lead, they would make the playoffs as a wild card team, forcing them to play a one-and-done elimination game against the league's other wild card team. A first-place finish would allow the team to skip that crapshoot game.

But the Braves, who had been chasing the Nats since late May, were making things interesting. Atlanta had swept a three-game series against the Nats in mid-September, reducing Washington's lead to five and a half games. On September 25, the Braves pulled to within four games with a home win over the Marlins and a Nationals road loss to the Phillies. The next day, the Braves kept the pressure on, winning their fourth straight game as the Nationals again battled the Phillies in hostile territory. Clinging to a 5–4 lead in the top of the ninth inning, the Nats knew a loss would drop their lead to three games.

With two runners on and one out, Danny Espinosa came up with a chance to pad the lead. But the real action—at least in the eyes of Phillies fans—would take place a few feet away, in the on-deck circle. A ball rolled to the Nats' on-deck batter, Jayson Werth, who picked it up and fake-tossed it to a fan, then rolled it into the Washington dugout instead.

After Espinosa struck out, Werth came to the plate with boos raining down from the Phillies faithful, who already disliked him for leaving the Phillies as a free agent two years earlier. On a 1–2 pitch, Werth grounded a ball up the middle to score both runners and break open a tight game. Harper followed with an RBI triple to right field, and suddenly, the Nats had a comfortable 8–4 lead. Storen retired the side in the bottom of the inning to preserve the win—and the Nats' four-game lead over the Braves.

Werth told reporters that earlier in the game, when he had flipped a ball into the right field stands, a fan reached into a woman's lap, grabbed the ball, and threw it on the field. And then in the ninth inning, he got the sense that there were drunk people behind the "innocent little children" he was going to throw the ball to. "So I just flipped it into the dugout, and evidently that rubbed some people the wrong way," Werth said. "But after the events in right field, I just felt that it was better to maybe not throw it into the stands."

Among those rubbed the wrong way was former Pennsylvania governor Ed Rendell. "I mean, Jayson Werth is a complete ass!" he said on WIP, a Philadelphia sports radio station. "We made him a star, and we got him that contract. Players are nuts."

Washington beat the Phillies the next night, too, behind Gonzalez's twenty-first victory. The Braves won their fifth straight game, but remained four games out with just six games left. The Nationals then went to St. Louis for a three-game weekend series against the Cardinals, the team they had manhandled about a month earlier. This time, St. Louis dominated, winning two of three games and outscoring the Nats, 26–12. "We've had rough outings before," Davey Johnson said at the end of the series. "We've bounced back. It's better to clinch it at home, anyway."

The Nats headed home for a season-ending three-game series against the Phillies, with a cushy three-game lead over the Braves. That meant that Washington's magic number was down to one—a single Nationals win or Braves loss would clinch the franchise's first division title since moving to D.C. On Monday night, October 1, a crowd of more than 35,000 came to Nationals Park for the opening game of the Nats–Phillies series, hoping to see history made against the team that had won the division title the past five seasons.

The Phillies jumped out to a 2–0 lead off John Lannan in the top of the second, and the Nats had trouble mounting any counterattack against Philadelphia pitcher Kyle Kendrick. By the time the game got into the late innings with the same score, Nats fans were focusing more and more of their attention on the scoreboard, which showed that the Braves were having trouble with Pennsylvania's other team, trailing the Pirates, 2–1.

In the top if the ninth inning, Nats fans started chanting, "Let's go Pirates," with Pittsburgh nursing the 2–1 lead in the top of the ninth inning. Just as the Nationals trotted off the field in the middle of the ninth, a spontaneous cheer erupted as fans saw the Pirates had wrapped up their victory over the Braves.

"NL EAST DIVISION CHAMPIONS," the scoreboards flashed. Fans immediately hoisted signs celebrating the achievement, with one blaring "Merry Clinchmas." Many pulled out their cell phones to record the moment. In the Nats dugout, players high-fived, embraced, and jumped up and down. Davey Johnson waved, blew kisses to fans, and held his arms up over his head in celebration.

Back on the field, the Nats were in the odd position of hitting in the bottom of the ninth inning already as victors—of the season, if not the now-meaningless game. Michael Morse led off to his tune of "Take on Me," with fans euphorically singing along.

"He just stood there at the plate, with the biggest smile," recalls Gregory McCarthy, the team's vice president for government and municipal affairs. "I gotta tell you, I actually got a little bit of goose bumps. I thought, 'I work here, I'm not going to get emotional.' But you kind of do."

The Nats went down one-two-three, wrapping up the Phillies victory, but that just got the full celebration started early. A submarine horn blared, fireworks lit up the black sky, and players sprinted into the clubhouse, where team owner Ted Lerner and CNN's Wolf Blitzer greeted them. After spraying champagne on one another, they came back onto the field and sprayed the stands, with fan favorite Morse leading the way. Players took a victory lap on the field—some exchanging high fives with fans, others holding their young children in their arms, pointing to the fans, as fans screamed in celebration.

Gio Gonzalez lifted owner Mark Lerner, squeezed him in a bear hug, and yelled, "The pimp with the limp right here!" as Lerner cracked up. "The pimp with the limp! And he came out. And he came out. That's the love right there!" Lerner earned this impromptu nickname—more commonly associated with a Miami DJ—because of a lingering limp from foot surgery over the summer.

"It was definitely a spontaneous thing," Gonzalez says now, adding,

> You're just so excited, words can't even come out. You just think of the first thing that comes out. It's an honor to represent Mark Lerner and his organization. . . . Even when times were getting tough and he had the surgery on his foot, he came out, and he showed so much love. And same thing with Mike Rizzo. In Rizzo we do trust.

Back in the clubhouse, players sported ski goggles to protect their eyes from all of the champagne and beer and circled the GM in celebration. Reflecting on the moment, Rizzo says, "It was very emotional. It was the culmination of a lot of years on the road, a lot of hard work, a lot of interaction with the players. It was their way of showing their appreciation of what we've built here. It was a great emotional time. And it was something I'll remember for a long time."

The victorious Phillies got to watch the other team celebrate. "Made me mad. Yes it did. Very much so. I'm a bad loser," said Phillies manager Charlie Manuel. "That's the first time I ever won and got beat."

Bryce Harper tweeted after the game: "I want to thank this city of D.C. and all the fans for the support you guys have showed us all year! NL East title, but not done yet!"

"Such an amazing feeling!" tweeted Stephen Strasburg. "So blessed to be a part of it! Now the fun begins!"

The Nats took the last two games of the season to finish 98–64 and claim the best record in baseball. Amazingly, after seven seasons in Washington where they failed to finish over .500, the Nationals finished with a .605 winning percentage. One of the biggest success stories for the Nationals was Ian Desmond. The shortstop hadn't hit above .270, or more than ten home runs, in each of his first full two seasons. But in 2012, his third full year, he hit .292 and led all major-league shortstops with 25 home runs, a .511 slugging percentage, and an .845 OPS. He also stole twenty-one bases in twenty-seven attempts.

Discussing the surge after the season, Desmond calls it part of his evolution as a big leaguer. "When you break into the big leagues, you obviously come in full speed ahead, you want to just take on the world," he says. He adds:

> My first year, I had a good year. And then I tried to reach down and dig for more the second year. My cup was kind of overflowing, everything was kind of out of control. And then last year, all the flowing kind of settled down, and I settled in nicely with the team, and I got my feet wet, and all that stuff was behind me and it was time to just go play.

Desmond had been with the franchise since the Expos drafted him in 2004. At the time, he says, the team was in "complete shambles . . . I've been with the organization for a long time. I was in the minor leagues kind of looking in. Those years were hard for me, going home, and having your friends and people saying, 'Oh, who do you play for?' And you say the Washington Nationals, and they're like, 'Who? Who is that?' But now, we've kind of made a name of ourselves and it's a little better."

As the top seed in the National League playoffs, Washington was slated to meet the winner of the one-game wild card showdown, which turned out to be the St. Louis Cardinals, after they defeated the Braves, 6–3, in Atlanta.

The Cardinals, the 2011 defending champions, had played inconsistently all season in 2012. The team's deep lineup featured five players who hit at least twenty homers, led by Carlos Beltran (thirty-two), and five regulars who hit over .290—including three over .300. But it was a sporadic offense, sometimes piling on runs by the bushels, and other times having a hard time scrounging up more than one or two. Only a late burst got the Cardinals to an 88–74 record, and only Major League Baseball's decision to add a fifth wild card in each league got them an invite to the postseason.

Still, the Cardinals were a dangerous team. The year before, they had also entered the playoffs as a wild card team and knocked out the Philadelphia Phillies, who had baseball's best record in the regular season. Despite losing star first baseman Albert Pujols, the 2012 Cards had finished second in the league in runs scored and batting average. And their pitching staff featured two aces in Adam Wainwright and Chris Carpenter; eighteen-game winner Lance Lynn; sixteen-game winner Kyle Lohse; and closer Jason Motte, who tied for the league lead in saves. They also had more players with playoff experience than Washington, although the Cardinals had a rookie manager, Mike Matheny, who had replaced legendary skipper Tony La Russa.

"Many in the Nationals organization believe the Cardinals are the toughest matchup for them in the entire field, American League or National League," wrote Adam Kilgore in the *Washington Post*. "If they get past the Cardinals, they may not face a tougher opponent all October, the World Series included. The best two teams in baseball—the ninety-eight-win Nationals and defending champs—could be facing off in St. Louis right now."

The Nationals were bringing plenty of firepower of their own. Adam LaRoche finished the regular season with thirty-three homers and one hundred RBIs; Ian Desmond and Ryan Zimmerman hit twenty-five home runs apiece; Bryce Harper slugged twenty-two in a memorable rookie season; and Michael Morse clobbered eighteen in just a few more than 100 games. The Nats also had three bona fide base-stealing threats in Ian Desmond (21 thefts), Danny Espinosa (20), and Bryce Harper (18), compared to just one for the Cardinals, Jon Jay (19). The Nats pitching staff, even sans Strasburg, was formidable, led by twenty-one-game-winner Gio Gonzalez (2.89 ERA), along with Jordan Zimmermann (2.94) and Ross Detwiler (3.40).

The only Washington team to win the World Series had been the 1924 Senators, and in trying to match that feat, the 2012 Nationals took a much more muscular approach. Four players hit at least twenty-two home runs, compared to twenty-two for the *entire* 1924 Senators team, last in the American League. Senators outfielder Goose Goslin, who hit a dozen homers, was the only player to hit more than three on the 1924 team, which instead relied on getting on base to manufacture runs.

Amazingly, one Washington baseball fan had seen both teams play, nearly ninety years apart. Bert Abramson went to the first game of the 1924 World Series as an eleven-year-old boy and saw the team play during the regular season as well. In 2012, he watched every Nationals game on television. "No question about it—this is a better team," the one-hundred-year-old Abramson says. "Washington was pretty good in those years, but nothing like this team. They couldn't hold a candle to this team. Everybody hits on this team."

The Nationals had won four of the seven regular-season games against the Cardinals, dominating at home, but getting roughed up in St. Louis. In the best-of-five playoff series, the Nationals had home-field advantage, but because of a scheduling quirk, the first two games would be played in St. Louis, with the remainder of the series returning to Washington.

The series started on a cool, sunny Sunday afternoon at Busch Stadium, with Gonzalez facing off against Wainwright. The Nationals took a 1–0 lead in the top of the second on an RBI single by Kurt Suzuki, but the team fell behind in the bottom of the frame when Gonzalez skidded out of control, walking four batters and throwing a wild pitch. The Cardinals scored two runs without even a single hit.

For the most part, Gonzalez settled down after that and was nearly unhittable when he wasn't walking guys. He wound up striking out five in five innings and left with his team trailing, 2–1, having surrendered two runs on just one hit. But he also walked a whopping seven Cardinals. Wainwright, meanwhile, scattered a bunch of hits but limited the damage with an impressive strikeout performance. In five and two-thirds innings, he fanned ten, while giving up just one run on six hits and three walks.

The Cardinals bullpen held the lead into the eighth inning, when the Nats put runners on second and third. With the pitcher's spot up and two outs, Davey Johnson sent left-handed hitter Chad Tracy up as a pinch hitter. Cardinals rookie manager Mike Matheny countered with lefty Marc Rzepczynski, but Johnson neutralized him by sending in right-handed hitter Tyler Moore. The move paid off when Moore poked a single to right, scoring the tying and go-ahead runs. Washington relievers Tyler Clippard and Drew Storen held the lead, giving the Nats the first game of the series.

The Cardinals evened the series the next day by jumping Nats starter Jordan Zimmermann for five runs in three innings, en route to a 12–4 thrashing. Cardinals starting pitcher Jamie Garcia was pulled after just two innings because of an injury, but five relievers finished the job. Carlos Beltran homered twice for the Redbirds, and Allen Craig and Daniel Descalso added one apiece.

After an off day, the teams retuned to Nationals Park for another historic occasion—the first postseason game in Washington in seventy-nine years. The last one had been the fifth and final game of the 1933 World Series at Griffith

Stadium. The New York Giants defeated the Senators in that game, 4–3, in ten innings, to claim the series four games to one. Only around 28,000 fans, a crowd probably thinned by the Great Depression, saw the Senators play their last postseason game.

The Nationals' first postseason game in Washington, played at 1 p.m. on a Wednesday afternoon, drew more than 45,000 fans. Dozens of red and white balloons and a giant American flag greeted fans outside the center-field gate. A band outside the ballpark added a little college football feel on the mild, sunny autumn day. Nationals Park was dressed up for the occasion, with bunting unfurled and a giant "MLB Postseason" logo painted on the grass behind home plate.

In the team magazine and scorecard on sale at the ballpark, Nats owner Ted Lerner tried to connect the old and new for fans. He recalled working as a peanut vendor at Griffith Stadium as a child. "Today, hosting postseason baseball for the first time since before World War II, marks a milestone in which we can all take great pride," he writes. "While a few memories may have faded since the last playoff series contested here in 1933, when I was just seven years old, the palpable excitement of October baseball remains as indelible as ever."

Some fans were irritated that the Nats were not getting prime-time coverage. "Washington a powerful city?" tweeted Gerald F. Seib, Washington bureau chief of the *Wall Street Journal*. "First postseason game in seventy-nine yrs Wed, and we get worst start time, no network coverage. Pretty outrageous." (The game was broadcast on the MLB Network, which some fans didn't get on their cable systems.)

Fox News analyst Juan Williams, a Nationals season-ticket holder, was one of many working Washingtonians to make the game. He recalls:

> For me, what stood out was the number of people who had clearly had just bailed on work. Because much like me, they had the baseball cap or a jacket or something, but you could see from the shoes and the pants they had taken off the suit jacket. And the other thing was the number of kids with their dads—I thought to myself, everybody thinks this is a really important moment, and so they've taken the kids out of school. To me that was another sign—dads wanting to share this moment with sons or daughters, but overwhelmingly sons—in starting a tradition, which is, "We're Nationals fans."

Fans started arriving at the ballpark hours before the first pitch, many in Strasburg, Harper, and Zimmerman jerseys. One fan wore a shirt that said, "Don't be a clown, bro," while another sported a Montreal Expos jersey.

In another throwback, the Nats had their first manager, seventy-one-year-old Frank Robinson, throw out the first pitch. Robinson, wearing his Nationals jersey and black pants, got a rousing ovation as he walked onto the field and made his toss from a makeshift mound between the real one and home plate. His throw to Ian Desmond, who had played for Robinson in spring training in 2005, made it on a fly. Robinson tapped Desmond in the chest in a "go get 'em" gesture. F-16 jets roared overhead.

Steve Bergsbaken, a fifty-nine-year-old fan from Washington's Capitol Hill neighborhood, near the stadium, had a Nats cap signed by Gio Gonzalez, Ross Detwiler, and Craig Stammen. He's been a season-ticket holder since the team arrived from Montreal, and only missed two games in 2012. Bergsbaken said he hadn't thought the team would make the playoffs when the season started. "This has been exhilarating," he said before the game. "It shows you have to keep faith."

JoAnn Sieve, fifty-four, and her father, Joe Giuliani, eighty-seven, both Virginia residents, had suffered through the Senators of the 1960s and were now finally able to see a Washington postseason game. "It's just unbelievable," said Giuliani. "I didn't think it would come this quick. It makes you forget about the Senators." "Maybe D.C. will finally get respect as a baseball city," said his daughter.

The Nationals sent Edwin Jackson, who had pitched for the Cardinals the year before, to take on playoff-tested Chris Carpenter. The year before, Carpenter won the fifth and deciding game of the National League Division Series by defeating Roy Halladay, 1–0.

In the regular season, Jackson had gone 10–11, with a 4.03 ERA. One of his best performances came in an August victory against the Cardinals at Nationals Park, when he gave up just four hits and one unearned run in eight innings, striking out ten. But a month later, he had been throttled by the Cards in St. Louis, giving up nine runs (eight earned) in just one and a third innings.

With the fans at full throttle as the game started, Jackson got the first two outs and looked like he'd get the Nats off to a good start. But the Cardinals struck quickly with a single by Matt Holliday, followed by an RBI double by Allen Craig down the left field line, to take an early lead.

The red-wearing, red-rally-towel-waving Nats fans got recharged in the bottom of the inning. They cheered wildly when the Nats put two runners on base with one out and were so amped up that they booed Chris Carpenter when he slowed down the action momentarily to tie his shoes. But the Nats left both men on base and came up empty. Carpenter later extolled the D.C. fans, saying, "The crowd was amazing. This is what you play for, and I took it in a little bit, yeah, no question."

In the top of the second, the Cardinals' eighth-place hitter and fill-in rookie shortstop, Pete Kozma, stunned the Washington crowd by slamming a three-run homer to the left field seats, setting the tone for the rest of the game. (A Nats fan threw the ball back.) Washington threatened in the bottom of the fifth inning, loading the bases with two outs, but Carpenter got Morse to fly out to end the rally, subduing the previously rollicking crowd.

David Gregory, host of NBC's *Meet the Press*, tweeted from the game: "This is not the playoff game I signed up for."

Carpenter pitched around seven hits in five and two-thirds innings, and the Cardinals cruised to an 8–0 victory. That made twenty runs in the past two games for the Redbirds, who now led the best-of-five series, two games to one. The Nationals, who left eleven men on base, were now one game away from elimination.

"We are not out of this by a long shot," Davey Johnson said after the game. "Keep us in the ballgame tomorrow, get a few key hits, and we're right back in it. Shoot, I've had my back to worse walls than this."

The Nats turned to Detwiler, a twenty-six-year-old native of suburban St. Louis, to face off against the veteran thirty-four-year-old Lohse, who had led the National League with an .842 winning percentage. Nats fans could be forgiven for being nervous, as Detwiler had been racked for seven runs (three earned) in just two and a third innings in his last start of the regular season, which came against the Cardinals.

Meanwhile, a local financial institution with the unfortunate name of Cardinal Bank had to make some quick revisions to an advertising campaign that appeared to root for the enemy. The bank's Cardinal logo, which bore some resemblance to the one on the Cardinals' uniform, had been plastered all over the Navy Yard–Ballpark Metro station outside Nationals Park. But the bank, in a bit of masochistic civic duty, painted the words "LET'S GO NATS! STOMP THE CARDINALS" over a giant decal of its own logo fixed to the floor near the station's exit, in time for Game 4.

In the Nationals clubhouse, thirty-seven-year-old reserve Mark DeRosa used his Karaoke machine microphone to try to motivate his teammates. DeRosa, who wasn't even on the roster for the playoffs, read part of Teddy Roosevelt's "Man in the Arena" speech. "With our backs against the wall, I wanted to say something that brought us together, a little band of brothers to go out and fight and see what happens," DeRosa told reporters. "I feel that was fitting." Jayson Werth came running into the clubhouse to hear the inspirational words. Drew Storen called the call to arms "epic," adding, "It's the stuff movies are made of."

Ironically, Teddy Roosevelt didn't care much for baseball. But his words in that speech, delivered in Paris after he served as president, fit the occasion. The oft-quoted lines from the speech include:

It is not the critic who counts; not the man who points out how the strong man stumbles, or where the doer of deeds could have done them better. The credit belongs to the man who is actually in the arena, whose face is marred by dust and sweat and blood; who strives valiantly; who errs, who comes short again and again, because there is no effort without error and shortcoming; but who does actually strive to do the deeds; who knows great enthusiasms, the great devotions; who spends himself in a worthy cause; who at the best knows in the end the triumph of high achievement, and who at the worst, if he fails, at least fails while daring greatly, so that his place shall never be with those cold and timid souls who neither know victory nor defeat.

With late afternoon shadows crossing the infield, Game 4 immediately had more of a playoff game atmosphere than the previous day. The Nationals took a quick lead in the bottom of the second on a solo home run by LaRoche. The Cards tied it in the top the third on a sacrifice fly by Carlos Beltran. And then the game settled into a classic pitching duel.

Detwiler was brilliant for the Nats. He pitched six innings, surrendering just that one run (which was unearned) on three hits. Lohse lasted an extra inning and had a similar final line: one run on just two hits in seven innings.

With no guarantee of a game the next day, Davey Johnson plucked a starting pitcher, Jordan Zimmermann, to relieve Detwiler. Zimmermann continued to mute the Cardinals' potent offense, striking out the side in the seventh. Then Tyler Clippard came in to face the heart of the Cardinal order: Carlos Beltran, Matt Holliday, and Allen Craig.

Charles Krauthammer, a Nationals season-ticket holder who had left the game in the fifth inning to get to Fox News for his television appearance that night, recalls watching this unfold on a monitor at the studio. The host, Brett Baier, was in Danville, Kentucky, the site of that night's vice presidential debate.

"Now I'm kind of a nervous Nellie when it comes to Clippard, 'cause I've been there for two of his meltdowns," Krauthammer says. So before he went on the air, the already-miked Krauthammer said to no one in particular, "I think I'm going to be the first person on live television to have a heart attack on the air."

"Brett Baier is in Danville, and he hears that in his ear during a commercial," recalls Krauthammer. "He says, 'Charles, are you all right?' I said, 'Brett, they just brought in Clippard, it's a tie game.' So he thought I was going to have a seizure on the set."

Clippard struck out three of the four batters he faced, giving up just a walk. A little while later, Krauthammer looked at the monitor and saw Drew Storen on the mound with two outs in the ninth inning. "And I hear in my ear, 'ten seconds,'" Krauthammer relates, adding,

> So I said to the floor manager, "Turn off the monitor. I can't possibly watch with two outs, top of the ninth, while trying to make a coherent statement on television." But I said one other thing to him: "In the next five minutes, if I ask for any updates, lie to me. I don't want the truth. Just tell me Storen's got the side out."

No lies were necessary. On a 3–2 pitch, Desmond ran down Matt Carpenter's short pop near the left-field line with a stumbling catch to retire the side, after Storen had struck out two batters and walked one. Carpenter's pop out was the first time the Cardinals had put the ball in play in three innings.

In the bottom of the ninth, eighteen-game winner Lance Lynn came on in relief to face the top of the Nats order. Jayson Werth fell behind, 0–2, but worked the count to 3–2, following off a boatload of pitches, including four 97-mile-per-hour fastballs. On the thirteenth pitch, Werth turned on a fastball and drilled a line drive over the left-field wall, into the night sky and off the back of the Cardinals bullpen, for a game-winning home run. The Nationals exploded out of the dugout in celebration as fireworks went off and a submarine horn blared. Werth tossed his bat toward the dugout and pointed to his teammates. As he approached home plate, he threw his helmet into the air and jumped into a welcoming party of delirious Nats waiting for him at home plate.

It was the kind of clutch performance that the Nationals had invested in when they signed the playoff-tested Werth to a seven-year, $126 million contract two years earlier. His first season in Washington had been a bust, when Werth hit just .232. In 2012, he missed about half of the season with an injury and hit for a high average (.300) but had only five home runs. Werth had displayed a knack for finding the power switch in the playoffs; the home run marked the fourteenth of his postseason career in forty-eight games.

"When I came here last year, this place was empty," Werth said moments later to ESPN baseball analyst Tim Kurkjian. "And now, a year later, this place is packed. It's awesome. We got great fans, and D.C.'s a great place to play ball."

Months later, Kurkjian, who grew up a Washington Senators fan in the 1960s, recalls it as a fantastic moment. "And I couldn't help but say to myself, 'Oh my goodness. I'm in my own town here, and we've got this incredible game.' That night was the biggest win by a Washington baseball team in seventy-nine years."

Davey Johnson told reporters that Werth's performance had fit the script: "That's the way that game should have ended: Jayson Werth hitting a home run. He has not hit that many this year. What was it, a thirteen-, fourteen-pitch at bat, something like that? It was unbelievable."

On a cold and blustery Friday night, a record Nationals Park crowd of 45,966 came out to see a winner-take-all Game 5. Fans waved red rally towels and wore red jackets or red sweatshirts. Some pulled red hoods over their heads to block the cold; others had red knit hats, scarves, and gloves. David Gregory, appearing on the stadium's video screen, pumped his arms in the air and yelled, "Let's play ball!"

The Nationals were feeling confident, with their twenty-one-game winner Gio Gonzalez pitching and a revved up home crowd providing an emotional boost. For the Cardinals, it was a challenge similar to the one they faced the previous October, when they had to go up against nineteen-game winner Roy Halladay in Philadelphia in Game 5 of the National League Division Series. The Cards had won that game, 1–0, to claim the series. But it soon became clear that more offense would be needed this time around.

In the bottom of the first, Werth picked up where he left off the night before, leading off the game against Adam Wainwright with a double down the left field line. Harper, who had been just 1-for-18 through the first four games of the series, followed with a triple off the left-center field wall—the first teenager to hit a three-bagger in postseason history. Zimmerman continued the assault with a home run to right center, and the Nats had a 3–0 lead without a single out. Nationals Park erupted.

Two innings later, Harper turned on a Wainwright pitch and slammed it into the right-field seats for a home run, giving him seven total bases in just two at bats. Zimmerman doubled, and Morse crushed a home run into the

Cardinals bullpen in left field to knock Wainwright out of the game. The Cardinals pitcher had given up six runs on seven hits in just two and a third innings—nearly identical to his last game in Washington in August, when the Nats pounded him for six runs on nine hits in two and two-thirds innings.·

In less than three innings, the Nats had already scored as many runs as they had in the previous three games of the series combined. With a 6–0 lead and their ace on the mound, the Nationals looked well on their way to a National League Championship Series showdown with the Giants. During the regular season, Gio Gonzalez had been 19–1 when spotted three runs or more.

But the Cardinals slowly mounted a comeback. Gonzalez, who had walked seven batters in the first game, again struggled with control. In the fourth, he walked Beltran, who came around to score on a double by Holliday to make it 6–1. In the fifth, he walked three men and threw a wild pitch, helping the Cardinals narrow the lead to 6–3. Johnson pulled his starter after the inning and trusted his bullpen to get the final four outs.

Meanwhile, the Nationals' offense, which had pounded two doubles, a triple, and three home runs in the first three innings, had gone cold against a succession of young, hard-throwing relievers. "You got their bullpen coming in, and everybody throws a one hundred, so it's not the easiest bullpen to get to," LaRoche would later recall.

From the visitors' dugout, Cardinals reserve infielder Skip Schumaker noticed a lot of Nationals players with a "bright-eyed, deer-in-the-headlights look. And I'm not going to mention names, but we saw them taking a couple of deep breaths between pitches, and they were up four or five runs," he told *St. Louis Post-Dispatch* columnist Bernie Miklasz. "When we saw that, we started talking. We weren't taking any deep breaths. We were the ones trying to push. It felt like we had the momentum, which is crazy to say because we were behind. But it really felt that way."

Fox News' Juan Williams was getting the same vibe at the ballpark. He recalls dancing in his seat and waving his hat when the Nats went up early, feeling the kind of excitement he had when watching the 1969 Miracle Mets as a kid in New York. "You had Gio on the mound, and it was 6–0?" he says. "The Cardinals start chipping away, and then you start to sense it: Oh my God, we're the ones playing tight, they're playing loose. Every inning it's one or two, and then three runs—what the hell?"

Stephen Krupin, the Nats fan who had witnessed nineteen straight losses in 2009, saw his first Nationals home game of the 2012 season that night. Krupin lived in Chicago in 2012, and he had seen the Nats play three times that year—all victories on the road. "I get to my seat as the first pitch is being thrown," he recalls. He adds:

The Nats have this amazing first inning. But we still didn't feel confident at 6–0 that early. We felt like some other shoe's going to drop. In the sixth inning, I'm walking up the concourse and a buddy of mine from high school is in the crowd. And he sees me, and he has this look like, "What are *you* doing here?"

Washington relievers Craig Stammen and Sean Burnett combined to pitch a scoreless sixth inning. But in the seventh, in a move that would be second-guessed by some baseball commentators, Johnson brought in a starting pitcher, Edwin Jackson, rather than setup man Ryan Mattheus. Continuing an infuriating pattern, Jackson walked a batter, Jon Jay, who came around to score later in the inning to cut the lead to 6–4.

Then in the eighth, light-hitting Cardinals second baseman Daniel Descalso crushed a home run off setup man Clippard into the Nationals bullpen, shaving the lead to one run. It was Descalso's second homer of the series after hitting just four all season. The yells out of the Cardinals dugout could be heard in the hushed ballpark.

The Nats picked up some breathing room in the bottom of the eighth inning on Suzuki's RBI single, which made it 7–5. It was the first Nats run since the third inning. The crowd, on edge for six innings, erupted, perhaps out of relief as much as excitement.

Kurkjian was back at his post at the end of Game 5, standing about thirty feet from the Cardinals dugout and getting ready to interview the Nationals stars after an expected Washington victory. "But I looked in that Cardinal dugout before the top of the ninth, and I can't stress enough how much life there was in that dugout," he says. "They really thought that they were going to win, because they had been through all of this the year before when they made this miraculous recovery against the Rangers. As the inning unfolded, I said, 'They can't win this game. They've won too many of these.'"

The year before, facing elimination in Game 6 of the World Series, the Cardinals had rallied from two-run deficits in the ninth and tenth innings and then defeated the Texas Rangers, 10–9, on a walk-off home run by Davie Freese in the eleventh. St. Louis, which had been down to its last strike in two different innings, went on to win the World Series the next night.

Now, holding a two-run lead, the Nationals brought on closer Drew Storen for the third straight day. Beltran led off by crushing a one-hop double off the right-center field wall and moved to third base on a groundout by Holliday. After Storen got two strikes on the next batter, Allen Craig, fans got on their feet, waved red towels, and cheered in anticipation. They went nuts after Storen struck him out on a nasty slider that tailed away for the second out of the inning. They stayed on their feet as Yadier Molina came to the plate, and when the count went to 2–2, they raised the octave a pitch, waiting for that last strike to end the series. But Storen threw two straight balls to walk Molina—one low and one high—putting the tying run on base. Fans winced in exasperation, and the stadium quieted.

Up came Freese, the previous year's World Series hero. Storen got ahead of him, too, 1–2, and the Nats were once again a single strike away from winning the series. "One more!" some fans pleaded. On the next pitch, Freese checked his swing on a slider, and 90,000 eyes quickly darted to first base umpire Ed Hickox, hoping he'd rule that Freese had swung, which would end the game. But the umpire signaled no swing, and the stadium moaned. The next pitch was called a ball, prompting more protests from the hometown crowd. Then, on a 3–2 pitch, Storen missed outside to walk Freese and load the bases. Freese, resisting the temptation to be a playoff hero, had laid off Storen's slider, as other Cardinals did throughout the inning. Reserve outfielder Adron Chambers came in to pinch-run for Molina at second base, giving the Cardinals speed in the potential tying base runner.

Storen was now facing the bottom of the Cardinals lineup, the seventh-place hitter Descalso, with the eighth-place hitter Kozma on deck. Neither had been much of a threat for most of the regular season. Descalso hit just .227, and Kozma played most of the year at Triple-A, where he batted .232 and was almost cut from the forty-man roster. But they were peaking at the right time. Descalso had already doubled and homered in the game, and Kozma, who hit .333 in twenty-six games at the big-league level after filling in at the end of the season for injured starting shortstop Rafael Furcal, had launched a big home run earlier in the series.

Descalso scorched a one-hopper up the middle, and shortstop Ian Desmond lunged up the middle to try to stop it. But the ball careened off his mitt into center field, and the Cardinals scored two runs to tie the game. Stunned fans shook their heads.

"Fans are on their feet, they're ready to start throwing confetti—now look at them," said television color commentator Bob Brenly. Descalso stole second to put runners on second and third. With St. Louis pitcher Jason Motte on deck, Davey Johnson could have intentionally walked Kozma and forced the Cardinals to pinch-hit for their closer. St. Louis had only one position player on its bench, backup catcher Tony Cruz. But the Nats manager decided to go after Kozma.

Storen got ahead of Kozma, 0–2, and the Nats were still just a strike away from going to the bottom of the ninth tied—a good position for a home team, especially in the playoffs. There was some energy left in the crowd, hoping for a repeat of the previous night's walk-off victory. But that energy fizzled when Kozma lined a two-run single down the right-field line, giving the Cardinals a 9–7 lead. Motte, who had not batted once during the regular season, struck out to end the rally.

In a repeat of their 2011 World Series Houdini act, the Cardinals had been down to their last strike on five different pitches, but the Nats could not put them away. St. Louis scored four runs on just three hits, aided by two crucial walks. Overall, the Nats walked eight batters in the game—incredibly and inexcusably—all after taking a 6–0 lead.

Krupin, who was sitting behind the Nats dugout, remembers that when the umpire called a strike in the bottom of the inning, "We could hear the Cardinals players in the dugout cheer at the called strike. That's how quiet the stadium was. And ten minutes earlier, the roof was coming off."

In the bottom of the ninth, the Nats sent up the top of the lineup, which had staked the team to a 3–0 lead in the first inning. The crowd, still standing but muted, watched Werth fly out to right, Harper strike out, and Zimmerman pop out to end the game. At 12:30 a.m., the Cardinals streaked onto the infield to celebrate, as the Nats gazed silently from their dugout. It was the Cardinals' sixth straight victory when facing elimination in the last two seasons. The Nats fans continued standing, in a state of shock. Some had their arms folded across their chests. Others shook their heads.

"When Zimmerman made the final out, there was dead silence," recalls John Hughes, a fan who attended the game. He says,

> The place was like a tomb. No one seemingly knew what to do. Then, very quietly, you heard a little bit of clap-clap-clap. Then a little more. Then a little more. The ripple spread. Then soon the entire stadium was politely clapping—no hoots, no hollers, no yelling. Just polite clapping, as you would hear at the Kennedy Center after a symphony concert.

Nats television color commentator F. P. Santangelo, a relentlessly upbeat cheerleader from the broadcast booth, said during MASN's postgame show that he'd been involved in some tough losses as a player. "But I've never seen anything like that," he said. "That's as bad as they get. And it just goes to show you—you gotta knock out the champ. The champion's not going down easy. . . . I'm still trying to get over the shock of it all."

The Nats had actually blown an even larger lead three months earlier, when the Braves came back from a 9–0 deficit at Nationals Park for an 11–10, extra-inning victory. But that was the regular season, not the deciding game of a playoff series.

Former pitcher Dennis Eckersley, an analyst on TBS's postgame show, referred to Kozma as "this kid, Bucky Dent's little grandson." Dent, a light-hitting shortstop for the Yankees, hit a three-run home run against the Red Sox in a 1978 winner-take-all playoff game, the key blow in New York's 5–4 victory.

Washington Post sports columnist Mike Wise tweeted, "I'm not going to sugar-coat—I have little desire to go cover the wreckage in another losing clubhouse/locker room in this town."

Said Krupin, "That may be the most devastating spectator sports experience in my life—and I'm a Wizards fan, I see a lot of bad games. I saw a little kid behind me crying. He was probably six years old. Getting back on the subway was like a funeral."

Not surprisingly, the Nationals took it just as hard. "With all the adversity we've gone through this year, and then to give up that many free passes, that's not the way you win ball games," Davey Johnson said, adding, "To not go after them at the end was not fun to watch."

"We had the right people there," the manager said at his postgame news conference. "Just got a little too cautious." He said that he thought Storen was "trying to be too fine. I mean, he's got a great moving live fastball, he just needed to throw it over. He wasn't alone."

Johnson had been on the other end of such a game a generation earlier. In the 1986 World Series, his New York Mets were down two runs to the Red Sox in the bottom of the tenth inning with two out and nobody on. The Mets rallied for three runs to win Game 6. They went on to win Game 7 and the series.

Now, Johnson told reporters, with a two-run lead in the ninth, "You gotta make them earn it. And unfortunately, we didn't."

But Storen insisted he made good pitches. "I wouldn't change a thing. I have no regrets," the grim-faced pitcher told a crowd of reporters in the library-quiet clubhouse after the game. "The most disappointing thing honestly is that I just let these guys down. . . . There's a bad taste in my mouth. It's going to stay there for a couple months, and it's probably never going to leave, and it's going be motivating, and be a little fire every time I go out there." Storen added, "I'm sure it'll be a learning process. But gotta let that wound heal, I guess, first."

LaRoche said that the last three outs of the game are the hardest ones to get. "Crazy stuff happens in that ninth inning," he said. "You've got somebody like Drew, who's got some of the nastiest stuff in the game. To give up some runs—it just doesn't happen that often."

"It's unfortunate that some of this falls back on him," LaRoche said softly. "He's been so good since he's come back. . . . He's one of the best in the game. We all know it. And I hope he knows that."

Harper, still a few days short of his twentieth birthday, said he wasn't ready to go home. "Don't want to take off that uniform," he said.

Kurkjian says that in the course of covering 3,000 baseball games, he's never seen anything quite like the Nationals "nightmare" that night, but that he sees some positive in it for Washington:

> I really believe that someday when the Nationals get to the World Series or win the World Series, they're going to point to Game 5 and they're going to say, "We won because we lost that game that night." Drew Storen will never forget the feeling in the pit of his stomach on how he lost that game for the Nationals. And I promise you, as smart as he is, he'll go out there, in the next real pressurized situation in the playoffs, and say, "Damn it, that is not going to happen to me again." And I think every guy in that room will be better for the experience.
>
> Every franchise has to have a seminal victory somewhere, and they got one in Game 4. And sorry, every organization has to have a seminal loss, too, to teach them what winning is going to feel like someday. Well, they got 'em both back-to-back in twenty-four hours. Biggest win in seventy-nine years, biggest loss in eighty-seven years, whatever it is. Biggest win we've ever seen from a Washington team—most of us—followed by the worst loss we've seen by a Washington team. It was just unmistakable, and I'll never forget those two nights for the rest of my life.

At baseball winter meetings in December, Davey Johnson elaborated on his strategy that last inning. "I had the right guy in there, and I like giving guys an opportunity to pitch to hitters with the base open," he told reporters. He added:

That little phenom shortstop came up and got the game-winning hit, and everybody thought I should have walked him. But I like to give (pitchers) a chance, and I do it all year long. . . . I've done that my whole life, and I ain't changing.

So I don't relive it because I think enough about what I'm doing before I do it, and I have all the reasons. I go through that checklist, knowing what's going to happen an inning or two ahead of time. So I've never worried about anybody second-guessing me because they don't know all the options that I have and how I've managed all year.

Kevin Dowd, a lifelong Washington sports fan in his late sixties, recalls how when he was younger, he couldn't sleep nights after the Redskins lost. He wouldn't read the sports section for a week—because he didn't want to experience the loss a second time. "And that's how I felt after Game 5. I haven't felt that way in thirty years," says Dowd, a regular contributor to his sister Maureen Dowd's *New York Times* column. "There were two pitches that could have been the called third strike to end the game, and he didn't get them. And I'm sitting on the coach going, 'It's a home game, you dumb bastard! Give us the fucking call!' So that was heartbreaking to me."

Kurkjian says he went back and looked at the close two-strike pitches and determined neither were strikes. "They were really close," he says, adding,

But David Freese did check his swing, and the pitch to Yadier Molina was not a strike. So I know people were screaming at the umpire. It wasn't the umpire's fault. It was a tested, seasoned, postseason team—the Cardinals—that knew how to win that game against a really talented Nationals team that hadn't been there yet. And it showed.

Desmond came to the same conclusion, reflecting on the loss a few months later. "Being in the playoffs for the first game, you go into it thinking, 'Oh, this is just another game,'" he says. "When you get there, and the crowds are louder, there's towels waving, adrenaline's flowing even more than you've ever experienced. It's not something you can prepare for if you've never been there before. So I think we were a little bit caught off guard."

Desmond, who hit .368 in the series, adds that he thought the Nats played well: "I thought we made a good showing."

Senate Minority Leader Mitch McConnell, a Republican from Kentucky and a self-described Nats "fanatic," watched the game on television from Louisville. He calls the loss "like a death in the family," saying, "It affected me for days. It had a huge impact. And I felt so sorry for Storen, and I really hope it doesn't play with him and mess up his unique talent, because these things happen sometimes." McConnell says that fellow Republican Mitt Romney's loss in the presidential election was worse, but he adds with a laugh that the Nats' loss "was a close second."

On the other side of the political spectrum, Democratic political consultant James Carville took it just as hard. "It's one of the great searing moments of my life," he says. "I go out of my way to try to forget about it."

"The next morning, I felt really bad," recalls Lynne Filderman, who grew up rooting for the Senators in the 1950s and 1960s. "But what a great ride the season was. The Nationals had given us such a wonderful season, with heart and character."

The Cardinals' rally from a 6–0 deficit was the largest comeback in a winner-take-all postseason game in baseball history. The old record of four runs happened twice, most recently when the Boston Red Sox blew a 4–0 lead and lost Game 7 of the 2003 American League Championship Series to the New York Yankees.

The first time it happened, ironically, the Washington Senators coughed up a 4–0 lead to the Pittsburgh Pirates to lose Game 7 of the 1925 World Series. That was the last winner-take-all postseason game in Washington history, until Game 5 of the 2012 National League Division Series. Washington lost both games by the same 9–7 score.

Another echo of Washington's past: Pete Kozma was the first rookie to get the game-winning hit in a winner-take-all game since Game 7 of the 1924 World Series, when Earl McNeely drove in the winning run for the Senators in the twelfth inning for Washington's only championship.

Despite the tough end to the season, the Nats had plenty to be proud of. They had vaulted from a sub-.500 season to the best record in baseball in just one year. Their .605 winning percentage was fourth best in Washington baseball history, behind the pennant-winning Senators of 1933 (.651) and 1925 (.636), and a second-place 1930 Senators team managed by Walter Johnson (.610).

On an individual level, Bryce Harper made history as well, becoming the youngest position player to win the National League Rookie of the Year Award. Harper, who turned twenty a few days after the season ended, finished with a .270 average, 22 home runs, 26 doubles, and 18 stolen bases in 24 attempts, and he led the team with 98 runs scored and 9 triples. He had the most extra-base hits and total bases for a teenager in baseball history.

Rizzo calls Harper a "baseball junkie," stating, "He loves the game, he lives the game, he knows the history of the game. He made us a better team. With him in the lineup, we had a better lineup, we had better defense, we had better power potential."

Harry Reid, the Senate majority leader, says that he started following the Nats closely in 2012 because of Harper, his fellow Nevadan. The two men met on the field prior to a game at Nationals Park. "He looks more like a linebacker to me than baseball player," says Reid, who played catcher in high school. "I'm amazed he can run so damn fast. He runs like a sprinter around those bases. Man, I wouldn't want to get in that guy's way."

Kevin Dowd is amazed by Harper's hustle: "You see him run out meaningless ground balls at a hundred miles an hour—nobody does that. This guy is almost like Robocop—he has been bred to play baseball."

The day after the twenty-year-old Harper won his award, Davey Johnson, nearly seventy years old, won the National League Manager of the Year Award. Earlier that week, he and the Nats agreed that he'd return for one more season as manager and then work as a consultant to Rizzo.

"World Series or bust," Johnson told the MLB Network. "It's going to be my last year, anyway."

Fifteen years earlier, Johnson won the award in the American League after leading the Baltimore Orioles to a division title, but he resigned that same day in a dispute with O's owner Peter Angelos.

Rizzo's first hire when he was named permanent general manager in 2009 was Johnson, as senior adviser. "He's just taken the reins and run with it," Rizzo says, elaborating,

> He's an extremely intelligent baseball guy, with a great demeanor. He's a guy who speaks his mind, I'm a guy who speaks my mind, so we fit well together, and it's been a very happy friendship and marriage between a GM and a manager. Not that we don't have our disagreements and arguments, which we do.

Rizzo wouldn't bite when asked if he agreed with Johnson's "World Series or bust" motto for 2013. "That's Davey's job to make those kinds of prognostications," Rizzo says. "I try to put the best team that we can on the field, give ourselves the best depth. I'm looking at 2013, but with an eye toward 2013 and beyond."

The Nats made several significant moves in the off-season. First, they acquired speedy outfielder Denard Span from the Minnesota Twins. Span, who entered the 2013 season with a .357 career on-base percentage, takes over in center field, with Harper moving to left. Span also provides the Nats with the natural leadoff hitter they lacked.

With an extra outfielder, the Nationals traded fan favorite Michael Morse back to Seattle in a three-team trade. The Nats received A. J. Cole, a pitching prospect they had sent to Oakland the year before as part of the haul for Gio Gonzalez. Washington also received a minor leaguer and player to be named later.

The Nats bolstered their starting pitching as well, by signing three-time All-Star pitcher Dan Haren to a one-year, $13 million contract. The right-hander gives the team an upgrade over Edwin Jackson, who left as a free agent. In their most significant move, the Nationals signed free-agent closer Rafael Soriano to a two-year, $28 million contract. Soriano had saved forty-two games for the Yankees the previous season. The move was clearly made with an eye toward not repeating the National League Division Series Game 5 meltdown against the Cardinals. It also gives the Nationals bullpen superb depth, with Soriano joining Storen and Clippard, both of whom served capably as closers in 2012.

With a young nucleus, outstanding starting pitching, a refortified bullpen, and a dangerous lineup, the Nationals should be an excellent team for years to come. Perhaps they'll even inspire a new saying about Washington: First in war, first in peace, and first in the National League.

OLD SENATORS STATISTICS

Year	League	Record	Finish
1960	American Lg	73–81 (.474)	5
1959	American Lg	63–91 (.409)	8
1958	American Lg	61–93 (.396)	8
1957	American Lg	55–99 (.357)	8
1956	American Lg	59–95 (.383)	7
1955	American Lg	53–101 (.344)	8
1954	American Lg	66–88 (.429)	6
1953	American Lg	76–76 (.500)	5
1952	American Lg	78–76 (.506)	5
1951	American Lg	62–92 (.403)	7
1950	American Lg	67–87 (.435)	5
1949	American Lg	50–104 (.325)	8
1948	American Lg	56–97 (.366)	7
1947	American Lg	64–90 (.416)	7
1946	American Lg	76–78 (.494)	4
1945	American Lg	87–67 (.565)	2
1944	American Lg	64–90 (.416)	8
1943	American Lg	84–69 (.549)	2
1942	American Lg	62–89 (.411)	7
1941	American Lg	70–84 (.455)	6
1940	American Lg	64–90 (.416)	7
1939	American Lg	65–87 (.428)	6
1938	American Lg	75–76 (.497)	5

Year	League	Record	Finish
1937	American Lg	73–80 (.477)	6
1936	American Lg	82–71 (.536)	4
1935	American Lg	67–86 (.438)	6
1934	American Lg	66–86 (.434)	7
1933	American Lg	99–53 (.651)	AL 1
1932	American Lg	93–61 (.604)	3
1931	American Lg	92–62 (.597)	3
1930	American Lg	94–60 (.610)	2
1929	American Lg	71–81 (.467)	5
1928	American Lg	75–79 (.487)	4
1927	American Lg	85–69 (.552)	3
1926	American Lg	81–69 (.540)	4
1925	American Lg	96–55 (.636)	AL 1
1924	American Lg	92–62 (.597)	WS 1
1923	American Lg	75–78 (.490)	4
1922	American Lg	69–85 (.448)	6
1921	American Lg	80–73 (.523)	4
1920	American Lg	68–84 (.447)	6
1919	American Lg	56–84 (.400)	7
1918	American Lg	72–56 (.562)	3
1917	American Lg	74–79 (.484)	5
1916	American Lg	76–77 (.497)	7
1915	American Lg	85–68 (.556)	4
1914	American Lg	81–73 (.526)	3
1913	American Lg	90–64 (.584)	2

Year	League	Record	Finish
1912	American Lg	91–61 (.599)	2
1911	American Lg	64–90 (.416)	7
1910	American Lg	66–85 (.437)	7
1909	American Lg	42–110 (.276)	8
1908	American Lg	67–85 (.441)	7
1907	American Lg	49–102 (.325)	8
1906	American Lg	55–95 (.367)	7
1905	American Lg	64–87 (.424)	7
1904	American Lg	38–113 (.252)	8
1903	American Lg	43–94 (.314)	8
1902	American Lg	61–75 (.449)	6
1901	American Lg	61–72 (.459)	6

NEW SENATORS STATISTICS

Year	League	Record	Finish
1971	AL East	63–96 (.396)	5
1970	AL East	70–92 (.432)	6
1969	AL East	86–76 (.531)	4
1968	American Lg	65–96 (.404)	10
1967	American Lg	76–85 (.472)	6
1966	American Lg	71–88 (.447)	8
1965	American Lg	70–92 (.432)	8
1964	American Lg	62–100 (.383)	9
1963	American Lg	56–106 (.346)	10
1962	American Lg	60–101 (.373)	10
1961	American Lg	61–100 (.379)	9

NATIONALS STATISTICS

Year	League	Record	Finish
2012	NL East	98–64 (.605)	1
2011	NL East	80–81 (.497)	3
2010	NL East	69–93 (.426)	5
2009	NL East	59–103 (.364)	5
2008	NL East	59–102 (.366)	5
2007	NL East	73–89 (.451)	4
2006	NL East	71–91 (.438)	5
2005	NL East	81–81 (.500)	5

BIBLIOGRAPHY

ARCHIVAL SOURCES

Historical Society of Washington, D.C.

Library of Congress, Washington, D.C.

Martin Luther King Jr. Memorial Library, Washington, D.C.

National Archives and Records Administration, College Park, MD

ARTICLES

Ceresi, Frank, and Carol McMains. "The Washington Nationals and the Development of America's National Pastime." *Washington History* 15.1 (2003): 26–41.

Considine, Bob, and Shirley Povich. "Old Fox: Baseball's Red-Eyed Radical and Archconservative, Clark Griffith." *Saturday Evening Post*, August 13, 1940, 14–15, 127–34.

———. "The Old Fox Turns Magnate: Baseball's Red-Eyed Radical and Archconservative, Clark Griffith." *Saturday Evening Post*, August 20, 1940, 18–19, 91–98 (second of two articles).

Dowling, Tom. "The Uncensored Ted Williams." *Washingtonian*, March 1970, 36–39, 56–60.

Eisele, Al. "Bob Short: This Fast-Talking, Short-Tempered Promoter from Minnesota Is Not Likely to Keep Cool in the American League Cellar." *Washingtonian*, March 1969, 46–47, 65–69.

Fimrite, Ron. "Sam Lacy: Black Crusader; A Resolute Writer Helped Bring Change to Sports." *Sports Illustrated*, October 29, 1990, 90.

Griffith, Clark, as told to J. G. Taylor Spink. "Doesn't Sigh for 'Good Old Days' Return: Points to Game's Progress, Sees Balance Achieved in Pitching and Slugging." *Sporting News*, July 23, 1952, 11–12.

———. "Sale of Son-in-Law Cronin 'Nats' Financial Salvation': Owed Bank $124,000 at Time, Griffith Reveals; Decided on Big Deal 'for Good of Joe and Mildred.'" *Sporting News*, July 30, 1952, 11–12.

Lieb, Frederick G. "Griffith Canny as Hill Star, Pilot, Owner: Always a Battler, He Helped to Build A.L. as Major." *Sporting News*, November 2, 1955, 11–14.

Small, Collie. "Baseball's Improbable Imports." *Saturday Evening Post*, August 2, 1952, 28–29, 88–90.

BOOKS

Brashler, William. *Josh Gibson: A Life in the Negro Leagues*. New York: Harper & Row, 1978.

Cobb, Ty, with Al Stump. *My Life in Baseball: The True Record*. Garden City, NY: Doubleday & Co., 1961.

Gilbert, Bill. *The Seasons: Ten Memorable Years in Baseball and in America*. New York: Kensington Publishing, 2003.

Hartley, James R. *Washington's Expansion Senators (1961–1971)*. Germantown, MD: Corduroy Press, 1998.

Judge, Mark Gauvreau. *Damn Senators: My Grandfather and the Story of Washington's Only World Series Championship*. San Francisco, CA: Encounter Books, 2003.

Kerr, Jon. *Calvin: Baseball's Last Dinosaur*. Dubuque, IA: Wm. C. Brown Publishers, 1990.

Mantle, Mickey, and Herb Gluck. *The Mick*. New York: Jove Books, 1986.

Mead, William B., and Paul Dickson. *Baseball: The President's Game*. Washington, D.C.: Farragut Publishing, 1993.

Povich, Shirley. *The Washington Senators*. New York: G. P. Putnam's Sons, 1954.

Ruth, Babe, as told to Bob Considine. *The Babe Ruth Story*. New York: E. P. Dutton, 1948.

Snyder, Brad. *Beyond the Shadow of the Senators: The Untold Story of the Homestead Grays and the Integration of Baseball*. New York: McGraw-Hill, 2003.

Stuart, Jeffrey Saint John. *Twilight Teams*. Gaithersburg, MD: SARK Publishing, 2000.

Thomas, Henry W. *Walter Johnson: Baseball's Big Train*. Arlington, VA: Phenom Press, 1995.

INTERVIEWS

Bosman, Dick. Personal interview. April 2005.

Boswell, Tom. Personal interview. March 2005.

Brinkman, Eddie. Personal interview. April 2005.

Brotman, Charlie. Personal interview. April 2005.

Carville, James. Telephone interview. January 2013.

Davis, Tom. Personal interview. April 2005.

Dempsey, Joe. E-mail interview. May 2005.

Desmond, Ian. Personal interview. January 2013.

Dowd, Kevin. Personal interview. December 2012.

Durenberger, Dave. Personal interview. May 2005.

Espinosa, Danny. Personal interview. January 2013.

Fankhauser, Henry. Telephone interview. August 2005.

Farley, Jack. E-mail interview. April 2005.

Gilbert, Bill. Telephone interview. April 2005.

Gildea, Bill. Telephone interview. April 2005.

Gonzalez, Gio. Personal interview. January 2013.

Grzenda, Joe. Personal interview. April 2005.

Hannan, Jim. Personal interview. April 2005.

Hardage, Robert. E-mail interview. May 2005.

Hochberg, Phil. Personal interview. March 2005.

Holdforth, Bill. Personal interview. April 2005.

Howard, Frank. Personal interview. May 2005.

———. Telephone interview. November 2012.

Jageler, Dave. Personal interview. October 2012.

Kennedy, John. Telephone interview. April 2005.

Krauthammer, Charles. Telephone interview. October 2012.

Krupin, Stephen. Personal interview. December 2012.

Kuhn, Bowie. Telephone interview. May 2005.

Kurkjian, Tim. Personal interview. December 2012.

McCarthy, Gregory. Personal interview. December 2012.

McCarty, William. Telephone interview. April 2005.

McCraw, Tom. Personal interview. March 2005.

McConnell, Mitch. Telephone interview. November 2012.

Reid, Harry. Telephone interview. December 2012.

Rizzo, Mike. Telephone interview. December 2012.

Schneider, Brad. Personal interview. March 2005.

Sievers, Roy. Personal interview. April 2005.

Solomon, George. Personal interview. March 2005.

Stevenson, Bob. E-mail interview. January 2013.

Storen, Drew. Personal interview. January 2013.

Valentine, Fred. Personal interview. April 2005.

Vernon, Mickey. Personal interview. April 2005.

Walker, Ben. E-mail interview. July 2005.

Williams, Juan. Telephone interview. December 2012.

Wills, Maury. Telephone interview. April 2005.

Wolff, Bob. Telephone interview. April 2005.

Yost, Eddie. Telephone interview. April 2005.

NEWSPAPERS/WIRE SERVICES

Associated Press

Los Angeles Times

New York Sun

New York Times

St. Louis Post-Dispatch

Washington Afro-American

Washington Daily News

BIBLIOGRAPHY

Washington Post
Washington Star
Washington Times
Washington Times-Herald
Washington Tribune

NIXON TAPES (FROM NATIONAL ARCHIVES AND RECORDS ADMINISTRATION)

President Nixon on White House telephone with Robert H. Finch. September 22, 1971, 6:55–6:57 p.m.

President Nixon in Oval Office with Stephen B. Bull, Walter E. Washington, Jerry V. Wilson, John D. Ehrlichman, and Egil G. "Bud" Krogh Jr. October 13, 1971, 11:06 a.m.–12:02 p.m.

WEBSITES

Baseball Almanac. 2012. http://www.baseball-almanac.com

Baseball Hall of Fame. 2005. National Baseball Hall of Fame and Museum. http://www.baseballhalloffame.org

Baseball Library. 2005. http://www.baseballlibrary.com

Baseball Reference. 2012. http://www.baseball-reference.com

ESPN. 2012. http://espn.go.com

MASN. 2012. http://www.masnsports.com

Retrosheet. 2005. 2012. http://www.retrosheet.org